Oklahoma Project for Discourse and Theory

READING NARRATIVE

READING NARRATIVE

J. Hillis Miller

University of Oklahoma Press : Norman

Also by J. Hillis Miller

Fiction and Repetition: Seven English Novels (Cambridge, Mass., 1982)
Ariadne's Thread: Story Lines (New Haven, Conn., 1992)
Illustration (Cambridge, Mass., 1992)
Topographies (Stanford, Calif., 1994)

Library of Congress Cataloging-in-Publication Data

Miller, J. Hillis (Joseph Hillis), 1928–
    Reading narrative / J. Hillis Miller.
        p.   cm. — (Oklahoma project for discourse and theory ; v. 18)
    Includes bibliographical references and index.
    ISBN 0-8061-3097-0 (cloth : alk. paper). — ISBN 0-8061-3098-9
(pbk. : alk. paper)
        1. Narration (Rhetoric)   2. Discourse analysis, Narrative.
    3. Literature—History and criticism.   I. Title.   II. Series.
    PN212.M55   1998
    808—dc21
                                                            98-5734
                                                              CIP

Reading Narrative is Volume 18 of the Oklahoma Project for Discourse and Theory.

The paper in this book meets the guidelines for permanence and durability of the Committee on Production Guidelines for Book Longevity of the Council on Library Resources, Inc. ∞

1   2   3   4   5   6   7   8   9   10

For Barbara Cohen

CONTENTS

ILLUSTRATIONS

SERIES EDITORS' FOREWORD

The Oklahoma Project for Discourse & Theory is a series of interdisciplinary texts whose purpose is to explore the cultural institutions that constitute the human sciences, to see them in relation to one another, and perhaps above all, to see them as products of particular discursive practices. To this end, we hope that the Oklahoma Project will promote dialogue within and across traditional disciplines—psychology, philology, linguistics, history, art history, aesthetics, logic, political economy, religion, philosophy, anthropology, communications, and the like—in texts that theoretically are located across disciplines. In recent years, in a host of new and traditional areas, there has been great interest in such discursive and theoretical frameworks. Yet we conceive of the Oklahoma Project as going beyond local inquiries, providing a larger forum for interdiscursive theoretical discussions and dialogue.

Our agenda in previous books and certainly in this one has been to present through the University of Oklahoma Press a series of critical volumes that set up a theoretical encounter among disciplines, an interchange not limited to literature but covering virtually the whole range of the human sciences. It is a critical series with an important reference in literary studies—thus mirroring the modern development of discourse theory—but including all approaches, other than quantitative studies, open to semiotic and post-semiotic analysis and to the wider concerns of cultural studies. Regardless of its particular domain, each book in the series will investigate characteristically post-Freudian, post-Saussurean, and post-Marxist questions about culture and the discourses that constitute different cultural phenomena. The Oklahoma Project is a sustained dialogue intended to make a significant contribution to the contemporary understanding of the human sciences in the contexts of cultural theory and cultural studies.

The title of the series reflects, of course, its home base, the University of Oklahoma. But it also signals in a significant way the particularity of the *local* functions within historical and conceptual frameworks for understanding culture. *Oklahoma* is a haunting place-name in American culture. A Choctaw phrase meaning "red people," it goes back to the Treaty of Dancing Rabbit Creek in Mississippi in 1830. For Franz Kafka, it conjured up the idea of America itself, both the indigenous Indian peoples of North America and the vertiginous space of the vast plains. It is also the place-name, the "American" starting point, with which Wallace Stevens begins his *Collected Poems*. Historically, too, it is a place in which American territorial and political expansion was reenacted in a single day in a retracing called the Oklahoma land run. Geographically, it is the heartland of the continent.

As such—in the interdisciplinary Oklahoma Project for Discourse & Theory—we are hoping to describe, above all, multifaceted *interest* within and across various studies of discourse and culture. Such interests are akin to what Kierkegaard calls the "in-between" aspect of experience, the "inter esse," and, perhaps more pertinently, what Nietzsche describes as the always *political* functioning of concepts, art works, and language—the functioning of power as well as knowledge in discourse and theory. Such politics, occasioning dialogue and bringing together powerfully struggling and often unarticulated positions, disciplines, and assumptions, is always local, always particular. In some ways, such interests function in broad feminist critiques of language, theory, and culture as well as microphilosophical and microhistorical critiques of the definitions of truth and art existing within ideologies of "disinterested" meaning. They function in the interested examination of particular disciplines and general disciplinary histories. They function (to allude to two of our early titles) in the very interests of theory and the particularity of the postmodern age in which many of us find ourselves. In such interested particulars, we believe, the human sciences are articulated. We hope that the books of the Oklahoma Project will provide sites of such interest and that in them, individually and collectively, the monologues of traditional scholarly discourse will become heteroglosses, just as such place-names as Oklahoma and such commonplace words and concepts as discourse and theory can become sites for the dialogue and play of culture.

Robert Con Davis
Ronald Schleifer

Norman, Oklahoma

PREFACE

This book, along with several others, was first conceived on a cold morning in Bethany, Connecticut, in the winter of 1975, as my old notebooks show. I had been writing an essay on Wallace Stevens's "The Rock" and had become obsessed with the proliferation of line images in narratives and critical readings of narrative, as well as by the relation of such images to various forms of repetition. I wanted to write an essay intertwining readings of Elizabeth Gaskell's *Cranford* and Walter Pater's "Apollo in Picardy." This was to be preceded by a relatively brief preface that would outline the various regions, nine in number, I thought, of narrative analysis in which line images function. Yielding shamelessly to the fallacy of imitative form, I imagined a prefatory essay that would be structured like a labyrinth made of successively smaller and smaller windings ending with that single straight-line labyrinth Jorge Luis Borges imagines.[1] When I got up to over one hundred pages with the second section of this project, after a brief antechamber on the line as letter, I realized my plan was in deep trouble. It has taken me all these intervening years to finish the project, which has undergone many mutations along the way. A sequence of books has emerged from the plan: *Ariadne's Thread* (1992), *Illustration* (1992), and *Topographies* (1994). *Fiction and Repetition* (1982) was closely associated with the project. This present book should have been first, or at least all of the part before the readings of *Cranford* and "Apollo in Picardy" in chapter 14. The latter was to have been last in my original plan. All those other books must be imagined as sandwiched between beginning and ending here. The finishing at long last of *Reading Narrative* completes the cycle and frees me from the promise I made to myself to work my insights out in detail on paper.

This book has a logical backbone of theoretical questions about the ends, beginnings, and middles of the narrative line. The Greeks called this line a "diegesis." *Reading Narrative* may be thought of as an extended commentary on what is problematic about Aristotle's formulations about beginnings, middles, and ends. What Aristotle says is cited and discussed in the first chapter, which raises all the issues of the book through an analysis of Aristotle's *Poetics* and Sophocles's *Oedipus the King*. This is followed by separate discussions of ends, beginnings, and middles, in that order. The sections on middles make up by far the longest section of the book. This, I claim, is appropriate, since middles, depending somewhat on how they are defined, take up most space (or time) in a narrative. Middles have also perhaps been less discussed as a separate problem in reading narrative than beginnings and endings. The chapters on middles take up various complications of narratives as they proceed from here to there, from start to finish. Such complications include shifts in narrators or speakers; anacoluthons, that is, abrupt shifts in syntax; indirect discourse; multiple plots; the use of tropes in narrative; and the master narrative trope that is not a trope, irony. These chapters are uneven in length. They just came out that way, according to the principle that one should say what one has to say and then stop. A more extended interleaved discussion of *Cranford* and "Apollo in Picardy" ends the book with a demonstration of how all these complications of the narrative line work together to generate meaning (or a suspension of meaning) in two salient examples.

Reading Narrative proceeds through analysis or invocation of a long series (or line) of citations and examples. Which takes precedence over the other, theory or example? It is impossible to answer that question. On the one hand, the theoretical formulations are important for me in their sequential development. On the other hand, the examples have received my full and fascinated attention. The strangeness of Aristotle's *Poetics* and the madness of Sophocles's language in *Oedipus the King*, the Sternean free arabesque that turns into a snake in Balzac, the portmanteau word "Ariachne" in *Troilus and Cressida*, Albertine's lying anacoluthons in Proust's *À la recherche du temps perdu*, sundials facing north in Pater's "Apollo in Picardy," hats on top of hats in Gaskell's *Cranford*—

each of these has demanded an attention that exceeds their role as mere examples of some theoretical point, until I might say what Yeats says in "The Circus Animals' Desertion": "Players and painted stage took all my love / And not those things that they were emblems of."[2] Yielding joyfully to them in this exclusive way and following them as far as they lead allows them fittingly to play their role as examples and put in question the theoretical points I use them to exemplify.

ACKNOWLEDGMENTS

As I have said in the preface, *Reading Narrative* has been many years in the making. Several segments have been previously published in preliminary form. All have been reworked to fit the general argument of the book and my current understanding. I am grateful for permission to reuse the following essays in this way: "Ariachne's Broken Woof," *The Georgia Review* 31 (Spring 1977): 44–60; "The Problematic of Ending in Narrative," *Nineteenth Century Fiction* 33 (June 1978): 3–7; "Narrative Middles: A Preliminary Outline," *Genre* 11 (Fall 1978): 375–87; "The Figure in the Carpet," *Poetics Today* 1 (Spring 1980)1: 107–18.

READING NARRATIVE

ONE

ARISTOTLE'S OEDIPUS COMPLEX

The God at Delphi neither quite explains nor hides; he gives a sign.

—Heraclitus, fr. 93

Aristotle is a skeleton.

—Wallace Stevens, *Adagia*

King Oedipus has an eye too many perhaps.

—Friedrich Hölderlin

Multicultural approaches in the humanities have recently proliferated in the United States. One motive is a desire to win freedom from the dominance of the so-called hegemonic culture supposedly buttressed by the canonical works of Western civilization. One inadvertent effect of multiculturalism may be to establish a perspective by incongruity that may allow a glimpse of the strangeness and heterogeneity of the dominant culture. Careful study of that culture's works remains as necessary as ever. To tell the truth, most United States citizens are still dispossessed of it after years of schooling. Relatively few of us have it by birthright or by early training. We are born outsiders to the "Western tradition." We remain outsiders throughout early family and school training. At best we are most likely inside ideological misinterpretations of our culture's major canonical works. That culture and the often reductive accounts of it must be studied in order to be contested. Otherwise we risk replicating its presuppositions and even its injustices. Those who do not study history are condemned to repeat it, though studying is also a form of repetition.

For the purpose of cultural studies, investigating what people have made of canonical texts is as important as reading those texts themselves. It is the misreadings that have often been historically effective. Far more people, for example, have been decisively influenced by Schiller's mis-reading of Kant in the *Letters on Aesthetic Education* than have read Kant himself, no easy task. In the case of such texts "reading" means studying them with care, word by word, taking nothing for granted beforehand.

Even the most familiar and canonical of texts in Graeco-Roman-Hebraic-Christian culture turn out to be exceedingly strange when they are read this way, that is, when they are looked at with a candid eye, or at any rate with an eye sharpened by the concurrent study of non-Western cultures or of minority discourses within the hegemonic culture. The canonical texts are as strange as any texts uncovered by anthropologists or by students of minority cultures. They are so odd, in fact, that one wonders whether they can ever really have been dominant at all, that is, whether they have ever actually been read. Has what they say ever been, or could it ever be, or ought it ever to be, institutionalized in social practice? Something else may have been put in their place all along. Some courses in "Western civilization," one is almost tempted to believe, are more a cover-up than a revelation of what "our" tradition really is. I begin this book by turning back to take another look, from the perspective of our current cultural situation, at two indubitably canonical texts of Western culture, Aristotle's *Poetics* and Sophocles's *Oedipus the King*.

All careful readers of the *Poetics* notice that Aristotle takes Sophocles's *Oedipus the King* as exemplary of tragedy in general. At key places Aristotle makes specific reference to it. Sophocles's play was clearly in his mind as a salient example of what his theory of tragedy would have to explain. That attempt to explain produced in the *Poetics* one of the great founding documents of the Western tradition. Almost all subsequent varieties of literary theory and criticism in the West down to the present day are in one way or another anticipated in the *Poetics*: formalism, structuralism, reader-response criticism, psychoanalytic criticism, mimetic criticism, social criticism, historical criticism, even rhetorical or so-called decon-structive criticism. Freud follows Aristotle in making Sophocles's *Oedipus the King* originary. For Freud, Sophocles's play presents the paradigm of the "Oedipus complex" that is, for him, universal in men. Claude Lévi-

Strauss's reading of the Oedipus story is exemplary for structuralist method and its results. Jacques Derrida's rereading of the *Poetics* in "La Mythologie blanche" is a crucial text of so-called deconstruction.[1]

The *Poetics* is exemplary in another way. If someone were to ask, "What do you mean by 'Western logocentrism?'" a good answer might be "Aristotle's *Poetics* is an example of what I mean by logocentrism. It is also a good example of what I mean when I say all logocentric texts contain their own undermining counterargument, their own deconstruction woven into them." Aristotle conspicuously assumed that everything can and should be explained rationally, returned to its presiding reason, or "logos." That may be what Stevens meant by calling Aristotle a skeleton. Aristotle also, notoriously, assumed that a good tragedy must itself be rational in the sense that everything in a good tragedy makes sense because everything is referred back to a single action and meaning. Nothing extraneous may be included. This rational unity is what one might call the "logos" of the play, taking that word in several of its chief meanings: as reason for being, as end, and as underlying ground. "Logos" in Greek also means mind, word, and order, arrangement, ratio, or proportion, as Aristotle's usage shows. "The tragic plot," says Aristotle in his imperturbably rational way, "must not be composed of irrational parts [meron alōgon]. Everything irrational should, if possible, be excluded; or, at all events, it should lie outside the action of the play."[2] Aristotle's example of the latter is, "in the *Oedipus*, the hero's ignorance as to the manner of Laius's death" (97; 24:1460a). Aristotle is right, as usual, or rather he is wrong but in an interesting way. It *is* absurd to suppose that Oedipus's wife, Jocasta, or someone else around the royal palace would not have told him about how Jocasta's first husband died. That might long since have started Oedipus putting two and two together. Yet the whole play depends on Oedipus's ignorance. Aristotle tells us what to do in such a situation, in a formulation that anticipates Coleridge's "willing suspension of disbelief." We must invest the irrational with a virtual rationality. We must take the irrational as rational, as one of the founding presuppositions of the play: "once the irrational has been introduced and an air of likelihood imparted to it, we must accept it in spite of the absurdity" (ibid.). Aristotle is wrong, however, as I shall show, in implying that this is the only irrational thing about *Oedipus the King.*

Aristotle's desire to banish or rationalize the irrational, to put it out of sight or to turn it into its opposite, explains his insistence on the need for a good tragedy to be "perspicuous" (33; 7:1451a). Reason is the power of clear seeing, according to Aristotle's epistemology. It is the process whereby the essence of a thing passes into our minds in perception and can be clearly understood there.[3] A play will therefore be rational only if it can be completely seen through. It must be able to be held in the memory all at once, from beginning to end. We must, in addition, be able to see to the bottom of it, so to speak, to understand why things have happened in the play as they have happened. The play must have none of the opacity of the irrational.

Aristotle's formulation of this is one of the many places where he makes an analogy between a good tragedy and a natural organism. About this appeal to nature ("physis") there would be much to say. One important goal of the *Poetics* is to make tragedy a natural growth and to provide its taxonomy. Tragedy is, as it were, one more animal or plant determined by nature for which the rational and encyclopedic philosopher needs to account. Both a good tragedy and a natural organism are reasonable. Both are governed by the "logos." Hence one can be used as a model for the other: "As, therefore, in the case of animate bodies and organisms a certain magnitude is necessary, and a magnitude which can be easily embraced in one view;[4] so in the plot, a certain length is necessary, and a length which can be easily embraced by the memory. . . . But the limit as fixed by the nature of the drama itself is this: —the greater the length, the more beautiful will the piece be by reason of its size, provided that the whole be perspicuous" (31, 33; 7:1451a).

The bigger the better, or at any rate the more beautiful, but only so long as you can see through the whole thing from one end to the other. The reasonable is the perspicuous. For Aristotle being reasonable, as I have suggested, is the highest value in a tragedy, the one thing most needful. Why is this? The function of a tragedy is to arouse the irrational emotions of pity and fear by a fictitious spectacle and then to purge them when the discovery ("anagnōrisis") makes everything clear, subjects everything to reason, so the spectators can say: "I see it all now." This is analogous to the way the pleasure in solving a riddle or in seeing the appropriateness of a metaphor, in Aristotle's view, comes from seeing through it. Anagnōrisis is like solving a riddle, like seeing why a raven is like a writing desk or why Oedipus is like a ship and a plow. I shall return later to this analogy of analogy. Just as the pleasure derived from mimesis is, for Aristotle, a result of the natural human pleasure in learning, so the performative effect of a tragedy, the catharsis of pity and fear, is brought about by the knowledge it gives. The affective and performative are subordinate to the constative or brought about by it.

A reader of the *Poetics* who had seen all this and understood it (but seeing *is* understanding, for Aristotle) might then want to turn to *Oedipus the King* to see just how it exemplifies tragedy as Aristotle defines it. That the *Oedipus* is mentioned so often promises further illumination by reading it. Is this play really what a reading of the *Poetics* would lead us to expect it to be? Or is the relation of *Oedipus the King* to the *Poetics* not rather a spectacular example of the way great philosophers choose examples that put the greatest strain on the doctrine they are propounding? The examples they choose perhaps even confound and dismantle that doctrine. Aristotle was smart enough (he was nothing if not intelligent) and courageous enough (he had great intellectual courage) to see that if he could make *Oedipus the King* support his project of rationalization, then he would, so to speak, be in business. One might say that Aristotle had an Oedipus complex, in a way not entirely different from what Freud meant by the term. Aristotle was obsessed by *Oedipus the King*. The whole effort of the *Poetics* is an attempt to displace the *Oedipus*, to put his own confident rationality in place of its threatening unreason. That displacement would make Aristotle the "master of those who know," as Dante called him, and the father of Western concepts of poetry.

Though Aristotle's *Poetics* is in many ways an extremely odd document, the repeated appeal by Aristotle to *Oedipus the King* as a confirmation of what he is saying is one of the oddest aspects of this strange text. *Oedipus the King* is the uncanny guest within the domestic economy of the argument Aristotle is making. Far from assisting him in his attempt to return everything in tragedy back to its home in reason, the references to that play, as I shall show, introduce something irreducibly irrational into what Aristotle says. It may be that Aristotle returns to the *Oedipus* so often because it is a nagging reminder that something is not quite right in what he is saying. The references to *Oedipus the King* are a kind of return of the repressed. If Aristotle is a skeleton, he is, it may be, one of those fearsome skeletons that walk abroad on Halloween and frighten anyone who sees them. He is not the skeleton as fleshless rationality but the skeleton as ghostly revenant. The *Poetics* manifests the presence of the repressed irrational in the act of attempting to rationalize it. In this the presence of *Oedipus the King* in the *Poetics* is like Oedipus himself in the play. Oedipus has come back from the dead, so to speak, to fulfill the oracle's prophecies. The play can be taken as an allegory of the doom that awaits attempts to rationalize the irrational—including perhaps this present essay.

Just what is there about *Oedipus the King* that does not fit Aristotle's prescriptive description of a good tragedy? As any one who has read the *Poetics* knows, Aristotle gives primacy to plot ("mythos") in a tragedy. It takes priority over all of the other elements of tragedy, for example, character ("ethos") and diction ("lexis"): "The Plot, then, is the first principle and, as it were, the soul [psyche] of a tragedy" (27, 29; 6:1450a). This is because tragedy is an imitation of an action. You could, says Aristotle, have a tragedy without character but not one without plot. Why is action "the end of a tragedy" (27; 6:1450a), meaning by "end" the "telos," the purpose of the whole thing? This is because the action produces the anagnorisis (discovery) and the "peripeteia" (reversal of fortune). These in turn produce the catharsis of pity and fear that are the reason for being of tragedy. The whole purpose of the play is to bring about that catharsis. This priority of plot leads to Aristotle's prescription of the proper "structure" of the plot:

Now, according to our definition, Tragedy is an imitation (mimesis) of an action that is complete, and whole, and of a certain magnitude; for there may be a whole that is wanting in magnitude. A whole is that which has a beginning, a middle, and an end. A beginning is that which does not itself follow anything by causal necessity, but after which something naturally is or comes to be. An end, on the contrary, is that which itself naturally follows some other thing, either by necessity or as a rule, but has nothing following it. A middle is that which follows something as some other thing follows it. A well-constructed plot, therefore, must neither begin nor end at haphazard, but conform to these principles. (31; 7:1450b)

As I said in my preface, this book might be described as an extended commentary on these formulations. Aristotle's sentences sound so familiar and so commonsensical to most readers, even if they have never read them before, that it is difficult any longer to see how odd they are. They are an elegant formulation of notions about origin, end, and intermediate continuity—all governed by some underlying cause—that are essential to "logocentrism." We take such notions about continuity for granted. It would be irrational not to do so. Where then is the oddness? For one thing, Aristotle's concept of wholeness, as the paragraph following the one just cited makes explicit, is modelled on the unity of a living organism, an organism "of a certain magnitude." The concepts of beginning, middle, and end, however, are temporal, not spatial. What are the beginning, middle, and end of an elephant, to choose an example with a certain magnitude? Does the middle of an elephant follow the beginning by "causal necessity"? Perhaps, but it is an odd way to say it. As a description of a well-made plot's temporality, however, Aristotle's language makes good sense. An action is temporal and might, so it seems, have a beginning, middle, and end connected by causal necessity as Aristotle prescribes.

Is this ever the case? Are Aristotle's definitions not suspiciously tautological, like saying morphine puts you to sleep because of its dormitive virtue? A beginning begins. An ending is where the play ends. The middle is what is between and connected to both ends. But we knew that already. Is there really ever a beginning of a play that does not itself follow anything by causal necessity? Or is there is an ending that nothing follows? Are all the middle elements ever connected by a clear causal necessity to what comes before and after? I shall raise these questions again later on with other examples, in subsequent sections of this book.

Oedipus the King, in any case, by no means exemplifies Aristotle's stipulations. As Thomas Gould observes, "This play has no plot in the ordinary sense of the word."[5] The "action" the *Oedipus* "imitates" is made up almost exclusively of people standing around talking or chanting. Whatever happens during the course of the play happens through language, through the give-and-take of dialogue, often of question and answer. The frequent use of brief sentences in rapid interchange (sticho-mythia) intensifies the reader's or the audience's sense of the way language is action in this play, as do many other ways in which the language calls attention to itself, most signally in all the repetitions of words and figures, as I shall show. By means of all this talk Oedipus gradually puts together the data that will bring him quite suddenly to discover the awful truth (if indeed it is the truth). He has murdered his father and slept with his mother. His children are also his brothers and sisters. His crimes are the cause of the plague in Thebes. Apollo has, for no apparent reason, inflicted a horrible punishment on him.

The real action of *Oedipus the King*, if one means by action decisive physical occurrences, has either taken place before the play begins (Oedipus's abandonment as a baby on Mount Cithaeron, his murder of his father, his solving of the Sphinx's riddle, his sleeping with his mother) or takes place offstage (Jocasta's suicide, Oedipus's self-blinding) after the "discovery." The play begins long after the real action has taken place. It presupposes that the audience already knows about that beginning before the beginning. The audience of course also already knows the end. Like a good detective story, of which it is the prototype in our tradition, *Oedipus the King* moves forward through a time made up of investigative interrogation. It does this in order to create a retro-spective reconstruction of crimes that have occurred long before the play begins. The difference from present-day mystery stories is that the audience of *Oedipus the King* already knows who committed the crime, though the detective does not know. Moreover, the detective is the criminal. This pattern makes *Oedipus the King* an unconventional mystery, to say the least, though similar idiosyncrasies perhaps lie hidden behind many more conventional modern mystery stories.

If the *Oedipus* begins before its beginning, the play, far from being a seamless sequence of events each causing the next, is made up of more or less fortuitous and discontinuous encounters. Though the story in the past may be an ineluctable chain of events (even that is debatable), the present action is a series of disconnected scenes. It is not rational that all of these should happen on a single day, however well they work as a concatenation leading Oedipus to his recognition. It just happens, for example, that the messenger from Corinth arrives that day announcing the death of the king of Corinth, whom Oedipus assumes is his father. It just happens that this messenger knows Polybus is not his real father. It just happens that the palace slave who saved Oedipus rather than carrying out the order to abandon him on Cithaeron is also the one person who survives the massacre of Laius and his retinue at Phocis, where the three roads meet, This means the same man can confirm that Oedipus is the child of Jocasta and Laius, that he murdered Laius, and that he is now married to his own mother. Of course the angry god Apollo manipulates all this, but that is just Sophocles's point. The gods are inscrutable, irrational. They make things happen in a way that defies reason, both in the sense of "gnōmē" and in the sense of "phrōnis," two words used frequently in the play in various forms for different kinds of practical intelligence. I shall return to this.

As for the end of the *Oedipus*, it is not really the end. It cannot be said that nothing follows causally from it. Oedipus is left at the end of the play uncertain about what Creon will do with him, whether or not he will allow him to go into exile. We know that something will follow next, as Creon consolidates his new power as king. Moreover, as the audience well knows, the events of this day are only an episode in a story that leads to Oedipus's own death and transfiguration at Colonus, and to the brother battle of his two sons leading to the death of Antigone. *Oedipus the King*, it could be argued, is not a self-sufficient whole but an arbitrarily excised segment of a larger action. This is true, that is, unless you accept the idea that in *Oedipus the King* the language is the action, that it is a play about the action language can perform.

I have stressed Aristotle's insistence on the necessity that a good tragedy be rational and on the subordination of diction to plot. A good tragedy turns on a discovery in which everything becomes clear, comprehensible by reason. That discovery leads to the reversal of fortune. Diction is all in aid of making the play a good imitation of an action. How well does *Oedipus the King* measure up to these prescriptions? Well, for one thing, if the action of the play proper consists almost exclusively of talk, this would seem to reverse the priority of plot over diction. The action of the play is an action performed by language. The plot is the language. Any careful reader of the play soon gets caught up in the complicated integument of recurrent complex words and figures, puns, double meanings, ironies. That is where the action is, in these details of language.

The use of the word "performed" above is more than nominal. It is a reference to speech-act theory. The diction of the play is full of speech acts: invocations, promises, curses, prophecies, anathemas. Examples are the chorus's invocation of the whole panoply of gods,[6] Oedipus's promise to find the murderer of Laius and rid the land of the plague, Oedipus's curse of the murderer, Tiresias's prophecy of the outcome, and Oedipus's anathema against Creon. Each of these is a different kind of speech act. Each would merit a full and discriminating reading, distinguishing its way of working from other kinds of speech acts. The climactic "discovery," finally, is brought about by what might be called Oedipus's performative reading of the data he has gathered. This is another speech-act aspect of the play. Reading is always performative, not passive reception of information. Reading, putting two and two together, as Oedipus does, is an active intervention, even if that intervention is guided by ideological assumptions about what the reader is going to find. Oedipus's "reading" actively puts data together. This brings about the discovery, along with the consequent reversal of fortune. The "cause" of all that happens is not some external determinism linking the events of the action in an inevitable chain but the (perhaps) arbitrary act of putting those (perhaps) disconnected events together to make a coherent story. Oedipus's concocted story convicts the detective story-teller himself of parricide and incest. "Whodunit" becomes "I dunit." The moral of the play might be: "Do not be too good a reader. It will get you into deep trouble." That is certainly what Jocasta repeatedly tells Oedipus, saying, "For the love of the gods, and if you love your life, / give up this search!" (ll. 1060–61). She also tells him, in a speech that has generated much commentary: "This marriage with your mother—don't fear it. / How many times have men in dreams, too, slept / with their own mothers! Those who believe such things / mean nothing endure their lives most easily" (ll. 980–83). This not only asserts the universality of what Freud was to call the Oedipus complex, but also tells Oedipus not to give it a second thought, if he wants to live easy. Modern appropriations like Freud's, however, tend to ignore the specific, culture-bound, theory of dreams that Athenians held in Sophocles's time.

All reading is performative, this play suggests. It makes something happen. Another example would be this present reading of *Oedipus the King*. My reading is also a piecing together of evidence to make a coherent story, as rational an account as I can make it, even though it is an account of the irrational. I want to see through *Oedipus the King* and write something perspicuous about it, as Aristotle did. What I write will have effects, though exactly what these will be is necessarily obscured for me, just as Oedipus had no way of knowing what his insistence on getting to the bottom of the puzzles he encountered would bring about, and just as Aristotle is not likely to have foreseen the importance his lecture notes on poetry would have for twenty-five hundred years in the West. Aristotle recognized this performative aspect of reading when he ascribed a purgative effect to watching and hearing a tragedy performed. A tragedy is not just an imitation of an action. It is an imitation for the purpose of making something happen, the catharsis of pity and fear in the audience.

If the Aristotelian relation of plot to diction is reversed in *Oedipus the King*, if in that play diction is plot, this would not in principle keep the play from being perspicuously rational. Perspicuity, however, is conspicuously lacking in the play, as I shall now show. This lack of transparency can be identified in two analogous regions: first, in opacities darkening the secret antecedent story that is gradually, so it seems, brought fully into the open by Oedipus's investigations; and, second, in the diction that makes up the action of the drama that unfolds before the spectator's eyes and ears.[7]

Oedipus is the embodiment of Aristotelian rationality in the play. He incarnates the desire to see to the bottom of things. He also is a surrogate for the rationality of the reader or spectator who wants to understand the action of the play, to see and comprehend what is revealed by that action. Oedipus is patiently and doggedly reasonable in trying to think things out on the basis of the evidence he is given. He is the incarnation of the desire to know, at all costs. The emblem for this is the way he has solved the riddle of the Sphinx when no one else could do so: "What is it that walks on four feet, then on two feet, and then on three feet?" "Why, man, of course," he replies. Oedipus's success with the Sphinx's riddle is the reason the priests of Thebes ask him to find out the source of the plague and make it go away. In his search for the plague's source, that desire to see and know is violently frustrated, both for Oedipus and for the spectator.

The desire to see through everything, as Aristotle's theory of poetry makes clear, is ultimately a desire to confront the underlying reasons why things happen as they do. That Oedipus himself is the cause of the plague can be figured out; thus the murderer is tracked down. What cannot be understood, what remains absolutely unfathomable, is why Oedipus has been punished by Apollo in this way. Everything that has happened and does happen to Oedipus is a response to the original oracular prophecy that predicted Laius's son would kill him and sleep with his wife. Tremendous efforts are made both by Oedipus and by his parents to keep that from happening. It happens anyway. Why? Assuming the gods are just, what have Oedipus, Laius, and Jocasta done wrong? What law have they broken? How have they offended the god? Why have they deserved this horrible punishment? Thomas Sutpen, in William Faulkner's *Absalom, Absalom!*, might be speaking for Oedipus when, after patiently recapitulating his life in a narrative presented to Quentin's grandfather, he asks: "You see, I had a design in my mind. Whether it was a good or a bad design is beside the point; the question is, Where did I make the mistake in it, what did I do or misdo in it, whom or what injure by it to the extent which this would indicate."[8]

Oedipus the King is deeply religious. This does not necessarily mean that a reading of the play, such as this one, must be itself religious, that is, ground itself on religious presuppositions. It does mean disagreeing with Freud, who saw in the religious aspect of the play a cover-up, an after-formation veiling the true subject, the universal double Oedipal desire to kill the father and take his place in the mother's bed. "Today, just as then," says Freud in the discussion of Oedipus in *The Interpretation of Dreams*,

many men dream of having sexual relations with their mothers, and speak of the fact with indignation and astonishment. It is clearly the key to the tragedy and the complement to the dream of the dreamer's father being dead. The story of Oedipus is the reaction of the imagination to these two typical dreams. And just as these dreams, when dreamt by adults, are accompanied by feelings of repulsion, so too the legend must include horror and self-punishment. Its further modification originates once again in a misconceived secondary revision of the material, which has sought to exploit it for theological purposes. . . . The attempt to harmonize divine omnipotence with human responsibility must naturally fail in connection with this subject-matter just as with any other.[9]

Against Freud, I claim that the religious terminology is so deeply embedded in the text of *Oedipus the King* that Freud's notion of a secondary elaboration distorting the original content cannot work in this case. A reading of the play must somehow take that religious terminology into account. Freud is right to say that the play fails to harmonize divine omnipotence with human responsibility. This, however, is just the point of the play and the source of its power, its exemplary ability to arouse pity and fear. Scholars have argued that the sequence of Sophocles's two Oedipus plays, *Oedipus the King* (produced around 437–436 B.C.) and *Oedipus at Colonus* (written in 406–405), register a profound change in Athenian concepts of the balance between divine and human responsibility. When *Oedipus the King* was produced, a more or less inscrutable divine power, or "daimōn," was assumed to be the ultimate cause of what happens, though men and women were held responsible for whatever they did "with their hands," whether intentionally or not. By the time of *Oedipus at Colonus*, "ethōs," or human character, was coming to be granted its own autonomous causal power and responsibility. Intentional human agency was coming to be important. Greek tragedy was made possible by the specific conflictual configurations of fifth-century Athenian thought about the relation of "daimōn" to "ethōs." These assumptions, moreover, were rapidly changing, from decade to decade, as the old religious awe was being replaced by notions of independent human responsibility. Far from being a cultural universal, *Oedipus the King* registers a particular historical moment in a single Greek culture.¹⁰

It might be better to say, however, not that *Oedipus the King* is deeply religious, but that it cannot be told whether *Oedipus the King* is deeply religious or sacrilegious. Though the play was initially performed on the occasion of one of the seasonal Dionysian festivals in Athens, that does not mean that it is necessarily piously orthodox, whatever that might have meant at that time in Athens. Works of art on religious themes that have survived and that have been canonized in the Western tradition tend to be transgressive in one way or another. This is certainly the case with *Oedipus the King*, as it is of many other Greek tragedies. This penchant for transgression is characteristic of the great canonical works of our tradition, for example, Shakespeare's plays. One might plausibly argue that the function of literature in the West is not to reinforce a reigning ideology but to put it in question, while at the same time demonstrating its power.

Oedipus the King has an uneasy relation to Athenian religion. It is both overtly pious and at the same time a challenge to the assumption that the gods are just. What can be told for certain is that its basic themes are religious questions. What is the secret cause that makes things happen as they do happen? Why is Oedipus fated, whatever he does to avoid his fate, to kill his father and marry his mother? Who is to be held responsible for his crimes? The play is religious in the specific, limited sense of seeking a rational knowledge of the hidden or transcendent reasons for the way things happen. A legendary story is chosen that takes a lot of explaining of that sort. Nevertheless, those hidden reasons, personified as the double-natured Apollo, destroyer and preserver, remain at the end altogether dark. Even the adequacy of their personification in Apollo is dubious. The hidden reasons are other than, "others" in relation to, human rationality and knowledge. The Greek word "daimōn," used more than once in *Oedipus the King* as a term for these "others," names an impersonal occult power, not a God with conscious intentions. Neither Laius nor Jocasta nor Oedipus has done anything at all commensurate with the suffering each endures. The play fails to give adequate reasons for their suffering. Sophocles includes nothing whatsoever in the play to indicate that Laius, Jocasta, or Oedipus is being punished for some crime." You cannot understand what happens to them by saying it was punishment by the gods for some sinful act. It just happened, like a bolt of lightning or like a beast springing on its prey, to use two of the play's own figures.

Attempts have been made to find some tragic flaw in Oedipus that would justify his fate, something like the "hamartia" Aristotle specifies as characteristic of the tragic hero. Oedipus's main characteristic is the rational desire to know that Aristotle praises and he himself typifies. Oedipus also has a tendency to get suddenly angry when his rational designs are thwarted. Can that combination be his tragic flaw? This would generate the irony that Aristotle's chief example of a good tragedy warns against the very characteristic that Aristotle most prizes. Oedipus is too rational. This would make the *Oedipus* truly a ghostly, disruptive presence in the *Poetics*. Oedipus's desire to know does not precede the god's decision and foreknowledge. It might be correct to say that Apollo punishes Laius and the baby Oedipus by endowing the latter with a gift for carefully figuring things out along with a quickness to anger. The combination will ultimately allow Apollo to destroy him. But why in the world did Apollo do that? What was the god's reason?

The only rational conclusion to draw from this play is that the gods are irrational, at least as measured by human reason. It is impossible to understand them, to see through their motives. The double bind in which this puts Oedipus, the citizens of Thebes, and any spectator or reader is forcefully expressed in one of the choruses at about the middle of the play. This chorus comes when Jocasta has been trying to persuade Oedipus that the oracles could not possibly be fulfilled because the son who was predicted to kill Laius was long dead when Laius was murdered. The chorus then asserts that "laws" governing proper human action and speech have been set forth "on high" by Olympus: "The god is great in them [those laws] and never ages" (l. 871). On the one hand, if the oracles are not fulfilled, then the validity of those laws will be put in doubt:

> No longer shall I visit and revere
> Earth's navel, the untouchable,
> nor visit Abae's temple,
>   or Olympia,
> if the prophecies are not matched by events
>   for all the world to point to. (ll. 897–902)

On the other hand, as the play shows that, if the oracles are fulfilled, the gods have treated men and woman with ferocious injustice, or at any rate in a way whose reason and justice are inscrutable. If there are "laws" permanently inscribed "on high" by the gods, those laws are so incomprehensible to humankind that they appear to be the lawlessness of unpredictable injustice. Like the countryman in Kafka's "Before the Law," Sophocles's play can be thought of as "before the law," piously responsive to it, demanding only that it manifest itself clearly so that we mortals can know how to behave. The play shows that neither the most careful thinking nor the most pious obedience avails to reveal what those laws are. One might be tempted to apply to the situation of Oedipus and the other characters in *Oedipus the King* Shakespeare's terrifying formulation in *King Lear*: "As flies to wanton boys, are we to th' gods, / They kill us for their sport" (4.1.36–37). Even this formula is too rational. It anthropomorphizes the gods. It ascribes to them a comprehensible human pleasure in cruelty. Nothing at all can be fathomed of the god's motive in *Oedipus the King*. For Sophocles, as for Heraclitus, "The God at Delphi neither quite explains nor hides; he gives a sign." The whole text of *Oedipus the King* might be seen as such a sign. Narration in general may be such a sign. We need storytelling, it may be, not to make things clear but to give a sign that neither quite explains nor hides. What cannot be explained nor understood rationally can be expressed in a narration that neither completely exposes nor completely covers over. The great stories in our tradition may have as their main function this proffering of an ultimately almost inexplicable sign.

The entire text of *Oedipus the King* can be seen as a sign (or a collection of signs) that neither reveals nor hides. The play offers itself as a narrative expression of the unfathomable otherness of the gods or of the "daimōn." I have said that *Oedipus the King* is a complicated integument of recurrent complex words, figures, puns, double meanings, ironies. What is most irrational about *Oedipus*, most antipathetic to Aristotelian rationality, is the way it gives evidence of gods who are wholly other or others. No way exists to understand them or to see through them. They are not perspicuous. No terms adequately define them. They are neither good nor evil, just or unjust, sadistic or sympathetic. These divinities are black holes. The reader or spectator can learn this only indirectly, through the words of the play, in an ever-unsatisfied torsion of the mind, as the words are read or recited before his or her eyes and ears. No way of seeing the ultimate cause face to face exists, as Oedipus's self-blinding implies. Like the sun, this truth cannot be looked at directly. You can neither stand it nor understand it.

A rational person, such as of course I am, resists reading this play. Such a reader instinctively refrains from looking *Oedipus the King* squarely in the eye, so to speak. The mind shies away from confronting *Oedipus*. It twists the mind to try to think it out. No doubt this is because the play resists the logical, analyzing intelligence, the Aristotelian rational mind. This is not surprising, since the desires for incest and parricide, the main motifs of the play, are things most people would like to suppress. They are things the less said about the better, like "the Queen of Spain's legs," as Elizabeth Gaskell says in *Cranford*.[12] We know she has them, but we should not talk about them. This resistance is experienced as a reluctance to perform the mental effort required for a careful reading of the play. Faced with a task of such difficulty, "the dull brain perplexes and retards," as Keats puts it.[13] Reading this play is like trying to think an indefinite multiplicity of incongruent things at the same time. This is a difficult, probably impossible, task, though it is the task that reading in general demands of the reader. No one, it may be, can look directly at *Oedipus the King*, for reasons for which the play gives signs.

One evidence of this resistance to reading is any translation of the play. The translator is forced continually to choose a single meaning for words that are ambiguous or have many meanings in the Greek. Subtle echoes from one word to another are necessarily lost because the roots of

the corresponding English words are often different. A translator, however anxious to be faithful to the original, covers over or suppresses much
in what Sophocles wrote. What Gould calls "a Greekless reader" (11), such
as I am, is like someone deprived of depth vision because of having one
eye too few, though knowing Greek would not be a guarantee against a
one-eyed reading. For a Greekless reader the admirable running footnote
commentary accompanying Thomas Gould's translation, with its continual discussion of complexities and nuances in the Greek, may serve as a
kind of prosthetic eye. This commentary allows a better look at these
signs that neither explain nor hide. Perhaps, however, such a translation
provides an eye too many, since it may be dangerous to confront this play
too directly. The "literal" translations Gould gives in his footnotes,
impossible English as they sometimes are, are often more useful than the
translation proper above on the same page. Gould has provided the
reader with a double text of *Oedipus the King*. This is a great help with a
text that is itself double, about doubling, and full of doublings of one
sort or another. Thomas Gould's statement about his policy as a translator scrupulously defines his way of dealing with these ambiguities:

Because *Oedipus the King* is the subject of so many and such intense disputes, I
have tried to translate it as literally as possible. Each line in the English
corresponds to the line with the same number in any modern text of the Greek;
and in each, those things that seemed most necessary for a close study of the
play have been rendered most exactly. . . . The thing I have found most difficult
to preserve is the manner in which Sophocles repeats a number of striking
words in different parts of the play, opening up to the audience a significance
or a level of action (usually demonic) of which the players are quite unaware. . .

  These key words are also often rich with overtones in the Greek, which
invariably means that no equivalent exists in English. I have discussed these
words in the commentary." (11)

The notorious example of Hölderlin's translations into German of
Antigone and *Oedipus the King*, however, shows that the problem may not be
even so resolvable as Gould's recognition of difficulties suggests. As
Walter Benjamin says of Hölderlin's Sophocles translations: "In ihnen

stürzt der Sinn von Abgrund zu Abgrund, bis er droht, in bodenlosen Sprachtiefen sich zu verlieren [in them meaning plunges from abyss to abyss until it threatens to become lost in the bottomless depths of language]."[14] As Gould's statement recognizes, it is often simply impossible "to be literal and still stay within the bounds of good English" (11). On the one hand, Gould's translation has by no means escaped what he calls "grotesque effects," which may explain why this admirable book is now out of print; on the other hand, to say, as he does, that he has treated particles and idioms "freely" is to confess that he has mistranslated. As I have said, the Greekless reader often feels that he or she is approaching closer to what Sophocles wrote, closer, for example, to the intimate ironic echoes of word and word or of figure and figure from one part of the play to another, in the footnote commentary where the confessedly "grotesque" literal translations are given.

One form of doubling in *Oedipus the King* is the notorious dramatic irony that pervades the diction of this play. (I shall return later to the larger question of irony.) Oedipus is continually saying one thing and inadvertently meaning another, as the audience, who knows the whole story beforehand, can perceive. The play opens with his address to the Thebans as "My children, ancient Cadmus's newest care" (l. 1). Oedipus thinks this is just a manner of speaking, but he really is the descendant of Cadmus; he says the truth without knowing it. A little later he says to them, "And yet, though you are sick, / there is not one of you so sick as I" (ll. 60–61), again without knowing the deeper truth of his own words. Another example is his saying of Laius, "I never saw him" (l. 105), when the audience knows he not only saw but was begotten by him and has killed him. Another is the famous line in which Oedipus says he will search for the murderer with as much zeal "as if [I were seeking vengeance] for my own father" (l. 264). Other examples are all the speeches in the play where Oedipus says he wants to see clearly while the audience knows that he will blind himself. The recurrent language in the play about seeing keeps the ultimate outcome insistently before the audience's eyes.

Oedipus the King is a fabric of such double meanings. Often these are figures of speech that mean more than the speaker intends, but sometimes they are words used literally that nevertheless have multiple meanings.[15] This perpetual current of double meanings adds up to what Gerard Manley Hopkins called an "underthought," or in this case to several underthoughts, second and third levels of thinking and action of which the characters are unaware.[16] The words and figures in question are irrational in the sense of being double in meaning, subject to a double logos, perhaps to an indefinite plurality of logoi, or, it may be, to no logos at all. What is said has the meaning that Oedipus and the other characters consciously intend to put in it. At the same time the audience sees other meanings put in them by. . . . Well, by what or by whom? By Sophocles, who remains above and beyond his creation, imperturbably in command of all these meanings? Or is it perhaps rather by an intrinsic and fundamentally uncontrollable capacity language has to mean different things in different contexts, to mean more or other than its user consciously intends? *Oedipus the King* seems to confirm Friedrich Schlegel's strange personifying dictum in "On Incomprehensibility [Über die Unverständlichkeit]": "Words often understand themselves better than do those who use them."[17] Or are the double meanings put in by what I would call the "others," the inscrutable gods? Is Apollo not what might be named a "polylogical" god, notorious for his doubleness, as both healer and destroyer? It may be Apollo who makes Oedipus continually say something different from what he means to say. Apollo, however, may be no more than a humanizing personification of powers that are utterly beyond human comprehension, exemplifying Jacques Derrida's terrifying sentence: "Tout autre est tout autre," which means, among other things, "Every other is wholly other."[18]

To ask these questions is another way of asking what is the secret cause of the action of the play, that is, the cause of the words the actors speak, since the action, as I have said, is in the language. It may be that it is in principle impossible to answer these questions. The language, whatever the answers given, whatever the cause assigned, would be exactly the same. No differentiae exist on which to base a decision. Moreover, for the reader to ask to see and to understand the reasons behind the way language works in *Oedipus* is perhaps to repeat Oedipus's own temerity in wanting to see and to know, to figure things out rationally.

Four complex, related, and recurrent words in the play keep before the reader contradictory, irreconcilable ideas about why things happen as they do, as well as about the various powers of the mind that might understand those causes. "Tychē" means luck as opposed to "moira," fate, but it also means "brought about by some demon." To say "tychē has caused it" is to say those two irreconcilable things at once, without necessarily choosing between them. "Gnōmē," thought, as opposed to "phrōnis," habitual intelligence, know-how, is conspicuously possessed by Oedipus. The words in various forms echo through the play. Oedipus thinks his "gnōmē" will suffice to understand things. (Has he not answered the Sphinx's riddle?) The play shows, as I have said, that this confidence in his problem-solving powers, along with his tendency to sudden uncontrollable anger, constitutes his double tragic flaw. For Sophocles to have claimed, even implicitly, that he was in control of the language of his play would have been to repeat Oedipus's fatal temerity. The unfathomable gods who bring it about that Oedipus fulfills the oracle's prophecies, in spite of his elaborate attempts to avoid doing that, are, perhaps, allegorical emblems of a mechanical quality in language that makes it escape the intentions of its user. Language will say and do something disastrously different from what the most rational, willing speaker means to say or to do with words. This fatality would apply to Sophocles too, in spite of his mastery of words. It would apply also to any reader of the play, such as this one.

Just why Oedipus's mental gifts are insufficient cannot be known for sure. All that can be said for certain is that one main horror of *Oedipus*, for anyone who reads it or hears and sees it performed, is the way Oedipus's words are taken away from him. He means to say one thing and says something else quite different. His words are not controlled by his conscious will to say what he wants to say. His logos, in the sense of "mind," does not control his logos in the sense of "word" or "meaning." His words are given meanings other than the one his rational mind intends. Two senses of "logos" are, for him, detached irrevocably from one another, logos as mind and logos as meaning. What Oedipus says is whisked away into the control of demonic polylogoi that make him say a truth he does not yet know. This is as great a cruelty to a rational man, a man such as Oedipus (or Aristotle), a man who prides himself on his clear thinking ability to figure things out and state them clearly, as is the god's cruelty in forcing Oedipus to do what he does not wish to do, what great efforts have been taken to keep him from doing, that is, kill his father and sleep with his mother.

This lack of control over language is one chief source of that pity and terror Aristotle says the play produces. I pity Oedipus for this alienation of what he says from what he means. I also fear that I may be subject, without knowing it, to the same double-speaking. How can I be sure my own language is not subject to the same alienation, even language, like mine, that tries to articulate that alienation? Since the play depends so much on questions of what language can do, it is difficult to see how *Oedipus the King* is cathartic, as Aristotle claims all tragedy is. It would be cathartic, one might argue, only if the peripeteia and anagnorisis also involve a discovery about language that is as clear as Oedipus's recognition that he has killed his father, slept with his mother, and fathered children who are his own brothers and sisters. This, however, is by no means the case, as I shall show. It is no more the case than finding out what he has done explains why he has done it.

Oedipus's promise to find Laius's murderer and his formal curse of the criminal near the beginning of the play are salient examples of the alienation from him of his own language. Both are speech acts that make something happen, something different from what he intends. His promise works to put him in a new situation. He must now either keep the promise or break it. He says, "because of this, as if for my own father, / I'll fight for him, I'll leave no means untried, / to catch the one who did it with his hand" (ll. 264–66). To promise to do this is unwittingly to promise to track down himself. His curse of the murderer, as well as of any who have knowledge of him and keep it secret, also has performative force. A curse is a way of trying to do something with words. What Oedipus does not know is that he curses himself, just as the promise commits him to catch himself as his father's murderer. The curse has, for the audience or for the reader who already knows how the story is going to come out, an ironic double meaning similar to that of Oedipus's promise:

> And this curse, too, against the one who did it,
> whether alone in secrecy, or with others:
> may he wear out his life unblest and evil!
> I pray this, too: if he is at my hearth
> and in my home, and I have knowledge of him,
> may the curse pronounced on others come to me. (ll. 246–51)

When Oedipus discovers he is the one he has cursed, he does not hesitate to insist that the conditions of the curse be carried out by Creon. A curse is a curse: once it has been uttered it cannot be withdrawn. It does not depend for its efficacy on the knowledge or intent of the one who utters it. It invokes the power of the god or gods in a magical incantation. The god, however, though he is in a way constrained by the curse uttered in his name, can always make use of the curse to make happen what he wants to make happen, whatever men or women say in his name. In this case Apollo, so it appears, wrests the curse from its intent and makes it an instrument of his own will. He uses the curse to punish Oedipus for crimes he did not intend to commit and does not yet know he has committed. Without at all wishing to do so or knowing that he does so, Oedipus cooperates in Apollo's plot to destroy him.

Men and women, *Oedipus the King* would imply, can never be sure their performatives will perform what they want them to perform. People can do things, and even do things with words, but they often do something other than what they mean to do. They say something other than what they mean to say. To speak is to be perpetually in danger of making a slip of the tongue. Human speech, as exemplified in Oedipus, manifests a horrible lack of control. Ordinary speech is like that of a brain-injured person who utters words different from those intended, or like the sounds made by someone with the sinister form of tic that causes its victim involuntarily to bark like a dog or speak blasphemies and obscenities, as if he or she were a mechanical talking head.

This equivocity of language in *Oedipus the King* takes two main forms that are different aspects of a single duplicity in language. One form is words, or word stems, that have what William Empson called a complex structure.

As I shall show, they rather manifest an antistructure, antimatter to Empson's matter.[19] The other form of duplicity is metaphor. Sophocles conspicuously exemplifies Aristotle's claim that a command of metaphor is the mark of genius in a poet. It is the one thing, says Aristotle, that cannot be imparted by another. It comes, or does not come, by nature, "for to make good metaphors implies an eye for resemblances" (87; 22:1459a). You either have such an eye or you do not have it. In Oedipus's case, his eye for resemblances may, perhaps, be the one eye too many that leads him to his self-condemnation. Correspondingly, Sophocles's eye for resemblances makes *Oedipus the King* into a text that can by no effort be rationalized in the way Aristotle wants to do with metaphor. A word, whether literal or metaphorical, does not have a fixed meaning in itself, as modern linguists and philosophers (especially Wittgenstein among the latter) have taught us. A word has the meaning given to it by the sentence in which it is used and by the context, both verbal and extra-verbal, in which that sentence is employed. Nevertheless, as *Oedipus the King* shows, all the other possible uses of the word in other sentences and contexts, especially in other places in the same text, are invoked as shadows or ghosts. This happens even when the word is used with a markedly different intent or meaning, as in the root meaning of the French expression for "mean": "vouloir dire," wish to say. Whatever I wish to say, I may be also saying something ironically, comically, or dangerously different.

The distinction between the two forms of equivocity I have named (complex words, metaphors) is to some degree artificial. The relationship among the various meanings of a complex word like "tychē" is a form of figuration, while the overtly metaphorical expressions in *Oedipus the King* often turn on key words that are complex in themselves even when detached from the overt metaphor of which they form a part. "Tychē," for example, as I have said, means both happening by chance and happening through the design of some daimōn." It is a double antithetical word, duplicitous in itself prior to any metaphorical transposition.[20] Nevertheless, the distinction between complex words and metaphors is useful. Complex words in the *Oedipus* often form parts of statements that are not in any obvious sense figurative, while metaphors are often overt comparisons between something or someone in the play and some other region of nature that may not play any role at all on the play's first level of reality. An example is the recurring metaphor of a boat or swimmer on the high seas to describe Oedipus or to describe the city of Thebes as governed by Oedipus (for example, ll. 22–24, 57). Boats do not figure at all in the story proper.

A restricted repertoire of terms makes up what Aristotle calls the "lexis," or diction, of *Oedipus the King*. Whatever any character says turns out, by some fatality or happenstance, some "tychē," to contain one or more of this limited set of terms and figures. Many of these are tactfully or casually introduced near the beginning of the play. They are like a set of notes in a scale to play melodies on later. Even a Greekless reader can, with the help of commentary like Gould's, get some sense of the complexity and purport of these recurrences. A simple list of these elements gives some idea of their range, but only a careful reading of the play, line by line, will grasp their complex interrelation. Many of the recurrent terms have something to do with the human body. This reflects the general importance of body parts as a resource for figures here (and in general), for example, in all those catachreses that give borrowed or "abusive" names to things in the outer world that have no proper names, such as "headland" or "face of a mountain." Body names also insistently keep before the reader the way the play has to do with Oedipus's body and those of his parents. Oedipus's injured ankles, for example, are given the same name ("arthra") as the eyeballs he pierces with his mother-wife's brooch pin. Hands ("cheiri") are often mentioned, for example, Oedipus's hands, which are polluted by having been the instruments of his father's death. A shadowy presence behind all these body terms is the image of two bodies joining in an act of incest in which Oedipus returns again to the womb that bore him.

Not all the recurrent words are names of body parts. The word for pollution ("miasma"), for example, recurs. It appears primarily in connection with the curse that has made the Theban land and women infertile, but "miasma" is subtly related to another word already mentioned, "cheiri," or hands. As Gould explains, the Greeks had a strong sense of the way a crime pollutes the hands of the one who performs it, even if he or she has not intended the crime. Oedipus may not have

intended to kill his father, but his hands are polluted by what he has
unintentionally done. The whole land, by a synecdochic contagion, is
consequently polluted through its king's crime. Until Thebes is purified
by Oedipus's punishment, the plague will continue. Hands and pollution
are, strictly speaking, not metaphors, since they refer to things literally
present in the play.

The overt metaphor of a ship being steered has, as I have said, no
literal referent in the play. The image of the plowed field often has no
literal referent, though in the background are the fields of Thebes
rendered infertile by Apollo's curse. Both ships and plowed fields often
seem brought in fortuitously from the available reservoir of poetic
comparisons. Aristotle's basic example of a metaphor based on a ratio
allowing a substitution of terms brings these two together: "The ship
plows the waves." The word "plows" is brought over from the realm of
farming to name the action of the ship's movement. The ship and
plowing figures, however, are more than nominal metaphors in the
Oedipus. Both are highly motivated. They are related to one another in
complex ways. The figure of plowing, since it is used as an oblique figure
for copulation, brings together the barrenness of the land and the
barrenness of women, both results of Apollo's curse. This connection
makes the particular form the plague takes a fitting punishment for
someone who has killed his father and slept with his mother, that is, as
the play says, "plowed the one who gave him birth" (l. 1497).

The ship is a traditional metaphor for metaphor, from Aristotle on
down through the centuries, since both a boat and a metaphor are forms
of transport. The word "metaphor" of course means "transfer," the
carrying over of a word from its literal use to a figurative one, as when we
say, "The ship ploughs the waves." Metaphor in *Oedipus the King* is,
however, transport in a more hyperbolic sense. What Oedipus and other
characters say is displaced, as I have said. It is carried over into a meaning
they do not intend. This is a general danger in metaphor. It always
exceeds the limited applicability to the referent it names by displacing the
literal word. The broader resonances of the borrowed word are brought
over willy-nilly with the word. When you use a metaphor you are always
likely to say more than you mean to say. In *Oedipus the King* those who use

the plowing and the ship metaphors are, without wishing to do so or knowing that they do so, also speaking of the way Oedipus has plowed his mother-field and has gone into the harbor of his mother's body. He has done this, the play tells us, like a ship coming back to its home harbor rather than entering the alien harbor for which it sets out and which it ought to reach (ll. 423, 1208–9). The latter stands for proper exogamy, marrying outside the immediate family. All this is inadvertently said by metaphors that at first seem to be no more than vivid and poetic ways of speaking, although their horrifying implications are ultimately made explicit. Contrary to Hopkins's sense of the "underthought" of Greek plays as something in poetic resonance with the main action of the play, the underthought in *Oedipus the King* is subject to a counter logos, in the sense of another alien mind controlling, or "steering," thought. What Oedipus or the others mean to say and what some other power makes them say are two radically irreconcilable things.

The degree of this irreconcilability exceeds the incongruities Empson accounts for as "the structure of complex words." However complex or even discordant the meanings encapsulated in a word like "sense" or "fool," they still, according to Empson's model, make a "structure." The word "structure" invites Empson's readers to think of the meanings in a complex word as distributed in a pattern, perhaps like vectors going out from a radiant node at the center. The meanings are set out in a spatial array that can in one way or another be rationalized, seen through, and grasped by the mind. The meanings in the complex words and figures in *Oedipus the King* do not make structures of this kind. They can neither be thought of together nor spatialized. They exceed the mind's grasp, in a species of irrational antistructure that exceeds even Empson's seventh type of ambiguity. This is because the various irreconcilable meanings are not centered on the radiant node of the complex word or figure. They are rather contradictory signs emitted by the black hole of the gods' or daimōns' unfathomable intents. As I shall show, the difference between Empsonian structure and Sophoclean antistructure is like the difference between adultery and incest.

Here are some examples of those contradictory signs. Images of feet, eyes, seeing, tracking, doubling, mounting, and plunging recur throughout the play, in complex permutations. Oedipus's feet were mutilated when they were tied together and he was abandoned as a baby on Mount Cithaeron. His name, according to one etymology, means "swellfoot." The Sphinx's riddle involves feet: "What walks on four feet in the morning, two at noon, and three in the evening?" This prophecy is echoed in Tiresias's prophecy of the way the blinded Oedipus will feel his way with a stick. Oedipus himself embodies the Sphinx's riddle as well as solving it. When the chorus says to Oedipus, "Do not stumble! Put our land on firm feet!" (l. 51), the audience will remember Oedipus's feet. Oedipus knows there is something wrong with his feet, though he only mentions that late in the play. The quite uncommon word used for Oedipus's eyes when he puts them out, "arthra" (ball joints), would normally name another part of Oedipus's body, for example his ankles. This ties his primal wound, bodily sign of his identity, to the ultimate punishment for being who he is. To stumble is a result of not seeing right. This connects feet and seeing to the images of tracking down. Oedipus asks "how can we ever find / the track of an ancient guilt now hard to read" (ll. 108–9). He has, he says, "tried many paths in the wanderings of thought" (l. 67), and in another place he says, "Alone, / had I no key [symbolon], I would soon lose the track" (ll. 220–21). To track down depends on clear seeing, for which the recurrent word is "skopein," to see, as in l. 291, where Oedipus promises he will scrutinize all stories. Seeing is of course emphasized all through the early part of the play in both its physical and epistemological senses. Oedipus sees things clearly. Apollo, however, is also in one of his epithets called the scrutinizer, as Gould observes. Oedipus promises he will track down the wild beast who killed Laius. The beast turns out to be himself. The god Apollo, however, also springs on Oedipus, as a wild beast, say, a mountain lion, springs on its hunter, the hunted hunting the hunter. Oedipus, in several ways made explicit in the play, duplicates Apollo. It is part of his "tychē" to do so. Oedipus's incest is linked to the Delphic oracle's placement at Mother Earth's "navel."[21] Like Apollo, Oedipus wants to see and to save. He looks upon himself as Apollo's agent: "In this way I ally myself in war / with the divinity and the deceased" (244–45). Apollo's spring on Oedipus and on Thebes ties the god's violence with Oedipus's violence of parricide and incest. The two violences are already implicit images of one another by way of the words for mounting or plunging: "enallesthai" (to leap on, rush at, lunge at) and "epenthrōiskein" (to mount and penetrate), used in both contexts. The figures of mounting and plunging mix violence and sexual congress. The words are used to name not only what Oedipus does to Laius and Jocasta, but also what the god does to Oedipus and to Thebes: "The firebearing god / has swooped upon the city" (ll. 27–28). The recurrent use in different contexts of "paiein" (to strike), and a single use of a novel compound, "eis-paiein" (to strike so as to enter), suggests that Oedipus is right, as Gould puts it, "to confuse the patricide, the incest, and the piercing of his eyes, as though all three 'blows' were one" (47). This is reinforced in another frightening symmetry Gould notices: the massacre of Laius and his retinue at Phocis, where the three roads cross, matches the incestuous penetration of Jocasta where legs and body join.

Figures of doubling, finally, keep insistently before the reader or spectator various forms of thematic duplicity that are mimed in the duplicity of words that say two antithetical things at once. Examples are the doubling of sex and murder, incest and parricide; the double nature of the god or gods, not only Apollo but the whole pantheon of deities to whom the chorus prays; the double pronged ax that Laius uses to attack Oedipus; Oedipus's two eyes that he pierces; the double doors of Jocasta's room, allusions perhaps to the double vulvae, the lips of his mother's genitals, that Oedipus has entered, like a ship returning to its home harbor, just as he enters her room through those double doors and just as she goes back through them to hang herself. The adept reader of *Oedipus the King* must struggle, without complete success, to keep all this immense tangle of connections in mind at once as they impinge on any given passage.

A connection deeper than a thematic one links all these verbal tangles to the central enigma of the play, that is, the question of why all these horrible events have occurred as they have occurred. As Paul Gordon has shown in a brilliant book building on Derrida's reading of Aristotle's *Poetics*, Aristotle's definition of "metaphora" as "epiphora"—that is, as

displacement, transference, transgression, or supplement—the ascription
to one thing of a word that belongs to something else ("onomatos
allotriou") makes metaphor and adultery analogous.²² As Gordon says,
the word Aristotle uses to say "belonging to something else" is "allotrios."
The same word is used by Aeschylus in the *Agamemnon* (l. 448) "to
describe courting another man's wife."²³ I claim that it is more correct, for
Oedipus the King at least, to say metaphor is like incest or, conversely, to say
incest is like metaphor. What is the difference between comparing
metaphor to adultery and comparing it to incest? How is incest different
from adultery as a metaphor for metaphor? Why is the former more
appropriate for *Oedipus the King*?

Adultery means, etymologically, adding something alien, something
other, as sugar or salt might be adulterated by adding some other
substance to it. The word "adulterate" comes from the Latin "ad" (to or
toward) plus "alter" (other, different), that is, "to or towards the other."
In adultery the man puts his seed where it should not be. Adultery
presupposes that there is a right place for the seed to be, since the word
adultery is properly used only for the transgression of a married man or
woman. In a similar way, Aristotle's theory of metaphor presupposes a
primary literal meaning that is then transferred to another use, as the
word belonging to one thing is ascribed to another alien thing that has
its own proper name. Adultery is unlawful, but it keeps the law and the
names of things firmly in place, just as a metaphorical transfer does not
put in question the literal meaning of the transported word. Aristotle in
the *Rhetoric* stresses the way a word may have a natural kinship with a
thing and puts it directly before our eyes. In his discussion of apt words
he says, "One word may come closer than another to the thing described,
may be more like it, and, being more akin to it, may set it more distinctly
before our eyes."²⁴ To put this another way, Aristotle's theory of
metaphor is entirely rational, and it is governed by the primacy of clear
seeing. It is consonant with the general commitment to reason I have
identified as Aristotle's main trait, however threatened it is by the ghostly
presence of the irrational.

In incest, on the other hand, all those certainties and stabilities are
confounded, just as the "metaphors" in *Oedipus the King* are not grounded

on the certainties of literal meaning but brought in to cover an ignorance, the impossibility of knowing the ultimate causes of things. Such metaphors are not really metaphors. They are rather catachreses, since the incestuous word does not displace a proper one but names something that has no proper name. One of the key words in *Oedipus the King* is "homosporus," meaning "sharing the same seed." The word is applied to the kinship of Oedipus, Laius, and Jocasta. What is horrible about the incest in the play is that Oedipus's seed both belongs and does not belong where he puts it when he begets on his mother-wife those children who are also his brothers and sisters. The irrational mixing up of kinship names, about which I shall say more later, corresponds to the undermining of Aristotle's theory of metaphor by the possibility of catachresis. This possibility Aristotle recognizes in those cases, like the phrase "the sun sows its seed," where the transferred word does not substitute for any existing literal word,²⁵ just as he recognizes the presence of the irrational in *Oedipus the King*, though in both cases he seems confident that his reason will be able to master these forms of unreason by putting them firmly in their places. As I have been showing, however, a reading of *Oedipus the King* shows that neither the use of figures in it nor the unreason of the story can be mastered by even the most powerful reasoning.

"Metaphora" is the name for an "epiphora," or displacement, in words like the movement into the wrong place of something that belongs to another, "allotrios." That, however, would still leave clear what really belongs to what. Metaphor for Aristotle is firmly grounded in literal language, in which the word belongs to the thing it names, as a wife belongs to her husband. Incest confounds those clear distinctions. What is displaced both belongs and does not belong to what it displaces, as Oedipus both belongs and does not belong in Jocasta's bed. This theme of displacement is picked up in the themes of crossing borders from Thebes into Corinth. What is in Thebes belongs to Thebes; what is in Corinth belongs to Corinth, just as a word belongs where it literally applies. Oedipus, however, belongs to both and to neither, just as he belongs and does not belong in Jocasta's bed. He thinks his parents are the king and queen of Corinth. Actually they are the king and queen of

Thebes. He thinks he is lawfully married to Jocasta in a properly exogamous union. Oedipus actually belongs, however, to the third place in the topographical configuration that organizes *Oedipus the King.* That place is Cithaeron, where Oedipus was abandoned as a baby. Cithaeron is trackless because it belongs neither to Thebes nor to Corinth. It is a kind of topographical nowhere, beyond all borders. It anticipates the nowhere to which Oedipus will belong when he is exiled by Creon and becomes a blind, homeless wanderer over the earth.[26] The problem of naming family relations when incest has occurred is a repetition of the alogical logic of metaphor. Metaphor is more incestuous than adulterous. Since no word belongs anywhere except by an initial performative fiat (as opposed to the natural belonging in which Aristotle believes), to use a word metaphorically is more like incest than like adultery. Since the word had no natural belonging where it was first applied, but was an arbitrary imposition, like giving Oedipus his name, "Oedipus," metaphor puts a word where it belongs and does not belong. It belongs as much in the new place as in the old, because it had no natural belonging in the old place. It does not belong in the new place either, because using it in the new place is against usage.

The paradoxes and aporias of metaphor are, it can be seen, like the paradoxes and aporias of incest. Incest is an allegory of metaphor. It might be better to say that incest reflects the human situation both in doing and in saying in relation to the gods. Metaphor breeches the law of noncontradiction just as incest does. This explains why Aristotle insists that the solving of a metaphoric riddle gives pleasure, just as do the anagnorisis and peripeteia of a tragedy. They give pleasure because both are moments when reason triumphs over the apparently unreasonable and everything becomes perspicuous again. Everything is put back in the place where it belongs. Aristotle recognizes in the *Rhetoric* what is initially obscure, irrational, and enigmatic about metaphor: "Clever riddles do, in general," he says, "furnish one with happy metaphors; for metaphor is a kind of enigma, so that obviously a metaphor taken from a good enigma will be good." The example is "A man I saw gluing bronze on a man with fire." The answer to the riddle is "cupping," the drawing of blood by a doctor for curative purposes.[27] Once you see that, the enigma is solved, and human reason is once again triumphant. That gives a burst of pleasure, the pleasure of seeing through. In the *Oedipus*, however, the enigma remains painfully unresolved, since it is entirely inscrutable why the gods, who are lawful and just, as the chorus says, should have done such an apparently unjust thing. In the same way, metaphor reveals and hides at once, by giving a sign. The play, both the plot and the language of which it is made, is made up of signs that both reveal and hide.

The double meaning of literal words throughout the play is perhaps the most sinister example of this supplementarity. Even if we try to speak with absolutely literal language, we are saying one thing and meaning another, as when Oedipus says, "I never saw him," while the audience knows the ironic double meaning of what he says. "Arthra," as I have said, is used both for ball joints of ankles and for eyeballs. To name one is unintentionally to hint at the other, whatever effort you make to limit the reference of the word. Since so many words are double or have supplemental meanings, we are metaphorical in spite of ourselves. In *Oedipus the King* an indefinite number of logoi govern a given word in place of one logos that would be the single source of meaning guaranteeing the single literal meaning of a word so that we could say what we mean and no more than what we mean.

The metaphoricity, or doubleness, of all language, even the most literal speech, is matched by the possibility of similar happenings in real life. Incest and parricide in family relations correspond to this duplicity in language. The result in the case of *Oedipus the King* is a striking example of the impossibility of straightforward, logical, clear storytelling. The unfathomable gods, the others that are wholly other, twist both language and events, as a black hole causes perturbations in whatever is nearby.

The rhetorical name for the duplicities of language and of represented events in *Oedipus* is "irony." What is meant by Sophoclean irony or by dramatic irony can be understood on the basis of what I have said so far. As the best recent work on irony has recognized, and as Friedrich Schlegel knew,[28] irony is never a benignly perspicuous way of saying one thing and meaning another. An ironic statement's truth cannot be identified by a simple process of decoding, putting a yes for a no, or a no for a yes. An example of such an apparently simple and decodable irony would be my saying "It's a beautiful day" as a way of saying "It's rainy, wet, and cold," when the person to whom I speak can plainly see it is raining. Even in such a case, however, I say something more and different from the truth that I ironically negate; I say two or more things at once. Ironic language is subject to not just a double logos (saying one thing and meaning another) but indefinitely multiple logoi, which in the *Oedipus* achieves anthropomorphizing catachresis in the contradictions of Apollo's epithets. He is called both Creator and Destroyer. Oedipus means to say one thing and instead says other things that he does not intend to say or know he is saying. He performs disastrous acts he does not intend to perform or know he is performing. The name given this kind of irony in *Oedipus the King* is "madness," just as Baudelaire was many centuries later to call irony a "folie lucide."[29] The word "madness" appears in the chorus's chant when Oedipus reappears after he has put out his eyes: "Oh man of pain, / what madness [mania] reached you? Which god [daimōn] from far off, / surpassing in range his longest spring, / struck hard against your god-abandoned fate?" (ll. 1299–1302). The word "madness" appropriately defines a play whose meaning is governed by alogical daimōns whose nature and motivations can in no way be rationalized or understood. Apollo is so double, so inscrutable, so much not just "other" but "others," that his darkness can never be made light, nor can any mortal bring speaking and knowing about him together. Apollo exceeds the grasp of Aristotelian rational thought. The chorus, moreover, does not dare to blame what has happened to Oedipus on Apollo, but says it was some "unknown god." To the question "which god has done this?" no certain answer is given by the play, though Oedipus continues to blame Apollo: "It was Apollo there, Apollo, friends, / who brought my sorrows, vile sorrows to their perfection, / these evils that were done to me" (ll. 1329–31). Oedipus may or may not be right. It is impossible to know. Apollo, moreover, as I have said, is perhaps no more than a name for the unsoundable mystery of those others who are wholly other.

Paul de Man's citation (three times) of Friedrich Schlegel's definition of irony as "eine permanente Parekbase" (a permanent parabasis)[30] is made in the context of his claim that irony differs fundamentally from other tropes. All other figures identify themselves by some verbal sign, "like" or "as" for simile, and so on. No linguistic signs, however, tell you whether a given piece of language is ironic or not. In addition, as de Man says, irony differs from other tropes in being capable of permeating an entire text, for example, Stendhal's *La Chartreuse de Parme* or Sophocles's *Oedipus the King*. Schlegel's striking phrase, "permanent parabasis," names the continuous suspension, all along the narrative line, of any single identifiable rational meaning. As de Man observes, however, "permanent parabasis" is an oxymoron, "violently paradoxical";[11] the formulation has its own ironic madness. Parabasis names the momentary suspension of the dramatic illusion in a play when some member of the cast comes forward and speaks in his own voice about the play, as in Prospero's speech at the end of Shakespeare's *The Tempest*. A parabasis makes sense only when it is measured against what it suspends, the primary level of mimesis that makes up the rest of the play. Parabasis is like a metaphor in this. Just as metaphor, in Aristotle's definition, depends on the indubitable existence of literal meanings, so a parabasis makes sense only if it suspends or interrupts a first level of representation that may be clearly identified. In *The Tempest* this is the story of Prospero, Miranda, Ferdinand, and the rest. A permanent parabasis, like a metaphor with no literal meaning, is irrational. It is a kind of madness insofar as it is a suspension that is not the suspension of anything that can be identified. It is, so to speak, a suspension in the void. "Suspension in the void" is an appropriate description of the radical indeterminacy of irony. If irony can pervade a whole text, then it is a diegetical, or narrative, element. It is an essential part of what de Man calls "the rhetoric of temporality." It may even be said that irony is the fundamental trope of diegesis in the novel as a genre, since all novels, even first-person ones, as I shall show later in this book, depend in one way or another on an ironic discrepancy between what the narrator knows and what the characters know. The "dramatic irony" that characterizes a Greek play such as *Oedipus the King* becomes in novels an ironic clash of perspectives introduced by the use of a narrator or narrators.

Might it not be the case, nevertheless, in spite of what de Man claims about the madness of irony,[12] that the "discovery" in *Oedipus*, and in tragedies generally, uncovers the true meaning of all the inadvertently ironic statements made prior to the anagnorisis? Can it not be said that when the scales fall from Oedipus's eyes, when his ignorance is reversed,[13] then his knowledge coincides with the gods' knowledge? He knows what they know? No, this is clearly not so, since the gods remain as opaque as ever. Oedipus's self-blinding is not only a displaced castration, self-punishment for his acts of incest, as Freud saw. It also expresses Oedipus's inability to see through what has happened to him. His blindness confirms a prior failure in perspicuity. Oedipus has represented just that power of clear thinking, clear speaking, and clear seeing that Aristotle uses as a model for a good tragedy. Since Aristotle so confidently prescribes it, he apparently has no doubt it can be attained. To show in Oedipus the fate of such a desire for clear seeing is Sophocles's proleptic way of saying, "What a purblind fool you are, Aristotle, to have such confidence in reason!"

The relation between *Oedipus the King* and the *Poetics* is a deeply ironic one. Aristotle has imported into his treatise a parasitical presence that radically undermines its premises. All Oedipus, the other characters, and the audience learn to see in *Oedipus the King* is that whatever we say or do may be subject to some entirely other logos than the one we intend, just as the events of a narrative may be put together in more than one way to make various different kinds of sense. Indeed Oedipus's sin, or "nefas," may be just that, putting two and two together, as Hölderlin, in his commentary on *Oedipus the King*, notoriously asserted.[14] The one eye too many that Oedipus perhaps has, in Hölderlin's view,[15] is, it may be, just his excessive power of reasoning. The deepest irony of *Oedipus the King*, especially when we think of it as a pervasive exemplary presence in Aristotle's *Poetics*, is the way Oedipus's confidence in that indefectible power of clearheaded reasoning Aristotle recommends leads Oedipus step by step to a confrontation with the madness of the irrational. It seems as though the irrational is hidden within the rational as a secret motivating force that will lead reasoning, if carried far enough, across the borders of reason into the no-man's-land of unreason and madness.

That Aristotelian or Oedipal putting of two and two together to make a perspicuous pattern is, however, just what a reader does, must do, from Aristotle to the latest reader today. We must read the text over and over trying to make sense of it. The text obliges us to make the best reading we can, to make the meaning of the text as clear as possible. This means that in order to understand Oedipus's crime we must ourselves commit a new version of it, perhaps. This desire to see through the play and to do better than Oedipus in figuring things out is particularly evident in several admirable modern essays on *Oedipus the King*, such as those by Sandor Goodheart and Cynthia Chase. These two critics in somewhat different ways follow Hölderlin in arguing that no firm evidence is given that Oedipus did commit the crime. Oedipus in his eagerness to get to the bottom of things may have misread the data. His self-condemnation is the result of a perhaps incorrect, and even impious, putting together of the data to make a coherent story. To put this another way, both these critics in different ways claim that Oedipus's crime exists only when he has organized what he has learned in a way that leads to his self-conviction. Such critics claim a rationality superior to Oedipus's, as no doubt I am also doing in my discussion of the play.[16] Making sense of a story is like putting two and two together to make four, but the same two and two may conceivably make five or minus four. Goodheart and Chase show how this is the case with *Oedipus the King*. To read is to respond to a demand for sense-making that any literary text, or indeed any text of any sort, makes on its readers. The text, however, whether of literature or of life, never unequivocally supports any reading we make of it. This means that reading is partly performative, rather than a purely cognitive act. The reader as a result must take responsibility for a reading that is always to some degree imposed on the text, just as Oedipus must and does take responsibility for the consequences of his reading of the data he is given. He keeps the promises and submits to the curses that have instigated that reading.

A recognition that the meaning of a whole line of narrative events may be changed by a change in a single one of them, especially by the last one, makes the chorus's celebrated concluding judgment in *Oedipus* more than just piously moralistic. To say the final episode in a life story can change the whole meaning of what came before also registers a deeply disquieting narratological insight. In Oedipus's case a sequence of events that seems clearly to show he is not only superbly intelligent but also "lucky," favored by the gods, is suddenly, in a single day, turned into the reverse, a recognition of his "madness" and "god-abandoned fate," as well as into a confrontation of the way it is impossible to understand why the gods have punished him in this way:

> People of Thebes, my country, see: here is that Oedipus—
> he who "knew" the famous riddle, and attained the highest power,
> whom all citizens admired, even envying his luck!
> See the billows of wild troubles which he has entered now!
> Here is the truth of each man's life: we must wait, see his end,
> scrutinize his dying day, and refuse to call him happy
> till he has crossed the border of his life without pain. (ll. 1524–30)

The language used by Oedipus and the others at the climax of the play is further evidence that the "discovery" in *Oedipus the King* does not bring about the perspicuity Aristotle sees as necessary in a good tragedy. At this moment the peripeteia, or change in fortune, should coincide with the discovery. Far from leading to rationally expressed clear seeing, the anagnorisis in *Oedipus the King* gives rise to the most violently irrational language in the play. Even, or rather especially, after the illumination of anagnorisis clear speaking is impossible. The end of this play is like a riddle, enigma, or metaphorical comparison that is not fully clarified when the riddle is solved or when the point of the comparison is seen. The most illogical, paradoxical, riddling formulations come at the end of the play. Here Oedipus and the other characters must find ways to say what ought not be said. The chorus speaks of "a marriage, not a marriage / where the begetter is the begot as well" (ll. 1214–15). The second messenger speaks of Oedipus "asking for his spear / and for his wife—no wife: where he might find / the double mother-field, his and his children's" (ll. 1255–57). Oedipus shouts: "O marriages! Marriages! / You gave us life and when you had planted us / you sent the same seed up, and then revealed / fathers, brothers, sons, and kinsman's blood, / and brides, and wives, and mothers, all the most / atrocious things that happen to mankind! / One should not name what never should have been" (ll. 1403–9).

Oedipus's suffering at the end of the play and the impossibility of naming it and thereby understanding it justify Hölderlin's assertion, just after he says King Oedipus has an eye too many perhaps: "The sufferings of this man, they seem indescribable, unspeakable, inexpressible."[17] Earlier the second messenger reports what Oedipus said just after he blinded himself: "He shouts that someone slide the bolts and show / to all the Cadmeians the patricide, / his mother's—O I can't say it, it's unholy—/ so he can cast himself out of the land, / not stay and curse his house by his own curse" (ll. 1287–91). Oedipus's formulations echo the dark prophecies of the riddle Tiresias propounds at the end of his encounter with Oedipus much earlier in the play. Hölderlin called this encounter the "caesura" of the play, the pause that breaks the rhythm of its forward-moving action in a suspended moment that looks before and after (for example, in echoing the Sphinx's riddle as well as prophesying Oedipus's end) and that holds the end apart from the beginning.[18] Tiresias pronounces a series of illogicalities: "A seeming stranger, he shall be shown to be / a Theban born, though he'll take no delight / in that solution. Blind, who once could see, / a beggar who was rich, through foreign lands / he'll go and point before him with a stick. / To his belovéd children, he'll be shown / a father who is also brother; to the one / who bore him, son and husband; to his father / his seed-fellow and killer. Go in / and think this out . . ." (ll. 451–61). Tiresias's ironical point in saying "Go in and think this out" is to indicate that Oedipus's kind of "gnōmē," or thinking out, will not work here. These events defy logical reasoning, though they have nevertheless happened. This means that the solution to the riddle has to be expressed in the same way as the riddle itself, that is, in more riddling language. The chief example of this is the violently irrational language by which Oedipus expresses his climactic insight. The end of the *Oedipus* does not function as a denouement untangling everything by giving the "answer" to Tiresias's riddle. The play is like an enigma that remains enigmatic. What has happened cannot be spoken of without defying the law of reason, the law of noncontradiction, as a metaphor does. To be son and father at once is to be an embodied metaphor, but to see this gives no pleasure as Aristotle promises solving a riddle or seeing the point of a metaphorical comparison will do.

Unlike Goodheart and Chase, I think we are meant to believe Oedipus did really kill Laius, and he obviously did marry Jocasta. He really was an example of those words the second messenger at the end of the play says it is impious to say, "his mother's . . . ." Nevertheless, he did not intend to do it or know that he was doing it at the time, so in a sense he did not do it—another irrational enigma. Goodheart, Chase, and Hölderlin, however, in different ways recognize that events in the past have power in the present only through speech acts in the present, acts of bearing witness that are performative rather than cognitive. As performatives they are a way of doing things with words for which the doer must accept responsibility, as Oedipus does accept responsibility for the revelation his desire to know has brought about.

Another way to put this is to say that the meaning of patricide and incest are social and linguistic. Paternity is, as Joyce's Stephen Dedalus said, a mystical estate. It depends on faith. Incest depends on kinship terms and does not exist without them. Animals cannot commit incest. Greek law and custom, as I have said, blamed someone as much for a criminal or unholy act done unintentionally as for one done deliberately. The hand or other body part that did it is guilty, polluted. Nevertheless, the play turns on a distinction between committing a crime and knowing that you commit it.

Oedipus does have an Oedipus complex. Since an Oedipus complex is like an ideological aberration, its efficacy depends on ignorance. Oedipus's crime depends on language in two ways. Without kinship names and the whole cultural system of taboos, prohibitions, and laws the crime could not exist. It also could not exist without Oedipus's linguistic activity of putting the data together and making a story of them. This activity is analogous to what Sophocles did in writing the play or to what we do in reading it. In this sense, the cause for what happens to Oedipus is not the gods as others, but Oedipus himself as speaker. Jocasta is right. If he had left things alone, all would have been well, or at least would have appeared to be well. This he cannot do. His speech responds to an implacable demand made on him by the "others," as we also respond in trying to make sense of the play when we read it. Nevertheless, the crime in a sense did not exist until he made a story of the data. His language, after the fact, "nachträglich," in Freud's terminology, is the cause of the cause.

This leads to a final question. Language always contains evidence of its own rhetorical activity. It thereby undoes, deactivates, or neutralizes that activity. Why is it that language always leaves exposed traces of its share in the crime? Why cannot it seamlessly cover its tracks? Why can its complicity in the tragic crime always be tracked down? No clear answer to that question can be given. The penchant of storytelling to undermine clarity by irony, however, may at least give a name to our ignorance.

In a crucial passage in *Allegories of Reading*, Paul de Man says, "The paradigm of all texts consists of a figure (or a system of figures) and its deconstruction." He goes on to say that this model "engenders, in its turn, a supplementary figural superposition which narrates the unreadability of the prior narration." These supplementary figural superpositions, de Man says, "we can call . . . *allegories.*"[19] That structure is somewhat like the Aristotelian one in that it depends on a double anagnorisis: first comes the deconstruction of the metaphor, that is, a discovery of what de Man calls "the failure to denominate," then the allegory of that narration's unreadability. In both cases a movement from ignorance to knowledge is made, even though the second knowledge is of that impossibility to know that de Man calls unreadability. De Man keeps scrupulously and prudently within linguistic terminology, though in later essays and even intermittently in *Allegories of Reading* he gives the name "materiality" to the other of language that also inhabits language, just as, for him, it constitutes a kind of rock bottom to history. "Materiality" is the place where language, especially performative language, and history converge. Following Sophocles, I have been less prudent and in a performative "calling" have assigned the epithets, "the complete otherness of the others," the "unknowability of the gods," and "black holes," phrases de Man would probably have found dangerously misleading, to what is the other of language, in both senses of the genitive. Nevertheless the de Manian sequence would seem to correspond, with appropriate metaphorical displacements, to the reading of *Oedipus the King* that I have proposed. First Oedipus discovers that the metaphorical names he and the others have given to things are inadequate. Then he discovers that this story of the movement from ignorance to knowledge is unreadable. First he thinks he knows all the horrible truth in a wholesale deconstruction of his former certainties. Then he knows that he does not know. At both levels, however, knowledge is attained.

The term "irony," however, is conspicuously absent in the passage I have cited as a key term from de Man's account of the way all texts are "allegories of reading." Irony adds another element, a kind of destabilizing wild card. Only in the final sentences of *Allegories of Reading* does de Man bring irony in, even though *Allegories of Reading* considerably postdates his eloquent treatment of irony in "The Rhetoric of Temporality." Irony is brought in at the last moment in *Allegories of Reading* as a kind of "tierce de Picardie" in a changed key recognizing the way irony undoes the neat pattern of "the deconstructive allegory of all tropological cognitions." To change the figure, the last sentences of *Allegories of Reading* are a kind of loose thread that will unravel the book's whole fabric if we pull on it hard enough—not all that hard, in fact. Irony is, as de Man says, "the systematic undoing . . . of understanding," including understanding of our lack of understanding. Irony, says de Man, in "a slight extension of Friedrich Schlegel's formulation," is "the permanent parabasis of an allegory (of figure)" (*AR*, 300–301). If irony is permanent parabasis, a suspension of knowledge all along the narrative line, it disables that structure of deconstruction followed by the allegory of its unreadability. Irony keeps us from knowing anything. It even keeps us from knowing for sure that we do not know. At first we think we know our pattern of achieved knowledge is unreadable because we can "see" that the deconstruction repeated the error it would denounce. But irony is the radical and permanent suspension of knowledge. We cannot, for example, know whether it is "just language" that makes *Oedipus the King* irrational or whether some demonic powers make the language of the play not perspicuous. All that can be known is that we cannot tell whether we can know or not. We also cannot know for sure that we will never know, nor whether or not we may already have stumbled on the correct knowledge without yet knowing it or ever being able to know it. Nevertheless, we can testify that all we say or do is a response to a demand made on us by a dark, plural otherness that cannot ever be faced or named as such. That demand imposes on us, as on Oedipus, an implacable but unfulfillable obligation to get definite knowledge and to act in a way that is justified by that knowledge. Our submission to the irrational, one name for which is "irony," repeats Oedipus's submission. That analogy is a way of saying that more than linguistic play is at stake when we read *Oedipus the King*.

I claim to have shown in two examples how unexpectedly strange and threatening to received ideas canonical texts in our tradition turn out to be. Aristotle has by no means completely subdued the ghostly irrational presence of *Oedipus the King* in the *Poetics*. One might say that unlaid ghost makes the *Poetics* inadvertently and savagely ironic, since the play shows the disastrous consequences of following the desire for rational knowledge that Aristotle recommends and exemplifies. *Oedipus the King* itself, moreover, so powerfully generates an unpurged, inexplicable, and inexpressible terror that one might hesitate to recommend it lightly as required reading.[40] In what follows I shall broaden my exploration of ends, beginnings, middles, and narrative ironies generated by complexities of storytelling. My examples come primarily, but not exclusively, from prose fiction during the post-Renaissance period, the era Henry Sussman calls "the broader modernity."[41] After a preliminary discussion of the way narratives are often figured as lines, I shall analyze first ends, then beginnings, and then, at much greater length, the various complexities of middles.

TWO

NARRATIVE LINES

The little story is all there. I can touch it from point to point; for the thread, as I call it, is a row of coloured beads on a string. None of the beads are missing—at least I think they're not: that's exactly what I shall amuse myself with finding out.

—Henry James, "Glasses" (1896)

As my discussion of Aristotle and *Oedipus the King* has shown, the logocentric presuppositions of the dominant Western tradition mean that narrative is, for that tradition, characteristically figured as a line of events causally connected. These have a beginning, middle, and end, like the beads on a string, to borrow Henry James's figure.[1] This chapter will investigate further the implications of that figure. The image, trope, or concept of the line threads its way through all the traditional Western terms for story-writing or story-telling. It is the dominant figure in this particular carpet. These terms differ from the words for the physical act, materials, or result of writing, which I have examined elsewhere.[2] The former are obviously figurative, or at any rate figurative in a different sense, while letters do literally form lines across a printed page. The sequence of events in a novel, whether it is thought of as the "real" events narrated or as the narration itself, is not a literal line. It is, for one thing, temporal rather than spatial. Writing, on the other hand, is "literally," in obvious ways, linear and spatial, even though writing is some use of a physical line so that it makes a figure that stands for something else and is open to repetition. A letter, word, or hieroglyph is already repetitive. It is already something other than itself, beside itself, since it refers to something other than itself. No sign, moreover, can exist without repetition, without being used more than once. In that repetition the second version becomes the origin of the sign-function of the first. The significance of both is generated in the space between, by what Jacques Derrida, notoriously, calls "différance." To speak of a "narrative line," then, is to transfer a process already figurative to new figurative uses, according to a regular displacing of "literal" referentiality that governs the terminology of narrative forms.

Narration both as a word and as an act (but my question here is what kind of act a story may be) involves lines and repetition. The word "narration" is from Latin "narrare," to narrate, from "gnarus," knowing, expert, from the root "gno-." The same root lies behind "anagnorisis," Aristotle's word for the "discovery" in a tragedy. The word "narration," meaning "to give an oral or written account of something, to tell (a story)," is a member of a family of words that includes "can," "con," "cunning," "ken," "kenning," "couth," "notion," "cognition," "gnosis," "diagnosis," "gnomon" (meaning pointer on a sundial, judge, indicator, a geometrical diagram made by removing from the corner of a parallelogram another smaller parallelogram similar in shape), physiognomy (meaning the art of judging character from facial features, or the facial features themselves, the "phiz"), "norm," "normal" (from Latin "norma," measuring stick, ruler). Within the concept of narration are obscurely inscribed the ideas of judging and interpretation, of temporality in its complexity, and of repetition. To narrate is to retrace a line of events that has already occurred, or that is spoken fictively as having already occurred. At the same time this sequence is interpreted, as a gnomon on a sundial tells the time, reads the sun, or rather reads the moving shadow cast by its own interruption of sunlight. A (g)narration is a gnosis, a retelling by one who knows. It is also a diagnosis, an act of identifying or interpreting by a discriminating reading of signs. A narrator is a kenner, but he or she often speaks or writes in riddles, kennings that must be unriddled in their turn by the reader even when they seem most perspicuously to point to what they tell of and name. This unriddling is another narration, that story all readers tell themselves as they read, for example, my own narration here of the aporias of narration.

Those aporias arise partly from the equivocations involved in thinking of a narration as in one way or another ideally a line from which there may be one kind or another of digressive deviation from the straight and narrow, the shortest path between two points. The aporias also arise in part from the equivocation between thinking of the narrative line as the sequence of events narrated and at the same time thinking of it as the sequence of the words or units of the narration itself, the repetition of external events in language. Gérard Genette, following the usage of Christian Metz in work on cinema, has, along with other narratologists, reintroduced a Greek word for narration: "diēgesis," anglicized to "diegesis." The word is used by Aristotle in the *Rhetoric* to name a "statement," for example, a deposition by a witness before a court. "Diēgesis" is also used in a crucial passage in Book 3 of Plato's *Republic*, discussed below. The word has not survived in the English vocabulary, though its close relative, "exegesis," of course, has. Both words come from the Greek "hēgeisthai," "lead," with an earlier sense of "to track down," from the root "sag-," to seek out. To any narration one could apply Dryden's admirable phrase: "The chase had a beast in view." This is another way of reaffirming what Aristotle says about the need to interpret any "mimesis" from the perspective of its end, or "telos." From the root sag- are also derived "seek," "sake," "seize," "ransack," "presage," "sagacious," and "hegemony." The Greek "exēgeisthai" means "to show the way," "expound." An exegesis leads or draws the meaning out of the text. The di- of diegesis is from dia- and means "through." A diegesis retraces a track already made, follows it through from beginning to end and so makes a story of it. Every telling is already a retelling. Even the most straightforward narrative is a repetition. It claims to repeat a journey already made.

Gérard Genette's "Discours du récit" in *Figures III*[3] is the fullest and shrewdest description I know of the complexities in order, tempo, temporal structure, narrative tenses, voices, and so on that have developed in prose fiction. These complexities follow from the fact that every diegesis is secondary and presupposes in one way or another the absence of what it relates. This first doubling, as Genette shows, gives rise to theoretically limitless complexities of redoubling, retracking, or retracing. Genette is one of the best of what I once called "canny" critics.[4] He is nowhere more shrewd than in his application of a descriptive intelligence to the untangling of narrative complexities. He may therefore stand by synecdoche for the small army of narratologists who have continued to work in the same region of descriptive intelligence. Genette is admirably inventive in finding or inventing names for the complexities of narrative form: prolepsis, metalepsis, analepsis, ellipse, analipse, diegesis, metadiegesis, and so on. The barbarity of these terms makes it unlikely that they would be adopted universally and so freeze into a machinelike system. Their cumbersome complexity may be an irony implicit in Genette's invention of them. On the other hand, by naming features of narrative not often seen, they lead to a recognition of how complex an apparently simple novel or short story actually is. Genette's work, like narratology in general, is misleading only to the degree it suggests that this elaborate act of naming will untangle the complexity of the narrative line and bring all its strands out into the full light of the logical sun. Narratology—the word means the knowledge or science of narrative. This present book, in its demonstration that this knowledge is not possible, might be called a work of ananarratology. Genette is shrewd enough and persistent enough to follow his line of analysis to the point where it occasionally reaches the borders of the uncanny or irrational, though he tends to draw back from such frontiers. The impossibility of holding the complexities he has identified clearly in one's mind all at once is in itself an experience of the alogical. Nevertheless, the patient sobriety of Genette's tone, like that of most of his fellow narratologists, tends to hide that he is walking throughout on the borders of those irrationalities of the narrative line that I am attempting to identify here. Genette too is walking down a corridor that leads ultimately to the blank walls of a blind alley. An analysis of the dependence of all language about narration on the self-contradicting image of the line is a good way to go far enough to encounter these latent aporias of diegesis.

I shall try here to untangle the narrative line from all those other lines discussed in *Ariadne's Thread*. This means following the working of all that family of terms by which we habitually coach ourselves or are coached, by novels themselves and by their critics, to spatialize the time of storytelling and to think of it as in one way or another picturable as a graph or plot, a line going from A to B or from A to Z, from womb to tomb, from adolescent awakening to happy tying of the marriage knot, and so on. Here are some of those terms: "curve of the action," "rise to a climax," "dénouement," "resolution," "ficelle," "plot," "subplot," "loose thread," "broken or dropped thread," "figure in the carpet," "tying up the threads of the story," "break in the action," "line of argument," "story line," "turn of events," "digression," "interpolation," "detour," "frame story," "spin a yarn," "come full circle," and so on. The list could be made more or less interminable. In whatever way one uses the image of the line to think about narrative sequence in a given novel, the image itself, instrument of the thinking, contains latent contradictions that lead to a specific kind of impasse that I shall identify.

This impasse in thinking may be variously encountered: in problems of closure; in problems of beginning; in problems setting curved, knotted, or broken line against straight; in problems involving the doubling of the narrative line, not only the doublings of multiple plot, but also doublings within a single story line, doublings of narrative voice by means of multiple narrators, citations, letters, diaries, and so on; in problems involving the means of producing the line and its relation to what it copies, its referent. These complexities will be investigated in more detail in subsequent chapters. Even the straightest narrative line, however, the most straightforward diegesis, is, as I have said, already the doubling of a preexistent or supposedly preexistent line of real historical events.

In all these areas the narrative line is traditionally thought of as ordered according to the unifying concepts of beginning, middle, end, and underlying ground, reason, or truth. Aristotle in the *Poetics* laid these down once and for all for our tradition. They are just the concepts encompassed by the Greek word "logos." The doubling of the narrative line, in any of the ways listed above (and these doublings, as I shall show, always occur), subverts the order of the logos and brings the eccentric, the a-centric, the irrational or the arational, the dialogical or the alogical into the centered, the logical, the monological. With that doubling, as my examples will demonstrate, comes death, an experience of the uncanny, a vanishing of the generative source, and a putting in question of the authority of the author. For male authors or narrators this means emasculation or the fear of emasculation, according to the Freudian law that says a doubling or division means an absence, an attempt to ward off a loss that creates the loss.[5] Such doubling is also Biblical. The exploration of line terminology for narration might take as text a strange passage in 2 Samuel 8:2: "And he smote Moab, and measured them with a line, casting them down to the ground; even with two lines measured he to put to death, and with one full line to keep alive." According to this strange apportionment life and death are measured with the line as a norm. In this Procrustean bed of measurement, survival lies in the single line. Death follows if one goes beyond that to two lines. It seems as if there is a fatality in the doubling of the line. The life line doubled becomes a death line. The narrative line in storytelling, however, is always already doubled. It is measured by death, or it is a measurement to put to death. This is a strange economy without balance, in which twice one, twice the finite life line, is the blank unreason of death, simultaneously desired and feared. Just as the multiplication of the penis or its symbols in the dreamwork expresses the fear of and secret wish for its loss, so in Freud's *Beyond the Pleasure Principle* the fear of castration, desire of castration, is a mask for the death wish, the end of the line. The death wish is desire for the limitless pleasure of the dissolution of the self.

THREE

THE END OF
THE LINE

I shall begin, then, with endings. It is no accident that endings in narrative are difficult to pin down, whether "theoretically," or for a given novel, or for the novels of a given period. The impasses of closure in narrative are present already in the terms most commonly used to describe endings. An example is the tradition, going back to Aristotle's *Poetics*, that uses the image of the knotted and unknotted thread to describe the narrative line.[1] "Every tragedy falls into two parts,— Complication (dēsis) and Unravelling or 'Dénouement' (lysis). Incidents extraneous to the action are frequently combined with a portion of the action proper, to form the Complication; the rest is the Unravelling" (65; 18:1455b).[2] Just where does the complication, folding up, tangling, or tying together end and the untying start? Aristotle suggests the possibility of a narrative that would be all unraveling, or dénouement. In such a narrative the "turning-point" from tying to untying would be the beginning of the narrative proper and all the complication would lie prior to the action as its presupposition:

By the Complication I mean all that extends from the beginning of the action to the part which marks the turning-point to good or bad fortune. The Unravelling is that which extends from the beginning of the change to the end. Thus, in the *Lynceus* of Theodectes, the Complication consists of the incidents presupposed in the drama, the seizure of the child, and then again . . . [the Unravelling] extends from the accusation of murder to the end. (65; 18:1455b)

By a strange but always possible paradox, the point where the ending starts here becomes displaced to the beginning. The entire drama is ending, so its beginning is the start of the ending. The beginning is a beginning/ending that necessarily presupposes something prior to itself in order to begin ending. The moment of reversal, when tying becomes untying, can in this model never be shown as such or identified as such because the two motions are inextricably the same, as in the double antithetical word "articulate," which means simultaneously putting together and taking apart. The tying/untying, the turning point, is not an identifiable point but is diffused throughout the whole action. Any point the spectator focuses on is a turning that both ties and unties. This is another way of saying that no narrative can show either its beginning or its ending. It always begins and ends still "in medias res," presupposing as a future anterior some part of itself outside itself.

These aporias of closure underlie disagreements among critics about whether a given novel or the novels of a given period exhibit closure or are "open-ended." Problems of closure are present also in the way a given apparently closed novel can, it seems, always be reopened. Virginia Woolf's seemingly definitive treatment of the Dalloways in *The Voyage Out* is reopened much later to produce *Mrs. Dalloway*. Anthony Trollope, a novelist of closure if there ever was one, nevertheless in the Barset series and in the parliamentary series reintroduces in later novels characters whose lives have seemingly been entirely closed in earlier novels. The apparently triumphant closure of Elizabeth Gaskell's *Cranford* has its unity quietly broken ten years later by the publication of a continuation story, "The Cage at Cranford." "The Cage at Cranford" is, it turns out, a story about the impossibility of closure or "caging." I shall present a reading of *Cranford* and its sequel at the end of this book

"Our tale is now done," says Trollope at the beginning of the last chapter of *The Warden*, "and it only remains to us to collect the scattered threads of our little story, and to tie them into a seemly knot."[3] For Trollope, the ending of a story is its tying up. For Aristotle, on the contrary, the ending of a narrative or dramatic action is its untying, its dénouement. The vogue in the seventeenth century of that story of Byzantine complexity, Heliodorus's *Aetheopica*, came from the pleasure of an untying. This ur-novel provides the sudden pleasure felt by one caught in a labyrinthine entanglement of mistaken identity and inextricably knotted narrative lines when suddenly he or she escapes into the full light of day. This pleasure is like the explosive release when one sees the point of a joke, or like the pleasure of solving a riddle or seeing the point of a metaphor, or like the pleasure in the final "éclaircissement," the "he done it," at the end of a detective story. The contrary pleasure, however, no less intense, is that of closure, the neat folding together of elaborate narrative materials in a single resolution leaving every story line tucked in.

Solve, dissolve, resolve—why this blank contradiction in dominant images of closure in narrative? Why cannot we describe unambiguously the moment of coming full circle in a final revelation at an end point toward which the whole story has been moving? Such a point would fix the characters in a new relation, their final destiny. Such a tying/untying would provide the sense of an ending[4] casting retrospective unity over the whole. Such endings are most commonly marriage or death. An ending that truly ends must however, so it seems, simultaneously be thought of as a tying up, a neat knot that leaves no loose threads hanging out, no characters unaccounted for, and at the same time as an untying, as the combing out of the tangled narrative threads so that they may be clearly seen, shining side by side, all mystery or complexity revealed.

The difficulty in deciding whether to call a given ending an untying or a tying up arises from the way it is impossible ever to tell whether a given narrative is complete. If the ending is thought of as a tying up in a careful knot, this knot could always be untied again by the narrator or by further events, disentangled or explicated again. If the ending is thought of as an unravelling, a straightening of threads, this act clearly leaves not one loose thread but a multitude, side by side, all capable of being knotted once more. If marriage, the tying of the marriage bond, is a cessation of the story, it is also the beginning of another cycle in the endless sequence of generations. "Every limit is a beginning as well as an ending," says George Eliot at the end of *Middlemarch*.[5] Death, seemingly a definitive end, always leaves behind some musing or bewildered survivor, some reader of the inscription on a gravestone, as in Wordsworth's "The Boy of Winander," or in Emily Brontë's *Wuthering Heights*, or in that mute contemplation of a distant black flag, sign of Tess's execution, by Angel Clare and 'Liza-Lu at the end of Hardy's *Tess of the d'Urbervilles*. Death is the most enigmatic, the most open-ended ending of all. It is the darkest dramatization of the way an ending, in the sense of a clarifying "telos," law, or ground of the whole story, always recedes, escapes, vanishes. The best one can have, as writer or reader, is what Frank Kermode, in his admirable phrase, calls "the *sense* of an ending" (my italics). Having no more than a sense of ending may be to be beguiled by an illusory finality.

Knotted, unknotted—there is no way to decide between these two images. The novelist and the critic of novels needs them both and needs them both at once, in a constant movement in place between two kinds of ending. Trollope, for example, goes on after his neat image of tying up in *The Warden* to consider opening up his story once more in a figure of speculative closure left free to the reader's imagination: "we have not to deal with many personages, or with stirring events, and were it not for the custom of the thing, we might leave it to the imagination of all concerned to conceive how affairs at Barchester arranged themselves" (259). Trollope both ties his novel neatly up and opens it to the imagination of the reader. He conspicuously also leaves it open to his own imagination, since the whole sequence of Barset novels follows over the years through a constant reopening of the apparently closed. The seeming closure of Eleanor Harding's story in her marriage to John Bold in *The Warden*, for example, is reopened again by the death of Bold and her courtship by Arabin in *Barchester Towers*. Septimus Harding's story seems neatly concluded at the end of *The Warden*, but it does not really end until many years later in another novel, *The Last Chronicle of Barset*.

All this problem of endings is neatly tied up within another double antithetical word: ravel. The word ravel already means unravel, as in Shakespeare's "Sleep that knits up the raveled sleave of care."[6] The "un" adds nothing not already there. To ravel up a story or to unravel it comes to the same thing. The word cannot be given a closure no matter how extravagant the series of doubling negatives attempting to make the initial opening into closure: ravel, unravel, un-unravel, un-un-unravel, and so on. In a similar way, no novel can be unequivocally finished, or for that matter unequivocally unfinished. Attempts to characterize the fiction of a given period by its commitment to closure or to open-endedness are blocked from the beginning by the impossibility of ever demonstrating for certain whether a given narrative is closed or open. Analysis of endings always leads, if carried far enough, to the paralysis of this inability to be certain whether a story has reached definitive closure.

FOUR

BEGINNINGS

So much for endings. I now turn to beginnings. If a storyteller cannot stop a story except by just stopping, if "they lived happily ever after" is always the hasty covering over of some gap or loose end, a narrator can also not begin except arbitrarily, by just beginning. Edward Said, in his admirable *Beginnings*, and Jacques Derrida, in "Hors livre,"[1] the introduction to *La Dissémination*, have identified the problematics of getting started. Though the problem is conceptual or theoretical, it also has to do with the inherence of figurative language in conceptual formulations. In addition it has to do with practical difficulties that arise in any act of storytelling. The examples of Hegel's prefaces and introductions, prefaces to introductions, introductions to introductions, discussed by Derrida in "Hors livre," manifest the problem in philosophical discourse, as does Paul Valéry's "Introduction à la méthode de Léonard de Vinci,"[2] though Valéry's subject is as much the problem of narrative coherence as the problem of beginning. The paradox of beginning is that one must have something solidly present and preexistent, some generative source or authority, on which the development of a new story may be based. That antecedent foundation needs in its turn some prior foundation, in an infinite regress. The novelist may be forced to go further and further back down the narrative line in an ever unsuccessful attempt to find something outside the line to which it may be firmly tied. Moreover, as Anthony Trollope observes at the opening of *Is He Popenjoy?* the traditional expedient of beginning in medias res only postpones the necessity of some recapitulation:

I would that it were possible so to tell a story that a reader should beforehand know every detail of it up to a certain point, or be so circumstanced that he might be supposed to know. . . . The plan of jumping at once into the middle has been often tried, and sometimes seductively enough for a chapter or two; but the writer still has to hark back, and to begin again from the beginning— not always very comfortably after the abnormal brightness of his few opening pages; and the reader who is then involved in some ancient family history, or long local explanation, feels himself to have been defrauded. It is as though one were asked to eat boiled mutton after woodcocks, caviare, or macaroni cheese. I hold that it is better to have the boiled mutton first if boiled mutton there must be. . . . A hundred and twenty little incidents must be dribbled into the reader's intelligence, many of them, let me hope, in such a manner that he shall himself be insensible to the process.[1]

Trollope's contradictions here reveal his uneasiness about beginnings. The reader must be given a virtual or pseudomemory, information at once boldly present, like boiled mutton at the beginning of a meal, and at the same time surreptitiously introduced, covertly dribbled in, like an intravenous feeding, so that the reader will feel always to have had the information, prior to beginning to read the book. The beginning is both inside and outside the narrative at once. If the novelist begins abruptly, with one character throwing another out the window, sooner or later he will have to explain who threw whom, and why. This explanation, as Sterne well knew, in principle involves an infinite regress forbidding a writer ever to establish, except virtually and by a fictive "as it were," the firm antecedent foundation necessary to get the story going. Narratives are in one way or another expedients for covering over this impossibility, which implies the impossibility of getting started. The beginning must be both inside the story as part of its narrative and at the same time outside it, prior to it as its generative base, the father of the line of filiation, or the mothering spider from whose belly the thread is spun. If inside, then the beginning is no base, no origin. It is an arbitrary starting, like beginning a bridge in midspan, with no anchor to the shore. If outside, then the beginning is not really part of the narrative line. It is disconnected from that line, like a tower piling or abutment of no help in building this particular bridge. Any beginning in narrative cunningly covers a gap, an absence at the origin. This gap is both outside the textual line as its lack of foundation and visible within it as loose threads of incomplete information ravelling out toward the unpresented past.

No one has more brilliantly expressed the impossibility of beginning or the way each beginning occurs over the chasm of its impossibility than Søren Kierkegaard, philosophical novelist or novelistic philosopher. Kierkegaard, or rather "A," his ironic alter ego, in the "ecstatic lecture" near the beginning of *Either/Or*, comically dismantles the certainties of Hegel's dialectic by showing that it depends on narrative terms or concepts like "aufgeheben," sublated. "A" establishes the mock eternity of an aporia before the division into opposites that generates dialectical or narrative movement. This paralysis makes nonsense of the movement generating oppositions. It forbids both philosophy and narrative from ever starting or going anywhere. This self-perpetuating paralyzed poise also forbids them, paradoxically, from ever stopping once they have, in defiance of logic, started. One could substitute the word "narrative" wherever the word "philosophy" appears in Kierkegaard's "lecture." The lecture can be taken as an expression of the impossibility of both storytelling and philosophizing. This does not prevent people either from doing philosophy or from telling stories. Far from it.

Thus [says "A," the "either" of *Either/Or*], when I say that I do not proceed from my principle, this must not be understood in opposition to a proceeding forth from it, but is rather a negative expression for the principle itself, through which it is apprehended in equal opposition to a proceeding or a non-proceeding from it. I do not proceed from my principle; for if I did, I would regret it, and if I did not, I would also regret that. If it seems, therefore, to one or another of my respected hearers that there is anything in what I say, it only proves that he has no talent for philosophy [read: narrative]; if my argument seems to have any forward movement, this also proves the same. But for those who can follow me, although I do not make any progress, I shall now unfold the eternal truth, by virtue of which this philosophy [narrative] remains within itself, and admits of no higher philosophy [narrative]. For if I proceeded from my principle, I should find it impossible to stop; for if I stopped, I should regret it, and if I did not stop, I should also regret that, and so forth. But since I never start, so can I never stop; my eternal departure is identical with my eternal cessation.

Experience has shown that it is by no means difficult for philosophy [narrative] to begin. Far from it. It begins with nothing, and consequently can always begin. But the difficulty, both for philosophy [narration] and for philosophers [narrators], is to stop. This difficulty is obviated in my philosophy; for if anyone believes that when I stop now, I really stop, he proves himself lacking in the speculative insight. For I do not stop now, I stopped at the time when I began.[4]

Kierkegaard (or "A") had begun this admirably comic demonstration that it is impossible to generate a continuous philosophical line with an example of beginning's aporia taken from that most central of fictional themes, courtship, marriage, and the line of generations: "If you marry, you will regret it; if you do not marry, you will also regret it; if you marry or do not marry, you will regret both."[5] If Kierkegaard (or "A") destroys dialectical philosophy by bringing into the open the narrative presuppositions of the figures "buried" in its concepts, one can turn the relation back the other way and dismantle narrative or show how it dismantles itself by observing how any story is a narrative version of a dialectical movement. Such a movement, as Kierkegaard demonstrates, cannot and does not move or go out from its beginning. Novels, like dialectic, depend on the cycle of generations, filiation from father to son, or from mother to son or daughter.[6] This mimes a movement of recollection that gathers the past to move into the future to make a retrospective prospect or future anterior. If philosophy is disguised storytelling, the organizing principles of narrative are philosophical, dialectical, "metaphysical" through and through. At the same time, Kierkegaard insists on the impossibility of escaping "regret," whatever you do, whether in philosophy, in storytelling, or in courtship. Kierkegaard knew whereof he spoke when he described the regrets of courtship, though he never found out from experience whether he would or would not regret marriage, only that he regretted not marrying. "Regret" here names the sharp anguish of the inability to go back and start again or not start, along with the pain of knowing that it would not matter, since starting and not starting come to the same thing. Both are matters of eternal regret, a sharp affect, not mere theoretical impasses. Whatever you do or think, you will regret both what you did and what you refrained from doing.

FIVE

MIDDLES

I turn now from endings and beginnings to middles. If Edward Said has shown what is problematic about beginnings and Frank Kermode has settled not for endings but for senses of ending, the coherence of the part in between is even more of a problem. A whole sequence of my chapters will now take up different aspects of all that part of narratives that comes after the beginning and before the end. I begin with general questions about the in-between in narratives. The middle may also be put, for the moment, like beginnings, under the friendly, but by no means entirely rainproof, umbrella of Søren Kierkegaard. "My life," says "A" in *Either/Or*, "is absolutely meaningless. When I consider the different periods into which it falls it seems like the word 'Schnur' in the dictionary, which means in the first place a string, in the second, a daughter-in-law. The only thing lacking is that the word 'Schnur' should mean in the third place a camel, in the fourth, a dust-brush."[1]

Meaning, whether in a narrative, in a life, or in a word, lies in continuity, in a homogeneous sequence making an unbroken line. The human need for continuity is so strong that a person will find some principle of order in any random sequence. One might note, for example, that a daughter-in-law is indeed a string, almost in the Jamesian sense of "ficelle." A daughter-in-law is an indispensable, though somewhat extraneous, means of maintaining the continuity of a lineage from father to son to grandson. No doubt one could, given a little ingenuity, assimilate the camel and the dust brush to the line of that "Schnur." A camel is certainly another way to get from here to there. Though it would be a little hard to imagine a dust brush made of camel hair, thereby making the dust brush a further displacement of the camel, it is certainly the case that daughters-in-law are supposed to be adept at wielding dust brushes to keep spic and span the house where the string of filiation is extended. Any random group can, with a little ingenuity, be made into an orderly line.

Part of the difficulty of making the series of elements in a narrative between beginning and end continuous is not the possibility of fragmentation or irrelevance, but the difficulty of establishing a principle by which one could be sure something is extraneous. "There should be no episodes in a novel," said Anthony Trollope, with a touching confidence that he could distinguish an "episode" from the straight and narrow path getting on with the main story.² Though Trollope is remarkably focused in his storytelling, his novels' masterly use of multiple plots means that from the perspective of any single plot they are full of "episodes" whose relevance to the given plot is primarily that of thematic relevance or echo. How can one be certain a given element is an inassimilable episode, or what might be called an "irrelevant detail," since, as Roland Barthes shows, with a little effort the most apparently irrelevant detail can be shown to be relevant?³ Whether one thinks of a novel from the point of view of the writer writing it or of the reader reading it, or as the mirroring of an objective series of historical events, or as the following of the line of a life, or as the making up "out of whole cloth" of a coherent story, one is likely to use models of causal chaining or of organic growth to describe the desirable hanging together of a narrative. So powerful is this assumption of linear continuity that it may easily be imputed to what from another point of view will appear as a random collocation of contiguous fragments.

Plot, double plot, subplot, narrative strands, graph or curve of the action, chain of events—these are versions of a compelling image. Such terms figure a story as a line that might be projected, plotted, graphed, or diagrammed as a continuous spatial curve or as a zigzag, in any case as some form of visible figure. This figure has a long history in Western thought, a sequence forming an extended line of lines, in genealogical filiation. The "origins" of this line of lines may be found in the double source of our culture: in the Greeks and in Judaic culture. The Psalmist's "The lines are fallen unto me in pleasant places; yea, I have a goodly heritage" (Psalms 16:6) is often echoed and has become almost a cliché. An example is the way Anthony Trollope's Josiah Crawley, in *The Last Chronicle of Barset*, reverses the figure for his own case when he has been unjustly accused of theft. "My God," he says, "what have I done against thee, that my lines should be cast in such terrible places?"[4] Greek lines include the twice-bifurcated dialectical line of the *Republic*, and the line image implicit in the Greek word for historical narrative, "diegesis." As I said earlier, the word implies that a history or a story is the leading out of events in a line or their tracking down later. To skip over such intervening lines as Dante's spiral track in the *Purgatorio* and Donne's compass lines, a modern sequence, closely adjacent to the genres of prose fiction, threads its way through the development of nineteenth- and twentieth-century literature. This more recent series goes from the Hogarthian lines of beauty and grace through the splendid parodies of these in Sterne, on to Edmund Burke, then to the aesthetic arabesques of Friedrich Schlegel and the spirals of Goethe, to the citation of Corporal Trim's airy flourish by Balzac as the epigraph to *La Peau de chagrin*, to Baudelaire's thyrsus, to Henry James's figure in the carpet, and to all those lines—genealogical, topographical, and physiognomic—in Thomas Hardy's work. In America a splendid branch line goes from Poe's arabesques to Emerson's "Circles" ("The natural world may be conceived of as a system of concentric circles"), through the shoreline in Whitman's "Out of the Cradle Endlessly Rocking" and elsewhere in his poetry, to Stevens's defiance of Emerson and Whitman in "The Stars at Tallapoosa" ("The lines are straight and swift between the stars. . . . / The mind herein attains simplicity" [ll. 1, 5]), to Ammons's admirably exuberant "Lines," where the line proliferates madly in its curvings, recurvings, and crossings: "lines exploring, intersecting, paralleling, twisting, / noding: deranging, clustering" (ll. 41–42).[5]

Laurence Sterne and Friedrich Schlegel will document an exploration of what is put on the line by this figure. Both authors think of writing or reading a novel, or a story's course, or a life's line, as the energetic production of a filament generated by the balance of antagonistic forces, within and without. This gradually produces a visible figure, open to theory, open, that is, to the speculative unifications of some onlooker, some narrator. "Theory" is from the Greek "theasthai," to watch, observe, from "thea," a viewing. "Theater" has the same source. Theorizing is a way of seeing clearly. Alternatively, writing, reading, or living, the making of a life or of history, may be thought of as the retracing of such a line already produced. As I have said, tracing, the making of a track; retracing, the following of a track already made; the ambiguity of a first that is already second, of an event that has always already happened in order for it to be retraced, of a pathbreaking that is always also a path-following—all these features are present in most formulations of the way the narrative line is a production, a performance, a happening. If even the first story is already a repetition, it always contains within itself the possibility of further repetitions—citations, parodies, subversions, doublings, subplots, counterplots to cross the main plot.

Behind Sterne's outrageous graphings lie Hogarth's lines of beauty and grace, referred to several times with apparent approbation early in *Tristram Shandy* and then hilariously parodied in two places. The Hogarthian line, whether in the two-dimensional form of the line of beauty, or in the three-dimensional spiral of the line of grace, was copied from antiquity. There it was already a sign, even the sign of a sign. The enigmatic representation of the line of grace, spiral form around a cone, in Hogarth's *Tailpiece, or The Bathos* (1764), is copied from "fig. 26," the first plate in *Analysis of Beauty* (1753). The enigma lies in the two inscriptions or legends in *Tailpiece* explaining the spiral around a cone, one from Tacitus, the other from Maximus Tyrius. The spiral stands for the cone around which it is wrapped in asymptotic yearning, sign for a sign. The cone in turn, surprisingly, stands for the perfection of the female body in its archetype, Venus. The inscription on Hogarth's Tailpiece speaks of "The Conic Form in wch the Goddess of Beauty was worshipd by the Ancients in ye Island of Cyprus." I say "surprisingly" because a cone might at first seem more a male than a female symbol, depending on whether one takes it inside out or outside in, as sword or as sheath. This cone, however, is a "pyramidal shell," and it tapers not to a point, but to a "small circumference." The first inscription, from Tacitus's *History*, book 2, chapter 3, reads: "Simulacrum Deae non effigie humana: continuus

William Hogarth, *Tailpiece, or The Bathos*. Reproduced with permission from the collection of Ronald Paulson.

orbis latiore initio tenuem in ambitum, metae modo, exsurgens, [s]et ratio in obscuro" ("The image [simulacrum] of the goddess does not bear the human shape; it is a rounded mass rising like a cone from a broad base to a small circumference. The meaning of this is doubtful"). The second inscription, from the *Dissertationes* of Maximus Tyrius, reads: "Venus a Paphiis colitur, cuius Simulacrum nulli rei magis assimile, quam albae Pyramidi" ("By the Paphians Venus is honored; but you cannot compare her statue [Simulacrum] to anything else than a white pyramid, the matter of which is unknown").[6] The key word in both these inscriptions is "simulacrum," meaning image, copy, icon, artificial or phantasmal likeness. The line of beauty in the flesh, seductively graceful curve of breast, waist, hip, and thigh, is represented by a hollow cone.

This is then further abstracted as a spiral line moving around that cone toward an effaced central point or axis at the blunted apex, sign of the missing interior. The line will never meet that virtual point, though it will approach closer and closer to it in infinite looping approximations.

This line is then taken by Sterne away from its "origin," the mysterious attractions of the female body, expressible in the Hogarthian curve only as the sign of the sign of an absence. The Hogarthian line is made by Sterne the image for spinning out a story, narrative line, or life line. Seduction becomes production, drawing from without becomes generation from within, or the following, after the fact, by some narrator, of that generation. The passages from Sterne are splendidly comic extrapolations of the Hogarthian line of beauty. The first is in chapter 40 of volume 6, the concluding chapter of that volume:

I am now beginning to get fairly into my work; and by the help of a vegetable diet, with a few of the cold seeds,[7] I make no doubt but I shall be able to go on with my uncle *Toby's* story, and my own, in a tolerable straight line. Now,

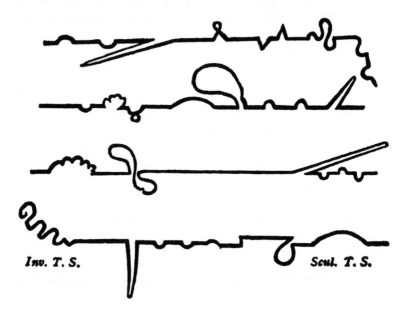

Inv. T. S.   *Scul. T. S.*

These were the four lines I moved in through my first, second, third, and fourth volumes.——— In the fifth volume I have been very good,———the precise line I have described in it being this:

A B   c c   c c c   **D**

By which it appears, that except at the curve, marked A, where I took a trip to *Navarre*,———and the indented curve B, which is the short airing when I was there with the Lady *Baussiere* and her page,———I have not taken the least frisk of a digression, till *John de la Casse's* devils led me the round you see marked D.———for as for c c c c c they are nothing but parentheses, and the common ins and outs incident to the lives of the greatest ministers of state; and when compared with what men have done,———or with my own transgressions at the letters A B D———they vanish into nothing.

In this last volume I have done better still———for from the end of *Le Fever's* episode, to the beginning of my uncle *Toby's* campaigns,———I have scarce stepped a yard out of my way.

If I mend at this rate, it is not impossible———by the good leave of his grace of *Benevento's* devils———but I may arrive hereafter at the excellency of going on even thus;

which is a line drawn as straight as I could draw it, by a writing-master's ruler, (borrowed for that purpose) turning neither to the right hand or to the left.

This *right line*,———the path-way for Christians to walk in! say divines

———The emblem of moral rectitude! says *Cicero*———

———The *best line!* say cabbage-planters———is the shortest line, says *Archimedes*, which can be drawn from one given point to another.———

I wish your ladyships would lay this matter to heart in your next birth-day suits!

———What a journey!

Pray can you tell me,—that is, without anger, before I write my chapter upon straight lines———by what mistake———who told them so———or how it has come to pass, that your men of wit and genius have all along confounded this line, with the line of GRAVITATION ?[8]

With admirably subversive wit, linking heterogeneities violently together, this passage gathers together many of the figures of the narrative line. It gathers them not to twine them into a unified chain or rope, but to play one figure against the others in a running, constantly interrupted series undercutting the possibility of an innocently solemn use of any one of the figures. Though the passage claims allegiance to the continuity of the straight line, its rhythm is abrupt, broken at every moment by Sterne's dashes and by the sudden shift to a new figure or topic. "What a journey!" The line of a narrative, Sterne assumes, should ideally be the production of a perfectly straight sequence going from beginning through middle to end, retelling with no digressions or episodes Uncle Toby's life and his own. This generation of a narrative line is conflated with the actual drawing of a straight line by rule or ruler, according to a norm ("norma": Latin for ruler). This conflation indicates the figurative, conventional quality of the image of the narrative line. At the same time it calls attention to its absurdity. It is a good example of Sterne's splendid gift for destroying a figure by taking it literally, with mock solemnity. He reminds the reader that a narrative is in fact nothing like a straight line drawn with a ruler, or that if it were it would be without interest. The interest of a narrative lies in its digressions, in episodes that might be diagrammed as loops, knots, interruptions, or detours making a visible figure.

What then happens to the concept of digression? The strangeness of any narrative line lies in the impossibility of distinguishing irrelevance from relevance, digression from the straight and narrow. *Tristram Shandy* as a whole is the magnificent demonstration of this, for example, in the way the passage promising a line henceforth as straight as a ruler can draw it is followed by the totally "digressive" journey of book 7. The peculiarity of the narrative line lies also in the incompatibility between moral rectitude and narrative interest. A wholly "moral" story would be a straight line without features, altogether boring, like a journey in which nothing happens, while every distinguishing feature of a given story is at the same time, Sterne implies, a moral transgression, since it turns away from the straight and narrow. "And make straight paths for your feet, lest that which is lame be turned out of the way," says Paul in the Epistle to the Hebrews (12:13).

The same contrast between the featureless straight line and the line curved to become a sign, and so carrying meaning and becoming a plot, but at the same time becoming transgressive, deviant, forms and reforms itself in the nine figurative lines Sterne superimposes on the seemingly innocent figure of a narrative as a linear series of events: the line of a journey, with its side trips and airings; the line of a logical argument, broken by digressions; the grammatical line of words in a piece of writing, which may be interrupted by parentheses, c c c c, and so on; the line of history with the zigzagging ins and outs of ministers of state; the ruled line of "moral rectitude," broken by lamenesses, wanderings, transgressions leading the feet away from the straight path; the straight line of a row of cabbages in a garden; the geometrical line defined by Archimedes in *On the Sphere and Cylinder*, I, Assumption 1 ("Of all lines having the same extremities the straight line is the least"); the line of gravitation, with a characteristic multiple pun on gravitation as Newtonian attraction, as the vertical descent of bathos or the art of falling, and as the grave solemnity of the horizontal line of moral rectitude, each meaning interfering with the others and "confounding" them; and finally, to come full circle back to Hogarth and the Venusian line, as the straight line of an ideally economical birthday suit, where an erotic pun that has been lurking throughout the passage may surface. The birthday suit is, as the notes to the Norton edition say, "clothes worn at birthday celebrations, especially that of the monarch" (334), but it possibly also already meant nakedness. The figure sets the dullness of a straight line drawn from one point to another on a female body against the Hogarthian curved line of beauty, which strays seductively from the straight road, following the contours of breast, waist, and thigh, to lead its beholder hopelessly astray in digressions, transgressions, parentheses, episodes, and airings, wanderings from the straight path like the episodes in *Tristram Shandy*.

A dazzling set of different linear figures gathered in a loose hank, superimposed, tangled, interfering with one another, like multiple incompatible signals graphed simultaneously on an oscilloscope—the passage in *Tristram Shandy* disarticulates the line, dissolves it, reduces it to fragmentary bits. It does this by showing its arbitrary or figurative quality and by showing the comic inability of this figure to account for or to plot the various regions of experience it is supposed to represent. The straighter the line, the more Archimedean it is, the less significance it has as a representation of anything human, the less susceptible it is to being repeated again as a recognizable sign, since all straight lines are the same, and the less it invites, unlike the line of beauty, to reproduction. On the other hand, the more information the line carries, the more curved, knotted, or hieroglyphic it is, the less it can any longer be called a line, and the closer it approaches toward the almost completely disordered state of broken yarn strands compacted in a ball or of a dust cloud in Brownian movement, impossible to graph by any line.

An erotic motivation, like that of the birthday suit, though with an opposing affect, generates the other literally represented line in *Tristram Shandy*. Corporal Trim warns Uncle Toby that marriage is confinement, like the inquisition: "once a poor creature is in, he is in, an' please your honour, for ever." Celibacy, the single state, the state of unattachment, is, on the contrary, liberty, the liberty of the arabesque:

Nothing, continued the Corporal, can be so sad as confinement for life———— or so sweet, an' please your honour, as liberty.

Nothing, *Trim*————said my uncle *Toby*, musing————

Whilst a man is free————cried the corporal, giving a flourish with his stick thus————

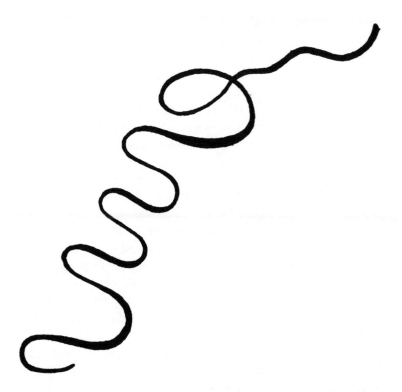

A thousand of my father's most subtle syllogisms could not have said more for celibacy. (9:4, 425–26)

Tristram Shandy throughout is a hilarious parody and undoing of the idea of a continuous and complete life story. It shows that all narrative lines come into existence in defiance of the fact that a narrative can neither begin nor proceed continuously once it has begun, nor ever stop or reach its goal once it has, in defiance of these impossibilities, begun continuing. As one example of this, Corporal Trim's flourish in its irregularity is a subversive parody of the Hogarthian line of beauty. Trim's flourish is still a line, however. If marriage is imprisonment, the immobilization of the stick, celibacy, is freedom, but freedom to move in response to "gravitational" forces. Freedom is not reaching the goal, that Venusian infinitely distant or absent point, apex of the cone. Corporal Trim's arabesque is rather the production of a life line generated by energies within in response to energies without, the moving point of the walking stick pulled this way and that by its own vital impetus in response to external attractions. The resultant line is the graph of these constantly changing vector forces. It is unlike Hogarth's line in being more wandering, reluctant, hesitant, given to turning back and looping over itself. It is unlike also in having no visible orientation or motivating goal. Does it go from bottom to top or from top to bottom? Which way did Corporal Trim flourish his stick? Presumably from lower to higher, but there is no way to be sure.

This wandering celibate line, which goes on producing itself only so long as it remains chaste, untied, has the paradoxical power of generating progeny, sons and grandsons bound to their sire in duplicating family resemblance. One such child is Balzac's "citation" of Corporal Trim's flourish as the epigraph to La Peau de chagrin, about which there is much to say. I shall return later to Balzac, but I want to follow first the lines of Friedrich Schlegel.[9]

Schlegel, in the "Letter about the Novel" from the Dialogue on Poetry (Gespräch über die Poesie) (1799–1800), puts the true novel (which includes for him Shakespeare and Ariosto, and which is more or less identical with "romantic" poetry as such) under the double aegis of Sterne and of Diderot's Sterne-inspired Jacques le fataliste. The link here is the arabesque. Corporal Trim's flourish is generalized as the free, natural, and irregularly curving contours of a genuine novel's narrative line, form par excellence, for Schlegel, of romantic literature. Schlegel's arabesque, however, like Hogarth's line of beauty, or even like Corporal Trim's flourish, is not entirely unmotivated. It is determined even in its grotesque wanderings by its relation to an infinitely distant or absent center. When he speaks of arabesques, Schlegel thinks as much of Raphael's arabesques, tangled, asymmetrical designs of fruit, foliage, animals, and flowers in the Loggias of the Vatican at Rome, designed by Raphael but executed by Raphael's associates, as of Moslem or Saracen designs. Every natural object was forbidden in the latter. In both cases, however, an absent point

Arabesque of acanthus designed by Raphael and executed by Giovanni da Udini, Loggias of the Vatican, pilaster 9. Reproduced from Nicole Dacos, Le Logge di Raffaello (Rome: Istituto Poligrafico dello Stato, 1977), pl. 17, 182.

of reference motivates the apparent disunities and wanton zigzags of the design. A novel like *Tristram Shandy* breaks the laws of dramatic unity. It lacks the Aristotelian unity of a mimesis copying an action with beginning, middle, and end. At the same time the arabesque narrative sequences of romantic novels are secretly controlled by their orientation toward that infinite and invisible center. Such narratives have the unity of figurative language, of "spirit" rather than "letter." The contrast with bourgeois, realist drama is a contrast between two kinds of unity, the unity of an immanent logos creating a direct and continuous diegesis (the letter), and the arabesque unity of a relation to an infinitely distant or transcendent logos (the spirit). Schlegel's name for that absent center is "chaos":

A novel is a romantic book. You will pass that off as a meaningless tautology. But I want to draw your attention to the fact that when one thinks of a book, one thinks of a work, an existing whole [ein für sich bestehendes Ganze]. There is then a very important contrast to drama, which is meant to be viewed; the novel, on the other hand, was from the oldest times for reading, and from this fact we can deduce almost all the differences in the manner of presentation of both forms. The drama should also be romantic, like all literature; but a novel is that only under certain limitations, an applied novel [ein angewandter Roman]. On the contrary, the dramatic context [der dramatische Zusammenhang] of the story does not make the novel a whole, a work, if the whole composition is not related to a higher unity than that of the letter [auf eine höhere Einheit als jene Einheit des Buchstabens] which it often does and should disregard; but it becomes a work through the bond of ideas through a spiritual central point [durch das Band der Ideen, durch einen geistigen Zentralpunkt].[10]

The contrast here is perhaps not entirely transparent at first sight. The wholeness of a drama, Schlegel is saying, is related to the fact that it is a visual form of art. This means that it must have the unity of the letter, that is of a literal representation, on the stage, of a continuous action, as Aristotle said. It also is often, for example, in much eighteenth-century bourgeois drama, straightforwardly mimetic of everyday life. A novel, on the other hand, is for reading. It does not depend on being a continuous, literally represented spectacle. It can and should therefore have discontinuities and changes of register that could not be represented on the stage. Its unity is the unity not of the letter but of the spirit, that is through an association of ideas relating each segment to the others by way of their common relation to a spiritual point, which can never be represented as such, but only represented indirectly, in figure or in allegory. As Ludovico, one of the characters in the dialogue, says later on: "All beauty is allegory. The highest, because it is unutterable, can be said only allegorically" ("Alle Schönheit ist Allegorie. Das Höchste kann man eben, weil es unaussprechlich ist, nur allegorisch sagen").[11]

This idea or image (it is image as idea) of a line that is fragmented and at the same time controlled by its relation to an infinitely distant center is expressed in a remarkable passage from the second ending of the essay "On Lessing": "Is there a more beautiful symbol for the paradoxes of the philosophical life than certain curved lines which, drawn out with certain steadiness and lawfulness, can nevertheless always appear only as fragments, since a center for them lies at infinity?" ("Gibt es wohl ein schöneres Symbol für die Paradoxie des philosophischen Lebens, als jene krummen Linien, die mit sichtbarer Stetigkeit und Gesetzmäßigkeit forteilend immer nur im Bruchstück erscheinen können, weil ihr eines Zentrum in der Unendlichkeit liegt?")[12] Hyperbole, tangent curve, parabola—these geometrical figures can be graphed, but never completely, and only in fragments, since one at least of their controlling points lies at an infinite distance, beyond the margin of any graph. A parabola, for example, is an ellipse with one focus at infinity, while a hyperbole is an ellipse inside out with two finite focii, and two more at opposite infinities, generating two opposing lines each moving doubly out toward infinity. The tangent curve, on the other hand, moves asymptotically toward an infinitely distant point, then reappears magically from minus infinity after a trajectory that no eye, theory, or logic can follow rationally in the sense of seeing through it. The names of geometrical lines, these visible paradoxes, are also names of figures of speech. Such tropes figure in one way or another the incommensurability between the vehicle of expression and its meaning. This is evident in the parables of Jesus in the New Testament or in the fragments of Friedrich Schlegel himself. An aphorism is another such figure. Etymologically, an aphorism is a definition established on the basis of a setting of boundaries. The word "horizon" has the same root.

The broken paradoxical line of Schlegel's romantic novel, ultimate permutation of the arabesque, is still, however, a line. It would still give the model of a narrative line that might be graphed, at least in part. In this sense it is a form of continuity or logic, however different this logic is from that of a line generated by a finite and visible center, the logic of the letter or of the mimetic representation of an action, as in Aristotle's definition of drama. Schlegel's theory of irony as "permanent parabasis," however, or his practice of irony in his fragments, suspends, interrupts, and disperses the narrative line altogether. It abolishes any conceivable center, finite or infinite, visible or invisible. Parabasis, as I said in the first section of this book, is the stepping forward of the chorus or an actor in a play to break the dramatic illusion and to speak directly to the audience, sometimes in the name of the author. If irony is parabasis, it is the one master trope that cannot be graphed as a line. Irony is the confounding, the point-by-point deconstruction, of any narrative order or determinable meaning. It does this by abolishing any identifiable controlling center, even at infinity. This explosion or powdering of the line can take place, however, only through the attempted production of the line. Irony is the basic trope of narrative fiction, for example in the perpetual discrepancy between author and narrator, or between narrator and character in "indirect discourse." All irony in narrative is one form or another of that doubling in storytelling that makes its meaning ultimately indecipherable, unable to be read even as what de Man calls "allegory of unreadability."[13]

Any work of fiction is in one way or another, or in several ways at once, a repetitive structure. Repetition is something occurring along the line that disintegrates the continuity of the line. This is true even though the series of repetitions may appear as the gradual covering over of some subversive implication, as the taming or organizing of irony back into a proper narrative sequence. Friedrich Schlegel himself was ultimately converted to Roman Catholicism. He then revised some of his earlier work in such a way as to make it less a putting in question of the certainties of Occidental metaphysics. The successive "repetitions" of Schlegel by his modern interpreters have tended to reintegrate what he disarticulated in his earlier work. Schlegel's critics, even Søren Kierkegaard, Walter Benjamin, or Peter Szondi, have tended to read him according to a Hegelian or romantic paradigm of historical dialectics.[14] The gunpowder remains along the line of repetitions, however, ready to explode again at any time, since the demolition power of irony does not spend its energy when it discharges the first time. As Friedrich Schlegel says, "Irony is something one simply cannot play games with. It can have incredibly long-lasting after effects."[15]

I have followed here a brief historical line going from Hogarth through Sterne to Friedrich Schlegel. The sequence indicates various possible uses for the image of the line as a figure for narrative continuity or discontinuity, for all that part of the story in the middle, between start and finish. My line is itself a middle, since Hogarth is not by any means its beginning, nor Friedrich Schlegel its end, as I began this section by indicating. The line stretches indefinitely before and after. Out of this truncated series I have made a little story line of my own, a line not apparently undermined, except retrospectively at the end, by irony. The sequence I have followed would need to be tested against representative narratives (if there are such things) in order to be confirmed or rejected as an adequate interpretative model giving a comprehensive range of possible middles. That testing remains to be done.

SIX

BALZAC'S SERPENT

One place to begin such testing is by following what happens to Corporal Trim's line when it gets cited by Balzac as the epigraph for *La Peau de chagrin* (1831). This will extend my discussion of middles with another somewhat disquieting example of a sequence that tells a story. Sterne's line was already itself the tangling or disintegrating of the Hogarthian line of beauty. In *La Peau de chagrin* the free arabesque traced by Corporal Trim's stick, sign of celibacy's liberty, is first turned from vertical to horizontal and then repeated from edition to edition of *La Peau de chagrin*. In each successive edition it loses more of its original characteristics. It ceases to be a line without beginning or end that approaches, in its relatively total detachment from any center of attraction, the dissolution of oriented linearity. In Balzac's successive citations, or perhaps it would be better to say, in those of his editors, Corporal Trim's flourish becomes motivated, organized, grounded. This happens in a process not unlike that of the gradual change of a word or phrase as it is whispered from ear to ear by a ring of children in the game called "Telephone" or, more suggestively still, "Operator." Why this particular transformation? What spontaneously motivates Balzac's line or draws it toward a goal?

In the first edition (1831) the figure appears as

(Sterne, *Tristam Shandy*, ch. CCCXXII)[1]

The line remained the same in the second edition of 1831 and in the editions of 1835 and 1838. It was suppressed in the 1833 edition, but appeared essentially the same in the editions of 1839 and 1846. Finally, in the posthumous edition of 1869, edited by Alexandre Houssiaux, the line became explicitly a serpent:

STERNE. *Tristram Shandy*, ch. CCCXXII [*]

As can be seen, Balzac's citations of Sterne's free line falsify the original text by turning the vertical line sideways, by unlooping the knot in Corporal Trim's line, and by thickening and narrowing the line here and there so that it already seems faintly to have the head and the tail added posthumously. This is a gross corruption of Sterne's text. It is false quotation, citation as misprision—an example of literary history as error or distortion, such as those distortions Gérard Genette has dissected in such detail in *Palimpsestes*.[2] Is there, however, ever such a thing as a correct and exact citation? Even a scrupulously accurate, photographic quotation, such as I have used here for Balzac's epigraphs, will perhaps be of a different size or a different degree of blackness from the original. In any case, it will have been cut by violence out from the mesh of its surrounding text. It is a quotation, not the original. Each successive figure in the various editions of Balzac's novel, after the "identical" repetitions of 1831, 1835, and 1838, was almost the same, but not quite. Ultimately the line is reversed (from left to right) and becomes a snake, forked tongue and all. This final distortion was apparently the work of the editor Houssiaux. According to Spoelberch de Lovenjoul, in an essay of 1907, Houssiaux "was persuaded doubtless that a *peau de chagrin* could be nothing but a *serpent's skin*, and probably had concluded that the epigraph of the work was intended to clarify this point!"[3]

What is the significance of this gradual distortion? What meaning did Balzac give to Sterne's line? The irregularity of Corporal Trim's line makes it a kind of natural sign or hieroglyph conveying, in its airy wantonness, more information about celibacy, as Tristram says, than "a thousand of my father's most subtle syllogisms." This power to embody and to convey information, fundamental property of any sign, always necessarily involves the possibility of repetition. Each sign invites its iteration. Each sign appears to have as its essence as sign the ability to carry over to its double the "original" meaning with which it was endowed. There is no sign without repetition. Even the "first" example of a given sign contains its implicit iterability, its implicit appeal to anterior and posterior duplications of itself. On the other hand, no iteration of a sign is exactly the same, if only in the way the context is different or the material substance of the sign is different. The chain of repetitions contains in itself the possibility, perhaps even the necessity, of gradual distortions of the original sign and therefore perhaps of its meaning. This is so however much the meaning of a sign may be thought to lie in its differences from other signs adjacent to it rather than in its differences from itself. Those other versions of itself form part of its surrounding mesh of differences. The meaning of a sign lies, in part at least, in its relation to erroneous duplications of itself before and after. The meaning is generated in the space between. It is generated by the differences. A curved or knotted line may always be cited, as in the series from Hogarth to Sterne to Schlegel to Balzac I am following here, but it is always cited with a difference, however slight or imperceptible.

The movement from one to another link in this chain of mis-quotations is not random or accidental. It is highly motivated. The free line of Sterne, sign of celibacy, of disarticulation, and subversive parody of Hogarth, becomes gradually transformed into a snake with a head and tail, a beginning, middle, and end. It changes into an exemplary model of Aristotelian narrative. It becomes the sign of an oriented sequence, archeological, teleological, grounded. Balzac's snake is a binding of continuous links presenting in miniature all the presuppositions of diegesis. Moreover, in this transformation the purely abstract or mathematical line becomes mimetic, "realistic," the picture of a snake. A powerful presupposition or preexistent paradigm has motivated this swerve bringing the line back to logocentricity. The permutation is more a return than a turn. The sequence from Hogarth through Sterne to Balzac is a sign of the tremendous power metaphysical preconceptions exert over any attempt to put them in question. The series is the story not of progress but of degeneration. The chain is a falling back into ancient assumptions repressing the acerb irony against traditional ideas of narrative coherence in this bit of *Tristram Shandy* and in Sterne's novel as a whole, if you can call it that.

Was this Balzac's intention or was it an unconscious reaffirmation of received metaphysical assumptions produced by Balzac's designers and editors rather than by Balzac himself? What did Balzac mean by citing Sterne's line as the epigraph to *La Peau de chagrin*? The text of the novel, with its strange story of a magic wild ass's skin that shrinks as the hero spends his forces to win more and more power, gradually exhausting himself in the process, leaves the application of the epigraph a matter of conjecture.[4] There is no reference to the epigraph within the body of the novel. The scientific background of *La Peau de chagrin* is the contemporary quarrel between mechanists and vitalists. Balzac comes down somewhat ambiguously on the side of the vitalists (since his concept of vitality was, if not mechanical, in any case strongly physical, whereas the vitalists were quasi-spiritualists). Balzac in this novel proposes a dynamic, voluntarist, economic conception of human life. A human being is will, but will is force. It is an energy capable of being hoarded or squandered. Will exists as a response to other, external forces, as its difference from them, plus against minus, in a balance always adding up eventually to zero in the equation of saving and spending. The horizontal undulations of Balzac's misquotation from Sterne would seem to describe not the celibate freedom of Corporal Trim's line, attracted only at an infinite distance by its pull toward the Venusian center, but precisely the opposite, namely the curve designated by a single human center of energy as it proceeds through life drawn this way and that by its own energy and by its responses to other energies. The resulting line is the graph of an immanently motivated life force that generates a continuous, goal-oriented story-line.

Just this meaning is given to the epigraph from Sterne in the introduction of 1834 to the "Etudes philosophiques." This introduction was written by Felix Davin but overseen by Balzac and corrected by him. Though Davin wrote it, it was an extension of Balzac's own will to power as the will to write, the will to manipulate the pen as an instrument of domination. "I conquer everything" was the inscription on Balzac's walking stick, to which Franz Kafka answered, "On my stick is written, 'Everything conquers me.'" Here is Davin's formulation:

But the critics have not seen that *The Wild Ass's Skin* is a definitive physiological judgment, passed by modern science, on human life; that this work is the poetic expression of this judgment, an abstraction made from social specificities. Is not the effect produced by desire, by passion, on the capital of human forces here magnificently indicted? [It is] a result of this moral theory that Corporal Trim outlines so energetically by means of the flourish that he traces in the air with his stick and that M. de Balzac has made into an epigraph so misunderstood by most readers. Few people have seen that after such a judgment passed on our organization there are no other alternatives, for most men, but to let themselves follow the *serpentine* movement of life, the bizarre undulations of fate. Therefore, after having poetically formulated, in *The Wild Ass's Skin*, the human system considered as a form of organization, and having disengaged from it this axiom: "Life diminishes in direct ratio to the power of desires or to the dissipation of ideas," the author takes that axiom as a guide, takes a torch to lead you into the catacombs of Rome; he says to you: Follow me! Examine the mechanism whose effects you have seen in the *Studies of Manners!*[5]

"L'allure *serpentine* de la vie"—the transformation of Sterne's free line into the oriented line of a snake's body was apparently intended by Balzac himself, since he allowed Davin's phrase to pass. Balzac's model of human life presents it as a dynamic balance of energies governed by the law of the conservation of force and by an implicit law of entropy fatefully determining the bizarre waverings of a life line or a story line until death stops it. Human life is the difference between the capital of interior energy and the waiting receptacles outside for those energies. As those energies are gradually spent, they tend to become more and more evenly distributed throughout the system until finally life ends altogether in a species of death by entropy. This model is a reappropriation of the line image for a new pseudoscientific version of an ancient metaphysical paradigm. Balzac's snakelike line is teleologically drawn toward a predetermined end. His misquotation of Sterne is, like all misinterpretation, a dismantling. It dismantles Sterne's ironic version of Hogarth's asymptotic line. Balzac's line is also, at the same time, the affirmation of an alternative metaphorical model. This model is open in its turn to further deformations, in a potentially endless line of substitutions.

Balzac's model, like all such dynamic systems, contains a latent opacity or uncertainty. It is impossible to distinguish between an intrinsic, self-contained "capital" of energy and an energy that has no intrinsic existence but is generated by its difference from other forces in a system of reciprocal forces. Is Balzac's life line the trajectory of an inner impulsion or is it a result, the effect of multiple exterior forces tracing an undulating curve? It is both and neither, in one of those uncertainties in which much hangs on deciding one way or the other, but in which a definite choice cannot be made. Since money and "economic forces" are other versions of this system, sociological or Marxist interpretations of literature and of human society are likely to come up against this undecidability.

SEVEN

"THE FIGURE IN
THE CARPET"

Balzac's transformation of Sterne's airy arabesque demonstrates, among other things, the enormous ideological power possessed by the metaphysical assumptions in Aristotle's formulations about beginnings, middles, and ends. These assumptions tend in one way or another to reassert themselves even when they have been put in question. I shift now to examples from Henry James to show the way that putting in question is nevertheless a recurrent feature of narrative, both in theory and in practice. Henry James's work combines in an exemplary way both subtle theory of narrative and subtle practice of the storytelling art. The leap I am about to make to Henry James's use of line images in his prefaces and in "The Figure in the Carpet" may raise a question about the relation among the items in my own line of examples. Are they themselves points on a fatefully determined historical line, with an origin, end, and continuous development leading from one to the next, a serpent with head, tail, and cloven tongue? No, they are somewhat randomly chosen moments of configuration gathering lines of thought and figuration inherent in the languages of Western culture. In saying this, I am aware I am apparently challenging some current assumptions about the specificity of a given historical and social context. That context has power, it is assumed, to determine or at least limit what can be written or thought at that historical moment and in that place, within that "episteme." Each new episteme has a new set of discursive possibilities. I agree that each literary work is embedded in an immense overdetermined network of historical, social, class, gender, and material forces. These include also the psychological peculiarities of the author. Taken together they constitute what we call the ideology of a given work. Nevertheless, that context does not have power to predict every work written within it. Who could have foreseen the idiosyncrasy of Sterne's *Tristram Shandy*, not to speak of the genius of Shakespeare, on the basis of their respective contexts? Nor can that idiosyncrasy or that genius be wholly explained, after the fact, by however exhaustive a retrospective repertory of the context, including the psychobiographies of the authors in question. It is this residue of the unexplained that most interests me here. I attempt to give the other half of the truth, the half different from what many people in literary studies are presupposing these days. Today's focus on historical or ideological configurations has the danger of over-emphasizing context at the expense of reading the work itself. The work may become a kind of hollow or vacancy overwhelmed by its context, just as my procedure has the danger of underemphasizing context through a fascination with verbal intricacies in the works read. Both, however, have the virtues of their defects.

One factor that has remained relatively constant, in spite of historical, social, and technological changes, has been the basic assembly of concepts and figures in the family of Western languages. This continuity makes it possible to feel that Sophocles and Shakespeare are our contemporaries as well as representatives of strange and to some degree opaque cultures that are "other" to ours. We can understand them because we are inhabited by similar tropological and lexical systems. These make translation possible, though always with some loss. They also make it possible for us to think and feel our way within these works. Such continuities, intrinsic to language, also especially interest me in this book. I claim that they are the matrix within which all the ideological changes from one historical moment to another must be expressed, if they are expressed in one or another of the family of Western languages.

My choices of works to read are to some degree accidental. They are works that seemed to me good places to investigate the complexities of diegesis as expressed in one way or another by line images. Nevertheless, my own sequence has its own conceptual rigor or logic. I have begun with a general exploration of the problems of narrative by way of two canon-ical urtexts in our tradition, Aristotle's *Poetics* and Sophocles's *Oedipus the King*. The book then moves to investigation of ends, beginnings, middles, and multiplications of the narrative line. The latter investigations will include indirect discourse as a fundamental procedure in modern narratives. The pervasive presence of irony as a feature of indirect discourse is the endpoint of this sequence. It is followed by a concluding section that reads two modern narratives, Elizabeth Gaskell's *Cranford* and Walter Pater's "Apollo in Picardy." These are read as texts where all the diegetical problems identified earlier are admirably exemplified. In the examples I have chosen there are, it happens, some cross-references and sequential influences, but an almost limitless number of alternative examples might have been found. Each of my examples is a node in an immense network. Each reforms, in a way at once unique and old, another version of the same contradiction, the capacity latent in the line image (concept, figure, and narrative model at once) both to express the logocentric paradigm and to put it in question. Each node or figure in the carpet is not so much a coming together in the sense of a tying up or resolution as it is the designation of a gap, a slip knot that disperses the threads once more. That dispersal prepares another later or displaced attempt at an impossible dénouement. This happens according to a law of repetition that Walter Pater admirably enunciated by means of the thread image. He is expressing a theory of repetition that is exemplified in his "Denys l'Auxerrois," as well as in "Apollo in Picardy": "That clear, perpetual outline of face and limb is but an image of ours, under which we group [these elementary physical forces]—a design in a web, the actual threads of which pass out beyond it. This at least of flame-like our life has, that it is but the concurrence, renewed from moment to moment, of forces parting sooner or later on their ways."[1]

To cite Pater, however, is to be besieged in memory by a swarm of analogous apposite examples of the line figure. These others have been omitted here for the sake of creating a fictitiously neat story line going from Hogarth through Sterne, Schlegel, and Balzac to James. To stay in the same historical period as that of Sterne and Schlegel, one thinks of the lines in Burke, Kant, and Blake, or of the red thread Goethe, in a strange passage about Ottilie's diary in *Die Wahlverwandtschaften* (*Elective Affinities*), says must snake or lace through any narrative as its organizing stem. As Goethe says, in an image that also appears in Melville's *Billy*

Budd, some common thread must unify a narrative sequence just as the "king's thread" is woven into any British naval rope. This red thread, like a dispersed signature, designates a given rope as royal property. The passage is cited here as a transition from the image of the single life-line in Sterne and Balzac to the image in James of a complex figure traced by many threads in a larger web of life. The latter involves a group of characters in their interaction. "Ein roter Faden," literally, a red thread, is a common German idiom for this idea of a pervasive, unifying theme. It has no match among English idioms, so far as I know. Here is the passage from *Elective Affinities*:

There is, we are told, a curious contrivance in the service of the English marine. The ropes in use in the royal navy, from the largest to the smallest, are so twisted that a red thread [ein roter Faden] runs through them from end to end, which cannot be extracted without undoing the whole; and by which the smallest pieces may be recognized as belonging to the crown.

Just so is there drawn through Ottilie's diary, a thread of attachment and affection which connects it all together [ein Faden der Neigung und Anhänglichkeit, der alles verbindet], and characterizes the whole. And thus these remarks, these observations, these extracted sentences, and whatever else it may contain, were, to the writer, of peculiar meaning. Even the few separate pieces which we select and transcribe will sufficiently explain our meaning.[2]

This spiraling red thread is something like a distinctive seal or stamp made of a line curved to form a monogram. Such a sign might be embroidered, for example, on clothing, say Desdemona's handkerchief. This monogram would unify by its mark disparate materials and designate them as belonging to a certain person, just as everything Ottilie writes in her diary is marked by her love for Eduard. In a similar way a melody may be identified as Mozart's by distinctive traits, though each melody by him is different from all the others. Gerard Manley Hopkins, in a splendid cascade of figures for figuring, signs for signature, speaks of the stigmata, the five wounds of Christ, as Christ's name or seal stamped on those he has "bespoken," claimed as his own by making them Christlike, what he elsewhere calls "AfterChrists."[3]

Those so sealed are remade by being re-marked according to Christ's own pattern:

> Five! the finding and sake
> And cipher of suffering Christ.
> Mark, the mark is of man's make
> And the word of it Sacrificed.
> But he scores it in scarlet himself on his own bespoken,
> Before-time-taken, dearest prizèd and priced—
> Stigma, signal, cinquefoil token
> For lettering of the lamb's fleece, ruddying of the rose-
> flake.[4]

One recurrent topic in Jacques Derrida's *Glas* and in other works by him is the problematic of signature. What is a signature? When is an apparent signature not really a signature? What is the difference between signing my name and inadvertently betraying my individuality by marks or rhythms of style in something I have written, or by leaving a fingerprint? What is the difference between merely writing my name, for example, in answer to a question on a form, and signing it, for example, in signing a check? Is it only a matter of a different performative intention? Is there such a thing as a forged signature? How does one tell a forgery from the genuine holograph? Might there be circumstances in which I could forge my own signature? The passages cited from Goethe and Hopkins, chosen for their relevance to the theme of the line curved back on itself to make a glyph, seal, or signature, could lead to a full discussion of that topic, or they could also lead to an analysis of *Elective Affinities* as a masterwork made of repeated configurations of figure and theme. The novel also overtly reflects on what is problematic about this procedure:[5] my transitional citation could easily become not a linking path but an endless detour, a side path in the labyrinth leading me perhaps permanently astray from the road going with apparent logic and rigor from Hogarth to James. Astray? That would assume that Henry James is the natural goal, climax, or endpoint of a line from which a discussion of Goethe or Hopkins would at this point be a deviation.

That is by no means the case, except within the logic of my sequence of examples. There is no being lost, but no being found either, in this exploration, since no predetermined goal exists. Each segment must in the end make its own separate claims to interest. No completeness is possible in analysis of the narrative line. The examples chosen form only the mirage of a single exclusive and determinate historical sequence. I stress this point to indicate that what I am saying about narrative lines in *Oedipus the King*, *Tristram Shandy*, and the rest, turns back to reflect on my own procedures in this book. Nevertheless, the distinction I have made between the conceptual logic of my sequence of chapters and the somewhat arbitrary nature of the choice of examples to illustrate each topic should be kept in mind.

I choose Henry James, then, as a salient figure in this carpet. His work will take me a step forward in this extended investigation of narrative middles. My choice makes James's work a momentary focus around which swirl lines of force gathering and regathering to form figures of the line figure. Other figures in the carpet, or crossroads in the labyrinth, have been cited from Sterne, Schlegel, Balzac, Hopkins, and Goethe. A multitude of other examples, as I have said, could be adduced.

Images of filaments, "ficelles," figures drawn with lines, tropes of woven or embroidered cloth, thread themselves through the dense metaphorical texture of Henry James's prefaces to the New York Edition of his works. These prefaces taken together form one of James's masterpieces, the most important treatise in English on the novel. A passage in the preface to *Roderick Hudson* is an appropriate place to begin, since it bears on the point just made about the impossibility of making a finite repertoire or neat historical story of the narrative line's branchings. The passage reflects not only on the difficulty of beginning but also on the even greater difficulty of stopping once one has begun. This present book traces a sequential line making a readable figure through a web that extends in all directions from any given starting place, in Daedalian complexity. On the surface of this web might be traced innumerable patterns, in an impossible attempt to achieve Apollonian reduction of Dionysiac materials. This tracing and retracing would be like that legendary dance of the rational egotist, Theseus. His dance, so tradition says, marked out ever-changing winding figures compulsively threading through a simulacrum of Daedalus's labyrinth laid out in a pattern on the ground, in an impossible attempt to master it.[6] Just this situation, from the perspective of the novelist, not the reader, is expressed with splendid eloquence in the preface to James's *Roderick Hudson*.

In the passage I shall cite, the issue is a double one. How, in writing a novel, can the author draw a line around the material to be treated, give it an edge or border that appears as a natural stopping place in all directions beyond which there is nothing relevant to the subject? Second, how, within those limits, can the author treat what is left inside the charmed circle totally and with total continuity, omitting nothing and articulating all the connections, all of what Tolstoi, in a splendid phrase, called "the labyrinth of linkages."[7] Continuity, completeness, and finite form—these, for James, make up the triple necessity of a satisfactory or satisfying narrative:

Yet it must even then have begun for me too, the ache of fear, that was to become so familiar, of being unduly tempted and led on by "developments"; which is but the desperate discipline of the question involved in them. They are of the very essence of the novelist's process, and it is by their aid, fundamentally, that his idea takes form and lives; but they impose on him, through the principle of continuity that rides them, a proportionate anxiety. They are the very condition of interest, which languishes and drops without them; the painter's subject consisting ever, obviously, of the related state, to each other, of certain figures and things. To exhibit these relations, once they have all been recognized, is to "treat" his idea, which involves neglecting none of those that directly minister to interest; the degree of that directness remaining meanwhile a matter of highly difficult appreciation, and one on which the felicity of form and composition, as a part of the total effect, mercilessly rests. Up to what point is such and such a development *indispensable* to the interest? What is the point beyond which it ceases to be rigorously so? Where, for the complete expression of one's subject, does a particular relation stop—giving way to some other not concerned in that expression?[8]

Completeness; continuity; finite form—James here gives masterly expression to the demands made on the author of a literary text, or at least on one who shares James's commitment to the ideology of shapely or organic aesthetic form. Where is the edge of a given subject or of a relation within that subject? It is obviously a matter of degree, of nuance. What is the difference between "directly" or "rigorously" ministering to interest and only indirectly or loosely doing so, beyond the margin, peripherally? The edge is no sharp boundary but an indefinitely extending gray area, no longer quite so rigorously relevant, but not irrelevant either. At what point does a bit of accrued "interest" become so small that it can be dispensed with, rounded off to the nearest zero, so to speak? What does James mean here by "figures," as opposed to "things"? The figures in the carpet? Figures of speech, embroidered flowers of rhetoric? Figures as the persons of the drama? Whatever the answers to these questions, it is clear that for James the necessity of completeness and continuity, reconciled with finite form, can never by any means other than a fictitious appearance be satisfied. The triple necessity is a triple bind. James is not only committed to the ideology of aesthetic form. He also shows that its demands are impossible to fulfill.

The reasons for this impossibility are multiple. On the one hand, no intrinsic limit exists for a given subject. To represent any subject completely would be to retrace an infinite web of relevant relations extending to the horizon and beyond, in every direction: "Really, universally, relations stop nowhere" (ibid.). It would appear, however, that this problem could be solved by the arbitrary drawing of a boundary line establishing a frontier beyond which the writer will not allow himself to go. The basic act of form-giving is the establishment of a periphery, a boundary. This border must be made to appear like an opaque wall beyond which there is nothing. Or rather it must not even be a perceptible wall, but an invisible enclosure. The frontier must make the work like a piece of music in which the note C cannot appear, or like the limits, no limits, of a universe that is finite but unbounded. In such a universe, one can go anywhere, in any direction, but one remains enclosed, without ever encountering walls or boundaries. If "relations stop nowhere," "the exquisite problem of the artist is eternally but to draw, by a geometry of his own, the circle within which they shall happily *appear* to do so" (ibid.).

Even when this fictitious reduction of the infinite to the finite has been accomplished, however, the problem of the limitless reconstitutes itself within the magic circle. Continuity and completeness are everything for the novelist. This means that every possible relation must be retraced within the circle, every figure drawn on its surface. Since each entity, "figure" or "thing," for James, exists *as* its relations, to represent the figure or thing completely is to represent all its relations. Each figure, by a cunning equivocation, is the figure made by the lines which may be drawn between it and other things, other figures. The multiplicity of these lines would be paralyzing if the writer consulted it directly. He or she has to know it and not know it in order to focus on one relation without being distracted by all the others. Here is another way in which the narrative line is spun out of its own impossibility. Even the tiniest temporal or spatial gap in the universal continuity would be a disaster. The writer has to be both aware of this necessity and force himself or herself fiercely to ignore it. This is as impossible a task as being told not to think of something without being given a positive substitute: "Don't think of your own name." The artist, says James, "is in the perpetual predicament that the continuity of things is the whole matter, for him, of comedy and tragedy; that this continuity is never, by the space of an instant or an inch, broken, and that, to do anything at all, he has at once intensely to consult and intensely to ignore it" (ibid.).

A new infinity of the narrator's task reforms itself within the arbitrarily closed line drawn to make the infinite finite. One way to see this infinity of the finite is to recognize an equivocation in the concept of representation. This equivocation is also present in the term diegesis. A diegesis, as I have said, is the following through of a line already there. A representation is a presenting again of something once present. Any telling is a retelling, a new line different from the first line. It contains within itself, however, the potentiality of further repetition or of renewed representations. One doubling invites endless redoublings. The tracks can be retraced over and over, though sometimes with significant differences, for example, in every act of rereading, as James specifies in the preface to *The Golden Bowl*: "It was, all sensibly, as if the clear matter being still there, even as a shining expanse of snow spread over a plain, my exploring tread, for application to it, had quite unlearned the old pace and found itself naturally falling into another, which might sometimes indeed more or less agree with the original tracks, but might most often, or very nearly, break the surface in other places" (23:xiii–xiv).[9]

In the passage that follows the one quoted above from the preface to *Roderick Hudson*, James speaks of life as a featureless canvas. The novelist's work is the embroidery of figures on this surface. Life itself is a woven texture, but an undifferentiated or unfigured one. It contains the possibility of many figures rather than being a single unequivocal figure already present. A given representation is the choice of one line to follow with new thread interlaced from hole to hole on the already woven canvas of life. This new thread makes a figure, a flower on that ground. The same canvas contains the possibility of an infinite number of slightly different variations on the "original" flower, set side by side on the canvas like the figures on a quilt, or superimposed one atop the other in a palimpsest-like embroidery. All these figures were intrinsically present as possibilities of the original finite square or circle. They were not only possibilities but necessities. The initial requirement, the reader will remember, was for total completeness in the retracing of all possible relations.

Here the figure of the embroidered canvas breaks down, like all such spatial figures for a temporal linguistic sequence. In its breaking down it reveals an impasse that was implicit both as a conceptual and as a figurative possibility in the original idea to be expressed. The narrative line, word following word, episode following episode, in linear sequence, makes a configuration. The latent possibilities of relation in the presupposed subject, however, demand an indefinite number of repetitive variations-with-a-difference on any embroidered figure that happens to come first. These must be thought of as superimposed or simultaneous, with no intrinsic priorities of originality and repetition, though in words they must make a temporal line. In the spatial figure of embroidered canvas they must falsely be imagined as separate flowers side by side, extending outward in every direction on the canvas. This canvas, at first a figure for the finite surface enclosed within the charmed circle the artist has drawn by that "geometry of his own," now must become "boundless" once more, since it is the paradoxical unfolding of the infinity implicit in the finite. All the flowers possible on a single circle of canvas cannot be represented in that circle but only thought of as an infinitely repeating pattern, each figure somewhat different from the last. "All of which," says James of his claim that the demand for absolute continuity must be both intensely consulted and intensely ignored, "will perhaps pass but for a supersubtle way of pointing the plain moral that a young embroiderer of the canvas of life soon began to work in terror, fairly, of the vast expanse of that surface, of the boundless number of its distinct perforations for the needle, and of the tendency inherent in his many-colored flowers and figures to cover and consume as many as possible of the little holes. The development of the flower, of the figure, involved thus an immense counting of holes and a careful selection among them. That would have been, it seemed to him, a brave enough process, were it not the very nature of the holes so to invite, to solicit, to persuade, to practise positively a thousand lures and deceits" (1:vii).

I say nothing of James's stress on terror here nor of the latent sexual implication in all this talk of little holes that solicit and must be perforated with a needle, though I shall return to the latter. I emphasize now the way the finite has here become magically infinite once more. This happens according to the paradoxical law governing all James's fiction whereby the more apparently narrow, restricted, and exclusive the focus, as for example, on the relations of just four persons (or six if the Assinghams are included) in *The Golden Bowl*, the more the novel is likely to extend itself to greater and greater length and even then to be unfinished in the sense of being disproportionate. Each work by James has what he calls a "misplaced middle." It has a lopsided shape that the novelist seeks to hide by consummate dissimulation so that the incomplete treatment of certain relations will not appear. *The Golden Bowl* was originally planned as a short story. Ultimately it became one of James's longest and most intricate novels. Even so, the last of the six books is only forty-eight pages long in the New York Edition, whereas book 4 is two hundred pages long. The last book hurries somewhat desperately to a conclusion, in order to keep the manuscript within publishable limits.

What, exactly, are the "flowers and figures" of which James speaks? Is it a question of a single all-inclusive linguistic design encompassing the totality of the story, or is it a question of a repeating figure specified and then varied throughout the story? The flower figure is an ancient trope for figure itself, that is, for what used to be called "flowers of rhetoric," the anthology of tropes that must be used as the indispensable means of expressing by displacement what cannot be expressed in literal language. "Anthology" originally meant a bouquet of gathered flowers, which then by displacement became a collection of choice passages. Of what are James's flowers the figurative expressions? What is the literal for these figures? James's figure is at once single and multiple. It is the figure of the whole and at the same time the figure of the details' repeated config-uration. Figure is at once a name for "figures" in the sense of characters in the story, and at the same time it is the name for their patterned relation. "Figure" names a design that emerges only from the retracing of "the related state, to each other, of certain figures and things."

"Flower" or "figure"—the figure as flower—is James's metaphor for the configuration made by the "realistically" treated human characters and relationships, with all their proffered abundance of psychological and social detail. The realistic human story is the literal of which James's figure of the flower is the metaphor. Nevertheless, the characters in their relationships are not the end of the story. They are themselves, in all their referential specificity, the material with which James creates the overall design of his story, like a repeated figure in a carpet. The human story is the metaphor of the figure, which, paradoxically, is the literal object of the story, though it is a literal which could never be described or named literally. It exists only in trope, as figure or flower, as a catachresis. Catachresis is the rhetorical name for the flower that is no flower that disfigures the anthology of tropes. Catachresis is the name for that procedure whereby James uses all the realistic detail of his work as a novelist to name in figure, by a forced and abusive transfer,[10] something else for which there is no literal name. Since it has no literal name, it has no existence, within the convention of referentiality that the story as a work of realism accepts. To exist, as Aristotle believed, means to be visible, open to the senses, and therefore literally nameable. This nonexistence that nevertheless exists, this "something else," is what the figure figures, as "The Figure in the Carpet" shows.

"The Figure in the Carpet" is James's most explicit allegorical narrative involving catachresis, though this procedure is the strategy of all his fiction. This is a strategy that must be sharply distinguished from those of so-called self-referential fiction. Self-referentiality does not subvert the assumptions and procedures of realistic fiction, since self-reference is still reference. As such it is assimilable within the assumptions of mimetic representation. Many writers, British and American, have traced the supposedly gradual development within the novel since Cervantes of self-reflection on the novelist's procedures. These studies remain, in spite of their considerable sophistication, caught in problematic assumptions about mimetic representationalism. Such books were influential back in the 1960s and 1970s but, in spite of their sophistication, they may now seem to some people quaint and outmoded formalisms. Examples are books by Robert Alter, Peter Garrett, and Alan Friedman." Self-referentiality is the mirror image of extra-referentiality. The former imperturbably reaffirms the assumptions of the latter, since the notion of self-reference depends for its definition on the assumption that there could be such a thing as a straightforwardly realistic novel, from which the self-referential novel is a deviation, modification, or development. Self-reference, moreover, is still a form of reference. Catachresis, however, is in one way or another present in any "realistic" narrative, not only in allegories of that "something" James's figures designate but also in the way there is no "literal" language for the representation of states of consciousness and interior experience. Catachresis constantly subverts the claims of literal reference made by any realistic narrative, even the claims of straightforward mirroring made by the most apparently simple stories.

"The Figure in the Carpet" (1896) dramatizes this situation on the thematic level, on the figurative level, and on the overall level of its organization as text. As Shlomith Rimmon-Kenan has argued,[12] the meaning of this story is fundamentally undecidable. It presents clues or narrative details supporting two or more incompatible readings. Therefore all those critics who have presented "monological" readings of it have fallen into a trap set not only by the story itself, in its presentation of an enigma that invites definitive clarification, but also by the critic's false presupposition that each good work of literature should have a single, logically unified meaning.

The notion of undecidable meaning must be distinguished, in one direction, from a definition of ambiguity in literature as plurisignificance or richness of meaning. In the other direction, undecidability must be distinguished from a perspectivism asserting that since each reader brings something different to a text, the text has a different meaning for each reader. The insight into ambiguity and irony among the New Critics, for example, in Empson (from whose writing, by the way, Rimmon-Kenan distinguishes her concept of ambiguity), goes beyond a simple idea of plurisignificance. Nevertheless, such insights tend to be covered over or controlled by assumptions of organic unity or of unifying "structure." The New Critics tend to assume that a work has total and totalizable significance, even if that totalizing is something the critic can never satisfactorily express in words. Empson in fact has conspicuous mastery in expressing the complex structures he finds in a word or a passage. Although a literary text is seen as having a richness of meaning that is beyond paraphrase, nevertheless, for the New Critics, even for Empson, the subtlest of them all, that meaning makes a complex whole.

Undecidability of meaning, on the other hand, is an effect of the play of figure, concept, and narrative in the work that forbids unification or any making whole. This effect the words of the work impose on the reader, so that it is not a result of "reader response." Moreover, instead of rich plurisignificance, the notion of undecidability names the presence in a text of two or more incompatible or contradictory meanings that imply one another or are intertwined with one another, but which may by no means be felt or named as a unified totality. "Undecidability" names the discomfort of this perpetual lack of closure, like a Möbius strip, which has two sides, but only one side, yet two sides still, in an interminable oscillation. The reader feels an urgent need to decide between two readings, but is unable to do so without ignoring other salient elements in the text.

There is nothing new about the experience of a disquieting power in literature to which the name "unreadability" is sometimes given today. The great writers themselves through all the centuries of our tradition have tended to experience this power, as their works show. Readers, however, sometimes even writers in their readings of their own work, have tended to be beguiled by the lure of a single and totalizable meaning. This is the lure of metaphysics as such. This lure is always present as the other side of the coin of unreadability. Unreadability is the generation by the text itself of a desire for the possession of a single meaning, while at the same time the text itself frustrates this desire. The text leads the reader to believe that he or she ought to be able to say what it means. This is the demand made on the reader by any act of reading. At the same time the text makes such a pronouncement impossible. This is what "The Figure in the Carpet" is about, though to claim that one can, in so many words, say what it is about is of course to succumb to the lure, to take the bait (to borrow James's own figures in "The Figure in the Carpet"). It might be better to say that the story dramatizes the experience of undecidability, or, rather, since this experience can only be named in figure, it presents figures for it, not least in the recurrent pattern of interpersonal relations that forms the human base for the story's allegorizing of its own unreadability.

The "figure in the carpet" in this story is on the "literal" level the figure used by the narrator to formulate his understanding of Vereker's claim that all his own work as a novelist is unified by the presence of a single inclusive design. None of his critics has noticed this, says Vereker, though it is what all his work is written to reveal. The reader of this admirably comic story must therefore figure out what is meant by this figure in the carpet. She or he must also figure out what is meant by the adjacent terms and figures for this figure that the narrator or Vereker, at one time or another, use:

"Isn't there," [asks Vereker in his midnight confidence to the narrator] "for every writer a particular thing of that sort, the thing that most makes him apply himself, the thing without the effort to achieve which he wouldn't write at all, the very passion of his passion, the part of the business in which, for him, the flame of art burns most intensely? Well, it's *that!* . . .

[T]here's an idea in my work without which I wouldn't have given a straw for the whole job. It's the finest fullest intention of the lot, and the application of it has been, I think, a triumph of patience, of ingenuity. I ought to leave that to somebody else to say; but that nobody does say it is precisely what we're talking about. It stretches, this little trick of mine, from book to book, and everything else, comparatively, plays over the surface of it. The order, the form, the texture of my books will perhaps some day constitute for the initiated a complete representation of it. So it's naturally the thing for the critic to look for. It strikes me," my visitor added, smiling, "even as the thing for the critic to find." (15:230–31)[13]

The unifying design is here spoken of as an "idea" behind, or below, the work and yet "in" it too. It existed first as a patronizing or paternal matrix (mother and father at once) in the mind of its author, a generative "passion" or "intention" that was then "applied." What, however, was the base of this idea in the mind of the novelist? "I wondered as I walked away," says the narrator, exasperated at their second meeting by Vereker's refusal to give him any clue to the figure in the carpet of his works, "where he had got *his* tip" (241). After the "idea" has been "applied," the intention fulfilled, it exists as an immanent and yet transcendent pattern within and also behind the work, present both in the part of it and in the whole, and at the same time above and beyond the work as its presiding paternal/maternal genius. The work as a totality, its "surface," "texture," or "form," what is superficially visible in it, is a gradually self-completing representation of the figure.

The structure in question, the reader can see, is the basic metaphysical one of the logos. God, as a paradigmatic example of this, is in Christian theology seen as the creative word who is present in all his creations as their ground as well as evident as a divine signature written everywhere in the creation. This signature, however, is always veiled, since God can manifest himself, by definition, only in disguised, delegated, or represented appearances, of which Jesus Christ is the model. In a similar way, the figure in the carpet is, on the one hand, visible; it is the overall pattern of Vereker's work that ought to stare any critic in the face. On the other hand it is necessarily hidden, since anything visible is not it but the sign, signature, or trace of an "it" that is always absent. In short, the figure is a figure, a trope of substitution.

The various figures for this figure, glyphs or hieroglyphs, are dispersed everywhere in "The Figure in The Carpet," whether in local verbal clues or in the design of interpersonal relations the story makes. All these figures reinforce or restate the traditional paradox of the creative logos, immanent and transcendent at once, as well as its always present subversive latent anaglyph, the idea that there is no idea, the idea that the figure behind the surface is a phantasm performatively generated by the play of superficial and visible figurative elements. Neither of these presuppositions is possible without the other. Each generates the other in a regular rhythm of undecidability, figure and ground reversing constantly depending on which feature is focused.

The development of the story in "The Figure in the Carpet" is punctuated by a wonderfully comic series of clues playing on the various contradictory possibilities latent in this logocentric image: that it is within, as contained within a container, that it is beneath, that it is behind, that it is a pervasive hidden thread, that it is all surface and no depth and so a fraud, that it does not exist at all, that it is the abyss, that it is a fatal lure, the appearance of food or of satisfaction that destroys the one who yields to its promise, and so on. These clues are always figures, since the "it" can only be expressed in a figure. There are no literal terms for the "it." This means that these figures are exemplary catachreses. Rhythm, ratio, or proportion, measure of all—the figure is an idea, a design, a general and organizing intention; subjective as latent theoretical possibility, and yet existing only as objective theatrical pattern; within, behind, below; hidden and yet revealed; ground, groundless abyss, and yet surface pattern; secret, perhaps phantasmal, thread, and yet the figure made by the visible beads strung on that thread—in short, logos in all the complexity of its various meanings.

"Is it a kind of esoteric message?" asks the delightfully obtuse narrator. To which Vereker replies, "Ah my dear fellow, it can't be described in cheap journalese!" (233). Vereker refuses to give any of his readers a clue to his labyrinth because, as he says, "my whole lucid effort gives him the clue—every page and line and letter. The thing's as concrete there as a bird in a cage, a bait on a hook, a piece of cheese in a mousetrap. It's stuck into every volume as your foot is stuck into your shoe. It governs every line, it chooses every word, it dots every i, it places every comma" (ibid.). Immanent law which governs every detail and is therefore present in that detail, as contained within container, foot in shoe, this "thing" has the power of punctuating the line of the narrative like a comma, establishing the rhythm of pauses in the chain of signs that is essential to its meaning. It also gives heads to what might otherwise be decapitated, without a ruling energy of capitalization: it dots every i. It gives a law to the minuscule detail by establishing a pervasive law or figure of the whole. At the same time, the "thing" leads the one who sees it by the false promise of satisfaction, of filling, a saturating of emptiness and desire. This promise, however, leads to a diabolical satire of fulfillment. It leads to the abyss of death. The beautiful caged bird changes in mid-chain of figures into the bait to trap the presumably safely theoretical spectator, watching at a distance, as in a theater. "It" is a food that becomes a means of execution, like cheese that baits a mousetrap. Vereker's images are as much a warning as a promise. "Give it up—give it up!" he mockingly, but also "earnestly" and "anxiously," says to the narrator at the end of their midnight dialogue (235).

The "general intention" of Vereker's work is, as the narrator guesses, "a sort of buried treasure" (ibid.), or it is faintly audible, or it is detectable as a faint odor, in "whiffs and hints . . . , faint wandering notes of a hidden music" (244). It is a veiled idol or goddess (251), and yet visible as a mode of behavior betraying the goddess in her mortal incarnation, in her gait: "vera incessu patuit dea! [her way of walking proved her a goddess]" (ibid.).[14] This revelation is made by the rhythm of the text itself. "It's the very string," says Vereker, "that my pearls are strung on!" (241). In short, as the narrator guesses, it is "something like a complex figure in a Persian carpet" (240). Inside, outside; visible, hidden, "it" is also absent, hollow, a hoax, a vacancy: "The buried treasure was a bad joke, the general intention a monstrous *pose*" (236), says the narrator, in exasperation, and later: "I know what to think then. It's nothing!" (266).

The best, and most comic, expression in the story for this last possibility is a significantly displaced one. It is shifted from the work of the strongly masculine, even male chauvinist, Vereker ("A woman will never find out," he says of his secret figure [239]) to the parody of that work in the first novel by Gwendolen Erme, the woman in the story who is fascinated by Vereker's work and who is passed from man to man among the critics who are fascinated by it in their turn. "I got hold of 'Deep Down' again," says the narrator, of her first novel; "it was a desert in which she had lost herself, but in which too she had dug a wonderful hole in the sand—a cavity . . ." (250). The title and the figurative description of this novel; the title of Gwendolen Erme's second, slightly better, novel, *Overmastered* (!) ("As a tissue tolerably intricate it was a carpet with a figure of its own; but the figure was not the figure I was looking for" [267]); the title of Vereker's last work, *The Right of Way*; the name of the journal for which the narrator, Corvick, and others write reviews, *The Middle*—all these are dispersed clues, names of absent and unattainable texts. These titles reinforce the image of a journey of penetration, crossing barriers, reaching depths, falling into abysses, but remaining always, precisely, in the middle, on the way, as all this part of this present book is an exploration of middles and comes in the middle. However much he enjoys a right of way the reader is never finally in the arcanum. The reader remains face to face with some mediating sign, obstacle as well as promise, trace of an absence.

This structure is repeated in the chain of interpersonal relations that organizes James's story. It is a chain so absurd, when the reader thinks of it, as to be one of the major sources of comedy in the tale. This chain is what the narrator calls "a series of phenomena so strangely interlaced" (260). Behind the whole series is Vereker's sick wife. Her illness, "which had long kept her in retirement" (246), is the reason the great novelist goes south, never to be seen again by the narrator. His friend, Corvick, however, identifies the figure in the carpet of Vereker's work in a flash of intuition. Corvick visits Vereker in the south to have his insight confirmed. Presumably Corvick passes his secret on to his wife, Gwendolen (or does he?). She in turn may or may not have given the secret to her second husband, the egregious Drayton Deane, though Deane appears to be honest in his denials of knowledge. One by one, after Vereker's death, and then after the death of his wife (who probably, the narrator says, had never seen the figure in the carpet anyway), the possessors of the secret die. They die so abruptly and so fortuitously as to suggest that possession of this secret is deadly, like looking on the goddess naked. The newly-married Corvick falls from a dogcart on his head and is killed on the spot, leaving his critical essay on Vereker, the essay that was to have revealed all, a mere useless fragment. Gwendolen, who has married Corvick and presumably received the secret as a wedding present, then marries Drayton Deane, but dies in childbirth without telling the narrator the secret and perhaps without having revealed it to her new husband either.

The passing on of the secret obviously has something to do with sexual intimacy and sexual knowledge. The narrator's "impotence" (273) seems connected to his celibacy, though both he and Drayton Deane at the end of the story are left equally "victims of unappeased desire" (277), although Deane was not celibate. "Corvick," says the narrator, "had kept his information from his young friend till after the removal of the last barrier to their intimacy—then only had he let the cat out of the bag. Was it Gwendolen's idea, taking a hint from him, to liberate this animal only on the basis of the renewal of such a relation? Was the figure in the carpet traceable or describable only for husbands and wives—for lovers supremely united?" (265). "The Figure in the Carpet" here crosses the same thematic intersection that is dramatized in the way the celibate narrator of "The Aspern Papers" is excluded from knowledge of Jeffrey Aspern's secret private life. What is revealed in sexual knowledge? Is it nothing at all or some deep insight? The presumably celibate Henry James had reason to be anxious about this. Is sexual experience, on the contrary, a figure of death? Does it figure a vacancy, the absence of any heading power, any law able to put dots on the i's, or does it unveil some ultimate presence, capital source or phallogocentric origin, yarn beam, loom (istos),[15] on which is woven the figured carpet?

Is that figure the figure of nothing, or is it the figure of the logos? There is no way to know for sure. James's story remains caught in the oscillation among these various possibilities. It remains a fabric of puzzling analogies, not least important of which is the analogy between the frustrated activity of decipherment performed on Vereker's work by the narrator and that performed on James's own figure in the carpet by any reader. The brilliant accomplishment of the story, however, is to provide both tropological and narrational figures for this predicament.

I return now, after this deviation (or is "The Figure in the Carpet" not smack in the middle, right in the right of way?), to James's preface to *Roderick Hudson*. There the figure of the figure in the carpet is, the reader will remember, both figurative and literal, a name both for the figurative design of relations among the human figures in the story and for the "it" which is the literal goal of the story, as the young author works away month after month at his "pale embroidery" (1:viii). The images of cloth and of the figures woven on that cloth reappear, both before and after the passage I began with from the preface, in obedience to the law of the compulsion to repeat that seems intrinsic to signs. It seems as though signs must have a genetic life of their own, like some viral energy of replication appropriating foreign conceptual material to their own shape, perhaps in defiance of their user's intentions.

The metaphor of canvas is first introduced as a name for a ship's sails. This happens by way of the metaphor describing *Roderick Hudson* as James's first adventure out of the short story's shallow waters into deep water in the novel's larger ship: "The subject of 'Roderick' figures to me vividly this employment of canvas, and I have not forgotten, even after long years, how the blue southern sea seemed to spread immediately before me and the breath of the spice-islands to be already in the breeze" (1:vi). After this figure, introduced so casually and so artificially (in the sense that its figurative nature is made obvious), is fully exploited in the theoretical paragraph I discussed above, it reappears once more in the subsequent return to reminiscences about writing *Roderick Hudson*. It returns as an image of the way the novel had not been finished when it began to appear in monthly parts. This fact "is one of the silver threads of the recoverable texture of that embarrassed phase" (1:viii). The sequence of paragraphs is like a quilt with squares in repeating patterns.

How can this series of compulsive duplications be stopped from proliferating endlessly? This is the question James addresses in concluding his theoretical development of the embroidered flower image. The image is of a seduction. The embroidering novelist, "masculine" perhaps in his activity of piercing all those little holes with his needle, is "feminine" in his act of "covering" them and in the passivity of his yielding to the invitation of the perforated surface. He follows it wherever it may lead. It is, the reader will remember, "the very nature of the holes so to invite, to solicit, to persuade, to practise positively a thousand lures and deceits." The problem, once the writer is led astray, seduced, is how to stop. He must initially assume that there is some loving fatherly power, paternal and patronizing. This father would govern the whole and give it visible boundaries, a beginning and an end. Such a power would act as the law or logos of the whole fabric. It would tell the writer where to start and when to stop.

Alas, no such power exists. The writer must act as his own father, in an act of self-generating that is at the same time a self-mutilation, an act of surrender and sacrifice. The writer can come to an end, make shapely literary form, preserve himself from the abyss of the interminable, only by his willingness to practice a cutting off at the moment of "cruel crisis." This crisis is an encounter at the crossroads that reverses the Oedipal murder. The artist as father, as patron, cuts off the potentially infinite power of the artist as (effeminate) son, as weaver, as artificer. Only this act of giving up can draw the line that makes narrative possible. Narration is here defined as a feminine and at the same time masculine activity of embroidery. It pierces the little holes on the prepared canvas with a threaded needle and makes the figure in the carpet:

The prime effect of so sustained a system, so prepared a surface, is to lead on and on; while the fascination of following resides, by the same token, in the presumability *somewhere* of a convenient, of a visibly-appointed stopping-place. Art would he easy indeed if, by a fond power disposed to "patronise" it, such conveniences, such simplifications, had been provided. We have, as the case stands, to invent and establish them, to arrive at them by a difficult, dire process of selection and comparison, of surrender and sacrifice. The very meaning of expertness is acquired courage to brace one's self for the cruel crisis from the moment one sees it grimly loom (1:vii–viii).

EIGHT

MULTIPLICATIONS
OF THE LINES

Le fil du texte disparaît, réapparaît, se tend jusqu'à la vibration, devient invisible par trop de rigueur ou de détours, se charge de tous les noms, porte la Mort et le mort.

—Jacques Derrida, *Glas*

The wire of the text disappears, reappears, stretches itself to the point of vibration, becomes invisible through too much rigor or too many detours, loads itself with all the names, bears Death and the dead man.

—Jacques Derrida, *Glas*, trans. John P. Leavey, Jr., and Richard Rand

So much for the middle as mediation between beginning and end. In previous chapters I have discussed complications in the narrative line that arise from discontinuities in sequence among all the segments that make up middles as they are generated by some putative beginning, drawn by some preexisting end, or sustained by some immanent or perhaps infinitely distant ground. I turn now to various doublings and tremblings of the narrative line itself as it makes its way from here to there. If a narrative cannot properly begin at a beginning, it cannot, having once begun in defiance of this impossibility, ever properly stop, though of course it can and does always stop, in one way or another, if only by just stopping. A narrative tends to continue forever as an indefinitely displaced middle. This continuation can only be cut off arbitrarily in midcareer, like an unfinished bridge jutting out into thin air. That middle, moreover, as I shall now show, is never a single straight line, never a single narrative account. It is always in one way or another double, triple, quadruple, potentially multiplied ad infinitum, like Derrida's vibrating tightrope,' a commentary on Genet's *Pour un funambule* ("For a Tightrope Walker"). The middle may therefore ultimately destroy itself as line. The narrative line is never a safe means of getting from here to there. It tends to give way beneath the weight of anyone who walks on it, like a frayed tightrope which, at the first pressure, breaks.

So far, in this discussion of beginnings, middles, and ends as they are expressed by the line figure, I have for the most part been talking as if the line of narrative were spoken by a single voice, a voice identifiable with a single generative consciousness, supported by a single logos (in the sense of "mind"). I have spoken, in short, as if the narrative line were monological. The problems of the narrative line arise, I have been suggesting, from interruptions of its continuity and from difficulties in beginning or ending it. That line, I have for the most part so far assumed, nevertheless remains, as long as it can be produced at all, safely tied to a single originating voice. This is of course by no means always, or even usually, the case. Additional complications of the narrative line arise from all its doublings: doublings of narrators and narrators within narrators; the enigmatic doublings of indirect discourse; repetitions in multiple plots; displacements effected by citations, epigraphs, prefaces, inserted letters, quoted signs (in the literal sense of signboards), inscriptions, gravestone markings—all that interpolated language in novels that is in different ways not at the same level of discourse as the basic narration. My interrogation of these is organized around a cascade of questions that are not rhetorical: I am really puzzled as to how these interpolations work and how they are to be differentiated from one another in their working.

What is the general effect of these graftings? They are aeroliths from some other planet, as one might call them, intruding into the enclosed atmosphere of the primary narrative language. Who speaks a given example of these, from what time or place? Are they inside or outside the story proper? How do they interact with that primary story-telling language to produce meaning? What is the effect, for example, in Anthony Trollope's *The Prime Minister*, when, after a prolonged immersion in the troubled inner consciousness of Plantagenet Palliser, the narrator shifts abruptly, in the gap between chapter and chapter, to the differently tormented mind of Ferdinand Lopez? What is the effect of George Eliot's citation, in Spanish and in English, as an epigraph to chapter 2 of *Middlemarch*, of the passage from *Don Quixote* about the wash pan that is taken by Don Quixote as Mambrino's helmet? Is that effect different from the effect of the epigraph to chapter 72, apparently composed by George Eliot herself: "Full souls are double mirrors making still / The endless vista of fair things before, / Repeating things behind"?[2]

Who is to be imagined as speaking, writing, citing, or signing these epigraphs? The author, Marian Evans? Or the narrator, George Eliot, the fictive persona of Marian Evans? What are the epigraphs' relation to the main body of the chapters on which they comment? Are they ironical? Straightforwardly interpretative? Superior in knowledge to the narrator, or equal, or inferior? Located just where in the psychic and scriptive space of the novel? Is the effect of such epigraphs different from that of citations inside the main body of the narration, as when Septimus Harding, in Anthony Trollope's *The Warden*, says to his daughter: "There is an old saying, Nelly: 'Everyone knows where his own shoe pinches'"?[3] Do citations made by characters in novels differ in function from those made by the narrator, as when Hardy cites Shakespeare in a title to place his rustics "under the greenwood tree," while those rustics presumably do not know Shakespeare?

What is the function of the odd phrase in parentheses after the title of Robert Browning's "The Glove": "(Peter Ronsard *loquitur.*)"?[4] The phrase in Latin tells the reader the poem is supposed to be thought of as spoken, now, in the present tense, by the French poet. The poem, however, is in English, except for two additional Latin phrases. It would never have been spoken by Ronsard in the way it is printed on the page. There is not one word of French in the poem. That language is effaced, as if it did not exist. Who speaks the parenthetical phrase in Latin, where, and to whom? Why in Latin? It must be another imagined voice or mask, neither Browning nor Ronsard but a different "dramatis persona," to put in the singular the plural title of a volume of Browning's poems (*Dramatis Personae*), or it must be imagined as a scribal clue, something written, not spoken. It would then be like the language in a playscript that gives names of characters, stage directions, and so on, words that are not spoken in the play's performance. Browning's poem, a short story in verse, in any case cannot be referred back to a single writing or speaking source.

What about letters in novels? I am thinking not so much of those letters that make up the main body of the text in an epistolary novel, but of those letters interpolated in the text of a novel told by an "omniscient" narrator. Such letters are like a living parasite within its host. Scarcely a Victorian novel exists that does not contain at least one such document, or pseudodocument, cited, inserted, often set off from the main text, with date, place, address, and signature. Such interventions of another hand, quoted, so to speak, by the narrator, far from straightforwardly reinforcing the verisimilitude of the novel, are more disturbing to that verisimilitude than letters in a novel entirely in letters, where a single convention is obeyed throughout.

Examples of quoted letters in novels are legion. Paradigmatic are those two letters of resignation Septimus Harding writes to his old friend the bishop in Trollope's *The Warden*. Both are given in toto in the text. One is a formal, public document in which Harding resigns the wardenship. The other is a private note to the bishop discussing the resignation's motives.[5] Another example is that letter from Hans Meyrick in chapter 52 of George Eliot's *Daniel Deronda*.[6] As Cynthia Chase has shown, this letter is an ironic subversion of concepts (for example, reversal of cause and effect in Daniel's belated discovery of his Jewish blood) that are essential to the narrator's interpretation of the main stories.[7]

Such letters can be seen as the externalization of an intersubjective relation, one person speaking to another at a distance. Do they differ in effect from other nonepistolary interpolated documents in novels? An example of the latter would be that "crumpled scrap of paper" the hero of Hardy's *The Mayor of Casterbridge* pins upon the head of his bed just before he dies. This is "Michael Henchard's Will," with its terrifying series of negative performatives, spoken from the grave. Henchard's strange speech acts attempt to order something not to happen. They are signed, in each copy of the novel, with the simulacrum of Henchard's signature. Here is another disquieting kind of language within language in novels. What is the linguistic nature of a signature's copy? Does it differ from the copy of other spoken or written words, for example, the copy of a holograph letter or a will? Here is "Michael Henchard's Will," with the line of quotation marks down the side as Hardy gives them. These emphasize the copied or secondary nature of the document that the reader actually has before his or her eyes:

> "That Elizabeth-Jane Farfrae be not told of my death,
> or made to grieve on account of me.
> "& that I be not bury'd in consecrated ground.
> "& that no sexton be asked to toll the bell.
> "& that nobody is wished to see my dead body.
> "& that no murners walk behind me at my funeral.
> "& that no flours be planted on my grave.
> "& that no man remember me.
> "To this I put my name.
>   "MICHAEL HENCHARD."[8]

The citation of these odd performative locutions by the narrator causes exactly the opposite of their intention to occur. Henchard attempts to insure the nonperformance of all those ritual markings whereby a community attempts to make certain that one of its members is both really dead and will nevertheless survive beyond the grave, at least in the memory of the survivors. This intention is contradicted anew every time Henchard's will is read. This happens according to a paradox of the remembering of an intention to forget that is pervasive in Hardy's fiction. To read or to quote "& that no man remember me" is to remember what one is commanded to forget. In a similar way all negatives in dreams are positives. For example, no man or woman can carry out Henchard's imperative, "Don't think of a dead body," unless a positive order ("Think of happy Elizabeth-Jane Farfrae!") supervenes. The effort of erasure by means of language's instrumental power infallibly turns into an iteration. It becomes a monumental perpetuation beyond or over death, undermining the happiness of the survivors, like a ghost at midday. The "not" maintains what is obliterated as the verbal phantasm of itself. The negative occurs and reoccurs in the perpetual present of the absence it commands: "& that no man remember me." The language of narration, even when what is narrated is not the story of a death, is always the maintaining of what is narrated in a posthumous survival, in a relation to death, beyond death, as a kind of ghostly negative that nevertheless has positive existence. All narration is a murmur from beyond the grave, the citation of something that has always already been spoken or written, killing it as living speech and resurrecting it at the same time as ghostly, remembered speech. The strange embedded languages—letters, citations, and so on—within the primary narrative language of novels work to bring this into the open.

Each form of these embedded languages works differently and would require a different analysis. What, to give another example, is the effect of interpolated stories in novels? These are places where the tale-teller suddenly shifts from one narrating voice to another. I have elsewhere discussed one example of an interpolated tale, "Die wunderlichen Nachbarskinder" ("The Strange Neighbor Children") in Goethe's *Die Wahlverwandtschaften*.[9] Much ink has been spilled discussing the interpolated tales in Dickens's *Pickwick Papers*. Is the effect of interpolated tales different from the shift by an omniscient narrator from following one mind in indirect discourse to following another mind? An example of the latter is the change, in Henry James's *The Golden Bowl*, from a primary focus, in the first half, on the mind of the Prince, presented in indirect discourse, to a primary focus, in the second half, on the mind of the Princess, also presented in indirect discourse. An example of the former is the substitution, in Joseph Conrad's *Lord Jim*, of Marlow's voice for that of the omniscient narrator who has told the story for the first four chapters. To give another case, Charles Dickens's *Little Dorrit* jumps, across the gap between the end of chapter 20 and the beginning of chapter 21, from one narrative domain to another. Chapter 20 ends with words spoken of Arthur Clennam by the omniscient narrator: "On the way [back to London], he unfolded the sheets of paper and read in them what is reproduced in the next chapter." The next chapter begins with the first words of Miss Wade's "The History of a Self Tormentor": "I have the misfortune of not being a fool."[10] The narrative switches from one speaker to another, from speech by the narrator in the third person past tense about the protagonist to speech (or rather writing) in the first person present tense by a character about herself. This transfer seems markedly different from the shift from one plot to another in a multiplotted novel. If chapter 20 of *Little Dorrit* is to be imagined as spoken, chapter 21 as written, what then of the phrase, "reproduced in the next chapter"? This phrase implicitly speaks of chapter 20 also as a chapter, therefore as written, not spoken. The phrase is a parabasis of the illusion on which it depends. It is another example of all the many forms of fissures, clefts, or shifts in strata of storytelling language I am identifying and discriminating. Any novel, however perfectly it maintains the fiction of being "told," contains multitudinous evidence, strewn here and there over the surface of the text, of being a fabricated document. The reader is constantly being reminded that what she or he reads was written down somewhere by someone in calculated simulation of imaginary speaking voices.

What of illustrations, those representations in another medium, interpolated, "tipped into," the printed text, like a white rose grafted on a red rose tree? They usually emanate from another hand, except in certain exceptional cases, like W. M. Thackeray's illustrations for his own novels. In either case, however, they are interpretations of the text in another medium. Do such pictures merely "illustrate," bring to light something already latently there? Do they thereby reinforce a continuity and consistency firmly maintained by the narrative line of the novel in question, or do they interrupt that line? If the latter, how does that interruption function, in a given case?"

Footnotes, prefaces, introductions, conclusions—all those bits of language in a novel that are peripheral, outside the main text—in one way or another function as a form of parabasis. They break the illusion on which the novel's power depends. It is as though the author has interrupted his or her role as narrator and has stepped forward to speak in his or her own voice of the novel as an artifice and of the novel's function in the real world of the reader. It is not clear who, exactly, speaks or writes these passages. What is their effect on the reader's response to the novel as a whole? Examples, again, are superabundant. A salient one is the "Finale" of George Eliot's *Middlemarch*. This ends with a direct address to the reader in which Dorothea is spoken of at once from inside the novel, as if she were a real historical person, and at the same time implicitly as a fictional personage who will have unpredictable diffusive effects on the readers of the novel. The passage is at once a parabasis and not a parabasis:

But the effect of her being on those around her was incalculably diffusive: for the growing good of the world is partly dependent on unhistoric acts; and that things are not so ill with you and me as they might have been, is half owing to the number who lived faithfully a hidden life, and rest in unvisited tombs.[12]

Marcel Proust's *À la recherche du temps perdu* contains another admirable example: "In this book in which there is not a single incident which is not fictitious, not a single character who is a real person in disguise [pas un seul personnage 'à clefs'], in which everything has been invented by me in accordance with the requirements of my theme [selon les besoins de ma démonstration], I owe it to the credit of my country to say that only the millionaire cousins of Françoise who came out of retirement to help their niece when she was left without support, only they are real people who exist."[13] The reader will see the vertiginous oscillation here. Françoise's generous cousins are real people, given their proper name (Larivière) by Marcel. But they help a character, Françoise, whom Marcel swears is fictitious, not modeled on a real person. As everyone knows, Marcel is lying, since Françoise was very much modeled on a real person. Or is this isolated sentence spoken not by the fictitious Marcel, narrator of the *Recherche*, but by the real Marcel Proust, who is inserting this palpable lie into a fictitious work? Alternatively, if the speaker is "Marcel," not Marcel Proust, then he is a fictive personage in any case, and everything he says is fictive, that is, a species of lie. That would seem to give him the right to say anything he likes, while at the same time depriving whatever he says of purchase on the real world. The Larivières themselves are fictionalized by this linguistic gesture or penchant of the language.

Another case in point is that strange footnote at the end of the next to the last chapter of Thomas Hardy's *The Return of the Native*. Here Hardy breaks the illusion that the novel is history. He steps forward to speak in his own voice, apparently, or rather to write in his own hand, in the "here" of an inscription at the bottom of the page. The footnote constitutes, it seems, a devastating indictment of his novel's authenticity. The footnote not only calls attention to the fictionality of the story, whereas the novel itself consistently maintains the illusion of its historicity. It also undermines the happy ending. That end is indicted as inconsistent with the original intention of the author. It is also, Hardy says, inconsistent with the story line's natural direction. The ending, says the footnote, in a kind of sardonic interruption from the bottom margin of the page, is a fraudulent capitulation to popular taste and to the demands of serial publication. Here the line of the narrative is broken by another voice or another hand asserting that the text proper is falsified by an ending that cannot be reconciled with what has gone before:

The writer may state here that the original conception of the story did not design a marriage between Thomasin and Venn. He was to have retained his isolated and weird character to the last; and to have disappeared mysteriously from the heath, nobody knowing whither—Thomasin remaining a widow. But certain circumstances of serial publication led to a change of intent.

Readers can therefore choose between the endings, and those with an austere artistic code can assume the more consistent conclusion to be the true one.[14]

After this footnote, the final chapter, "Cheerfulness again asserts itself at Blooms-End, and Clym finds His Vocation," takes on for its reader a phantasmal, hollow, factitious character. It is as though it were not really there, or as if it were there not because it really happened that way but by way of the fabricating false witness of the author. The whole story, however, is fictitious, and Hardy was free to end it any way he liked, according to any "intent" that was dominant at the moment, including the intent to satisfy popular taste. Or could it be, after all, that the happy ending is the consistent one? The reader is forced to choose, as Hardy says, just as in the cases of the two endings of Dickens's *Great Expectations* and of the two versions of Hardy's *The Well-Beloved*. The reader cannot choose, however, as Hardy says, except by the arbitrary imposition of one artistic code or another. The ending of *The Return of the Native* remains double. It oscillates ironically between the two possibilities. Hardy's footnote has permanently broken the unity of the narrative line.

What, finally, is the function of the prefaces or introductions that are parts of the texts of so many novels? Or are they safely outside the texts they preface? Is the voice who speaks or the hand that writes an introduction always that of the author, or can a preface also be written by a persona of the author? Is the preface's voice or hand always different from the narrator's? What happens in the fissure between the end of an introduction and the beginning of the text proper? For example, what happens in the space, indicated by a specific date and place ("Hermitage / 12 September, 1919") and by a list of chapter titles, between the end of the "Foreword" to D. H. Lawrence's *Women in Love* and the first words of the novel as such?

In point of style, fault is often found with the continual, slightly modified repetition. The only answer is that it is natural to the author: and that every natural crisis in emotion or passion or understanding comes from this pulsing, frictional to-and-fro, which works up to culmination.

Hermitage
12 September, 1919

[This is followed by the chapter list. Then the novel proper begins:]

Ursula and Gudrun Brangwen sat one morning in the window-bay of their father's house in Beldover, working and talking. . . ."[5]

The famous and still shocking figure at the end of the "Foreword" is an interpretation or even subversive deconstruction, before the fact, of the story. *Women in Love* has an episodic structure. Each chapter develops one "symbol" (the rabbit, the horse, the African statue, wrestling, the stoning of the reflected image of the moon, and so on) to a climactic revelation. Far from being asked to think of this sequence as a referential narrative oriented toward the imitation of men and women in society, the reader is invited by the foreword to think of the novel as the remaining traces, so to speak, of a series of autoerotic performances, or perhaps of fantasied sexual assaults on the reader. In each of these Lawrence, pen in hand, works himself up to a culmination through the frictional to-and-fro of a repetition that is natural to him. These episodes, far from imitating nature and human nature in the sense of mirroring them, imitate nature rather in miming, in the words on the page, the productive rhythms of nature. Or rather it mimes those productive rhythms onanistically short-circuited, shunted off on a detour from real satisfaction to the fantasy satisfaction provided by literature. The material world is reentered only when the book, much later, is read, "used" by its readers. That use, however, remains itself a detour from real life, another figurative or substitutive satisfaction. The detour of literature never returns to the main road.[16] Rarely has the way the physical act of writing can be a substitution for sexual activity been made so overt. This gives another center (the "natural" pulsations of the author) to the apparently monological story line of the fictional narrator. The story becomes a figurative substitution, not what it apparently is. The narrative voice, with its repetitive rhythms, becomes a stand-in for something else. It is, rather, a double stand-in, since it stands for the act of writing, which stands in turn for the sexual act of auto-affection.

A second example, among so many, of the subversive doubling effect produced by prefaces to realist novels, is that strange ending Dickens wrote for the preface to the Cheap Edition (1850) of *Oliver Twist*. Dickens cites from *The Observer* newspaper a statement by one Sir Peter Laurie in a vestry meeting of Marylebone parish claiming that Jacob's Island only exists in fiction, so need not trouble the city officials. "The Bishop of London, poor soul, in his simplicity," said Sir Peter, "thought there really was such a place, which he had been describing so minutely, *whereas it turned out that it ONLY existed in a work of fiction, written by Mr. Charles Dickens ten years ago* [roars of laughter]."[17] Dickens's commentary on this is comic enough. It is effective polemically in the vehemence of its irony. Its hyperbole, however, becomes a little disquieting as the paragraph proceeds. It is as though there were some alien energy in Dickens's irony causing him to say something more or different from what he apparently means to say. He inadvertently raises questions about the status of *Oliver Twist* in relation to the reality Dickens claims it copies:

When I came to read this, I was so much struck by the honesty, by the truth, and by the wisdom of this logic, as well as by the fact of the sagacious vestry, including members of parliament, magistrates, officers, chemists, and I know not who else listening to it meekly (as became them), that I resolved to record the fact here, as a certain means of making it known and causing it to be reverenced by, many thousands of people. Reflecting upon this logic, and its universal application; remembering that when FIELDING described Newgate, the prison immediately ceased to exist; that when SMOLLETT took Roderick Random to Bath, that city instantly sank into the earth; that when SCOTT exercised his genius on Whitefriars, it incontinently glided into the Thames; that an ancient place called Windsor was entirely destroyed in the reign of Queen Elizabeth by two Merry Wives of that town, acting under the direction of a person of the name of SHAKESPEARE; and that Mr. POPE, after having at a great expense completed his grotto at Twickenham, incautiously reduced it to ashes by writing a poem upon it;—I say, when I came to consider these things, I was inclined to make this preface the vehicle of my humble tribute of admiration to SIR PETER LAURIE. But, I am restrained by a very painful consideration—by no less a consideration than the impossibility of *his* existence. For SIR PETER LAURIE having been himself described in a book (as I understand he was, one Christmas time, for his conduct on the seat of Justice), it is but too clear that there CAN be no such man![8]

At first this seems no more than a single irony, saying one thing and meaning another. Dickens indignantly reaffirms the realist aesthetic that is used in the preface to the third edition (1841) to defend the presentation of the Dodger, Sikes, and Nancy: "IT IS TRUE."[19] *Oliver Twist* as a novel copies reality. It draws its authenticity from its accurate correspondence to reality, for example, the correspondence between the description in the novel of the slum, Jacob's Island, and the real slum in London. The purpose of the novel, or one of its purposes, is to make something happen in the real world, to persuade those in power to make sanitary reforms. As the passage, with its crescendo of ironic annihilations, continues, however, the other side of the truth about the power of writing appears. It seems to be unintentionally revealed by Dickens's intention to say something else forcefully by saying its ironic opposite. There *is* a negative power in fiction. Jacob's Island in the novel presupposes, at least for the time of the reading, the effacement of the real slum in London. The reading of a text, however referential that text may be, assumes, or rather creates, the nonpresence, during the reading, of what the text points to, as a signpost functions by saying the thing it names is somewhere else, over there, absent, displaced. We never encounter realities in any piece of writing, only their figments or simulacra. The two Jacob's Islands' modes of existence are different. One is physical, the other verbal. The two cannot dwell easily together. Each presupposes the effacement of the other. They are like a particle and its antiparticle, mirror images that annihilate each other on contact. The language of fiction is, as Joyce was to argue in *Finnegans Wake*, both a "lifewand" and a "deathbone." Dickens's paragraph, on the other side of its irony, is an exuberant exercise of the deathbone's magic power to turn things into fictions by naming them, so decreating them, one by one— Jacob's Island, Newgate Prison, Bath, Whitefriars, Windsor, Pope's grotto, ultimately Sir Peter Laurie himself. Dickens's full capitals for these proper names seem to correspond to the exercise of this magic power of annihilation. Name something in capitals and it vanishes. Among these annihilations, however, would be that of the two voices who speak in preface and novel. The author of the preface and the narrator of *Oliver Twist* are the same person, or seem to be. No one can miss the familiar voice of Dickens himself, full of generous rage against the mistreatment of the poor, in the polemical diatribes within the novel, as well as in the preface. Nevertheless, the author and the narrator are rather mirror images of one another than identical. Each is distinguishable from the other by specific traits of language, for example, in the way the narrator speaks of Sikes, Nancy, and the rest as having had a literal, historical existence, whereas the author of the preface speaks of them as true in the sense of being accurate simulations of real prostitutes and thieves in London. Each voice ironically suspends the existence of the other. If Sir Peter Laurie is nullified by being described in a book, the most striking version of this paradoxical life-giving, death-dealing power of fiction is the way it is impossible for Dickens the author and "Dickens" the narrator to dwell together within the same universe of discourse, just as Marcel Proust and Marcel, the author and the narrator of *À la recherche du temps perdu*, cannot be reconciled. This is the case however much they may succeed in dwelling uneasily together within the covers of the same book. Charles Dickens in creating the fictive narrator who tells the story of Oliver Twist by the same gesture threatens himself with annihilation. The ironic language of the preface of 1850 gives the reader power to see this.

I have given some examples of breaks in the single line of language in novels—epigraphs, prefaces, interpolated letters, footnotes, cited documents, chapter titles, and so on. Is it possible to develop a general theory to account for all of these, or does each work differently? It would seem that the concept of a single paternal authorizing consciousness should serve as a unifying principle. This singleness would allow the assimilation of all these disparate levels of language and their return to the foyer of a single mind. The author of the novel is the source and guarantee of all the language in the text. His is an embracing consciousness within which the minds of the various imaginary persons—characters, narrators, speakers or writers of titles, and so on—express themselves, within that safe unifying enclosure. A novel is a benign sort of ventriloquism, in which the novelist pretends to be this person or that, speaks for them or as them. The pretense, however, fools no one. The novel as a genre, this line of argument would claim, is originally and permanently monological. All the language within it can be returned to a single source, base, or logos. All dialogue within a novel, for example, that between character and character, or that penetration of the character's mind by the narrator's mind, registered in indirect discourse, is ultimately monological. It is based on a transparency of these minds to one another within a single mind that comprehends them all. That mind returns all the other minds to a single principle by which they may be fully understood and interpreted.

Would this reduction account for all the examples of narrative doubling I have identified? I think not. Perhaps there is an intrinsic possibility of what might be called "radical polylogism" in storytelling. This may happen as an effect, perhaps inadvertent, of language itself. It may happen as an effect of the human imaginative power to be, or to think of itself as being, someone other than itself and to speak for that other. "Radical polylogism" would mean the presence of an indefinite number of incompatible logoi in a text. By no effort of reduction could these be reduced back to the unity of a single point of view or of a single mind. These logoi would remain irreconcilable, heterogeneous, like planets with different atmospheres, different principles of life, different flora and fauna. Or one might think of this doubling (when there are only two) as an ellipse with two foci. The presence of two or more irreconcilable voices or measures of meaning may be encountered as the juxtaposition of two or more modes of language: preface against narration, epigraph against chapter, footnote against text. Or it may be the enclosure within the narrative of another alien narrative, like Miss Wade's "The History of a Self Tormentor" or the letter of Hans Meyrick in *Daniel Deronda*. Or it may be the overlapping, in a single stretch of discourse, of the language of two incompatible minds, for example in the superimposition of mind over mind in indirect discourse. In all these cases the reader is unable to bring the language back to a single all-embracing unified reading. Two or more incompatible readings, each drawn to the center of gravity of its own perspective, are possible. To make any one of these readings leaves something left over or left out, some remnant, morsel of text, some detail that cannot be assimilated to it. Such a text is like a conglomerate igneous rock that has embedded in the main mass bits of other kinds of rock that were not dissolved entirely by its molten heat. These remain enclosed there as foreign substances, alien crystals.

The great modern theorist of dialogue in this sense is Mikhail Bakhtin, or Mixail Baxtin (even his name transliterated into English is dialogical, as is his notorious [probable] use of pseudonyms). In "Discourse in Dostoevsky," chapter 5 of *Problems of Dostoevsky's Poetics*, and in "Discourse in the Novel," in *The Dialogic Imagination*,[20] Bakhtin recognizes, in a way ultimately subversive of his overt theory, that dialogism is not necessarily a matter of the juxtaposition of blocks of language emanating from different irreconcilable points of view or ways of speaking, but that it may focus on a single word in a text. Bakhtin calls this "microdialogue."[21] The possibility of microdialogue shifts the governing reference from logos in the sense of mind to logos in the sense of word. This would put in question, in spite of Bakhtin's use of the term "voice" in connection with microdialogue, all those discussions of Bakhtin's work that understand dialogue as exclusively a matter of minds, selves, or consciousnesses in interaction, not essentially as a matter of language. The single word may point simultaneously toward two different linguistic foci or be simultaneously a link in two different clashing sign systems. Each one of these would be an incomplete circuit of meaning without the word in question, but each appropriates the word in a different way.[22]

A fissure, moreover, something dialogical in Bakhtin's own argument, also opens between his recognition that dialogue in the radical sense of double-centered language is a universal possibility in narrative and his historicist claim that Dostoevsky brought something altogether new into the history of narrative types. All narrative prior to Dostoevsky, Bakhtin sometimes implies, was essentially monological, while at other times he allows for the possibility of dialogue at any time. Even the attempt to master dialogical doubling through theoretical reasoning seems to become dialogical, that is, no longer, strictly speaking, reasonable, just as rational discourse about irony seems infallibly to become itself ironical. Both attempts at mastery thereby undermine their claims to sovereign understanding. I shall return later to irony as the endpoint of my own rational sequence. My own sequence surely, I am confident, avoids the dangers I am identifying.

NINE

PLATO'S DOUBLE DIEGESIS

I now turn to a major means by which middles are doubled in narratives: citation of another's speech. An important passage in book 3 of the *Republic* sets single narration (diegesis) against double narration (mimesis or double diegesis).[1] The passage shows that the subversive possibility of dialogue, in Bakhtin's sense of diverse incompatible voices, multiple mental or linguistic centers in a single text, has haunted Western thought at least since Plato. According to contextual assumptions that have remained dominant throughout the centuries, Plato's condemnation of *mimesis* takes place in connection with specific theological and metaphysical concepts, in proximity to a discussion of lying, and on the basis of an opposition between male and female speech as well as of a distinction between speaking and writing.

The model, for Plato, of simple narration (diegesis) is the speech of God: "Then there is no lying poet in God. . . . Then God is altogether simple and true in deed and word, and neither changes himself nor deceives others by visions or words or the sending of signs in waking or in dreams."[2] Is the truth-telling speech of God perhaps modelled on the image of an authoritative masculine human voice that speaks directly from the foyer of its own presence to itself and says only what corresponds exactly, in unbroken continuity, to that self-presence? For such a voice there is no fissure, temporal or spatial, within which lies, dissimulation, or other base and baseless speech may enter. Which logos is the image of which? This insoluble problem arises whenever it is a question of the figure of speech, since speech is always, by definition, derived, secondary, a copy. It must be a figure for some literal act of production, for example, the creative performatives of God or of nature.

Those productions, however, can only be spoken of by analogy with the figure of human speech, in a torsion twisting the mind and constantly reversing original and copy.

The interdict against mimesis, or against a species of what Bakhtin calls dialogue, follows directly from this paradigm. The proper narration is one in which the poet speaks in his own voice (poets are generically male for Plato) and tells the story directly, like a man speaking to other men, or like the direct speech of God. This is "simple diegesis." Mimesis begins whenever the poet pretends to be someone else and mimes the voice of another. The example Plato gives is amusing enough. It involves the rewriting of a passage in the *Iliad* that is mimesis, therefore, according to Socrates, dangerous, lying, immoral. In the speech of Chryses in book 1 of the *Iliad*, Homer

delivers as if he were himself Chryses and tries as far as may be to make us feel that not Homer is the speaker, but the priest, an old man. . . . But when he delivers a speech as if he were someone else, shall we not say that he then assimilates thereby his own diction as far as possible to that of the person whom he announces as about to speak? . . . And is not likening oneself to another in speech or bodily bearing an imitation [mimesis] of him to whom one likens oneself? . . . But if the poet should conceal himself nowhere, then his entire poetizing and narration would have been accomplished without imitation. And lest you may say again that you don't understand, I will explain to you how this would be done. If Homer, after telling us that Chryses came with the ransom of his daughter and as a suppliant of the Achaeans but chiefly of the kings, had gone on speaking not as if made or being Chryses but still as Homer, you are aware that it would not be imitation [mimesis] but narration [diegesis], pure and simple. It would have been somewhat in this wise. I will state it without meter for I am not a poet. The priest came and prayed that to them the gods should grant to take Troy and come safely home, but that they should accept the ransom and release his daughter, out of reverence for the god, and when he had thus spoken the others were of reverent mind and approved, but Agamemnon was angry and bade him depart and not come again lest the scepter and the fillets of the god should not avail him. And ere his daughter should be released, he said, she would grow old in

Argos with himself, and he ordered him to be off and not vex him if he
wished to get home safe. And the old man on hearing this was frightened and
departed in silence, and having gone apart from the camp he prayed at length
to Apollo, invoking the appellations of the god, and reminding him of and
asking requital for any of his gifts that had found favor whether in the
building of temples or the sacrifice of victims. In return for these things he
prayed that the Achaeans should suffer for his tears by the god's shafts.
(638–39; 393a–e, 394a)

The reader will see what is at stake here. The trouble with mimesis is
that it is, in a specific sense, a lying speech. It is not based on a substantial paternal origin in the speaker's consciousness or selfhood. It is
language floating in the air, so to speak, detached from any immediately
present generative source. Such language contains the possibility of
infinitely proliferating lies or fictions. This proliferation would be a self-
generating production of language by language. It would be controlled
by no logos in the sense of an originating and grounding mind. The
interdict against mimesis is analogous to the interdict against writing in
the *Phaedrus*. Since mimesis and writing are deprived of any consciously
speaking authoring voice, both are like orphans deprived of their father,
wandering alone in the world, capable only of repeating themselves
mechanically.

Once this separation by mimesis of language from its immediate
source in a mind has been initiated, however, by even the smallest break
in diegesis pure and simple, there is, it seems, no way to stop it. Mimesis,
once begun, moves rapidly, Plato suggests, through a descending hierarchy
of lower and lower forms, beginning with women. Women, according to
Plato's phallogocentric assumptions, are naturally liars, mistresses of
veiled or misleading speech. Below women the hierarchy extends swiftly
downward through imitation of slaves, bad men, madmen, to the
imitation in language of senseless things, things with no mind at all, not
even that deprived or mutilated mind accorded by Plato to women. The
mimesis of senseless things is exemplified by James Joyce's echo of a
printing press's sound in the Aeolus section of *Ulysses*: "Sllt. The nether-
most deck of the first machine jogged forward its flyboard with sllt the

first batch of quirefolded papers. Sllt";³ or of thunder in *Finnegans Wake*:
"babababadalgharaghtakamminarronnkonnbronntonnerronntuonnthun
ntrorvarrhounawnskawntoohoohoordenenthurnuk!"⁴ Here is Plato's
litany of prohibitions against that sort of imitation:

> We will not [says Socrates] then allow our charges, whom we expect to prove
> good men, being men, to play the parts of women and imitate a woman young
> or old wrangling with her husband, defying heaven, loudly boasting, fortunate
> in her own conceit, or involved in misfortune and possessed by grief and
> lamentation—still less a woman that is sick, in love, or in labor. . . . Nor may
> they imitate slaves, female and male, doing the offices of slaves. . . . Nor yet, as
> it seems, bad men who are cowards and who do the opposite of the things we
> just now spoke of [things done by men who are "brave, sober, pious, free"],
> reviling and lampooning one another, speaking foul words in their cups or
> when sober and in other ways sinning against themselves and others in word
> and deed after the fashion of such men. And I take it they must not form the
> habit of likening themselves to madmen either in words nor yet in deeds. For
> while knowledge they must have both of mad and bad men and women, they
> must do and imitate nothing of this kind. . . . Are they to imitate smiths and
> other craftsmen or the rowers of triremes and those who call the time to them
> or other things connected therewith?
>
> How could they, he [Adimantus] said, since it will be forbidden them even
> to pay any attention to such things?
>
> Well, then, neighing horses and lowing bulls, and the noise of rivers and the
> roar of the sea and the thunder and everything of that kind—will they imitate
> these?
>
> Nay, they have been forbidden, he said, to be mad or liken themselves to
> madmen. (640–41; 395d–e, 396a–b)

At this point the reader of the *Republic* may remember that she or he is
reading a dialogue that is, as Nietzsche was to argue in *The Birth of Tragedy*,
in that mixed form Plato most condemns, since it combines all the genres
and obliterates their firm boundaries. The Platonic dialogue, says
Nietzsche, is the immediate precursor of that most mixed and debased of
forms, the novel:

If tragedy [says Nietzsche] had absorbed into itself all the earlier types of art, the same might also be said in an eccentric sense of the Platonic dialogue which, a mixture of all extant styles and forms, hovers midway between narrative, lyric, and drama, between prose and poetry, and so has also broken [durchbrochen hat] the strict old law of the unity of linguistic form. . . .

The Platonic dialogue was, as it were, the barge on which the shipwrecked ancient poetry saved herself with all her children: crowded into a narrow space and timidly submitting to the single pilot, Socrates, they now sailed into a new world, which never tired of looking at the fantastic spectacle of this procession. Indeed, Plato has given to all posterity the model of a new art form, the model of the *novel* [das Vorbild des *Romans*]—which may be described as an infinitely enhanced Aesopian fable [als die unendlich gesteigerte aesopische Fabel].[5]

The passages condemning mimesis in book 3 of the *Republic* are themselves mimesis of as complex a sort as can be found in any sophisticated modern novel told by multiple narrators, for example, *Wuthering Heights* or *Lord Jim*. In the *Republic* Plato pretends to be Socrates retelling to Glaucon and others a conversation he has had earlier with Adimantus. Socrates in this mimesis within mimesis plays the roles both of his own earlier self and of Adimantus, his interlocutor. He punctuates his imitative narrative with "he said" and "I said." The *Republic* is the archetype of all those narratives down to Borges and others that are fundamentally dialogical, double diegesis in Plato's radical sense.

Moreover, does not even that passage in which Plato in the guise of Socrates purifies Homer of mimesis by rewriting him as simple diegesis contain mimesis in spite of itself? Is not mimesis present in the report in indirect discourse of the language used by Agamemnon or by Chryses? Indirect discourse is always already a form of dialogue. I shall return to this important topic. Even the most objective report of the language of another is a double line of language. Its single narrative line is adulterated by mimesis. It is impossible to bring it back to a single logos. The unintentional comedy[6] of the passage in which Socrates expunges mimesis by rewriting Homer lies in its failure to succeed in doing what it seems so blithely to assume is easy to do by a simple change of grammatical person. Mimesis expelled from the city of discourse returns secretly to undermine even the language that performs the expulsion. Mimesis irremediably contaminates any diegesis. That makes its simplicity bifold, trifold, quatrefold. This happens not only in the irony that this condemnation of mimesis is performed by Plato pretending to be Socrates pretending to be an earlier self pretending to be Homer, but also in the concocted pseudo-Homeric passage itself, which still contains traces of mimesis, bits of free-floating language detached from any certain source. Can we even, finally, in the light of Plato's own procedure of storytelling in the *Republic*, blandly identify, as Socrates does, the narrator, speaker, or singer of the Homeric poems with Homer himself? Are not the invocations of the Muse at the beginning of the *Iliad* and the *Odyssey* reminders that all poems are spoken or sung by assumed voices? The voice of the poet is always a role. The poet invokes the Muse so that he can speak with a voice that is not his own. Mimesis, the poets' inveterate lying, is from the beginning, and inescapably, intrinsic to poetry as such. This is so however earnestly a writer tries to stick to simple diegesis and to the security of its authorization by a single mind.

TEN

ARIACHNE'S
BROKEN WOOF

A passage in Shakespeare's *Troilus and Cressida* brilliantly works out the implications of the division of the mind into two when the single narrative line of monologue becomes the doubled line of dialogue, when diegesis becomes mimesis. It is also a spectacular example of what Bakhtin calls "microdialogue," the presence of dialogue within a single word. As Shakespeare shows, when one logos becomes two, the circle an ellipse with two centers, all the bindings of Western logocentricism are untied or cut. "Logos" comes from "legein," to gather, as wheat is gathered into sheaves or as bits of string are gathered into hanks. In the passage in question Troilus has been watching Cressida dallying with Diomedes. I give the Variorum text, since the question is in part what Shakespeare wrote. It is necessary to get back as close to that as possible:

> *Troy.* This fhe? no, this is *Diomids Creffida*:
> If beautie haue a foule, this is not fhe:
> If foules guide vowes; if vowes are fanctimonie;
> If fanctimonie be the gods delight:
> If there be rule in vnitie it felfe.
> This is not fhe: O madneffe of difcourfe!
> That caufe fets vp, with, and againft thy felfe
> By foule authoritie: where reafon can reuolt
> Without perdition, and loffe affume all reafon,
> Without reuolt. This is, and is not *Creffid*:
> Within my foule, there doth conduce a fight
> Of this ftrange nature, that a thing infeperate,
> Diuides more wider then the skie and earth:

And yet the ſpacious bredth of this diuiſion,
Admits no Orifex for a point as ſubtle,
As *Ariachnes* broken woofe to enter:
Inſtance, O inſtance! ſtrong as *Plutoes* gates:
Creſſid is mine, tied with the bonds of heauen;
Inſtance, O inſtance, ſtrong as heauen it ſelfe:
The bonds of heauen are ſlipt, diſſolu'd and loos'd,
And with another knot fiue finger tied,
The fraɛtions of her faith, orts of her loue:
The fragments, ſcraps, the bits, and greazie reliques,
Of her ore-eaten faith, are bound to *Diomed*.
(V, ii, 162–85)[1]

The word "Ariachnes" leaps to the eye of the reader of this passage or to the ear of its hearer. Slip of the tongue or of the pen? Ignorance on Shakespeare's part? Error of the scribe or of the typesetter who has put in one letter too many? An alteration for the meter's sake? The extra "i" makes nonsense of the word. The letter too many, "prosthesis" in one possible meaning of that word, calls attention to itself almost as much as a gap, an ellipsis, a syncope, a letter too few, would do. The one letter too many or the one too few come strangely to the same thing. Both produce a gap in the meaning and call attention to the material base of signs, marks on the page that the eye interprets or acoustic disturbances perceptible to the ear. The little "i" in "Ariachnes" has the effect of a bit of sand in a salad or of a random sound in a symphony, the flutist dropping his flute, the snap of a breaking violin string. The harmony is broken, the string untuned.

The notes in the Variorum *Troilus and Cressida* give amusing evidence of the efforts by editors, emenders, and critics down through the centuries to remove the grain of sand, to root out the "i" and to return the dialogical "Ariachnes" to the monological "Arachnes" or, alternatively, to "Ariadnes." "Ariachnes" in the folios is "Ariachna's" in the quarto, but is "Ariathna's" in five copies of the latter. ". . . and Ariachne written by one so well read in Golding's *Ovid!* . . . The printer introduced Ariachne to complete the meter" (Keightley, 1860); "It is not impossible that

Shakespeare might have written 'Ariadne's' broken woof, having confounded the two names of the stories, in his imagination; or alluding to the clue of the thread, by the assistance of which Theseus escaped from the Cretan labyrinth" (Steevens, 1773); "Mr. Steevens hopes the mistake was not originally the authour's. . ." (Malone, 1790); "Shakespeare . . . might have written—'Arachnea'; great liberties being taken in spelling proper names" (Steevens, 1793); "The point [of how Shakespeare came to write 'Ariachne'] is of no moment. What is of moment for us to see is that by Ariachne Shakespeare meant the spider into which Arachne was transformed, and which in Greek bears the same name. . ." (Ingleby, 1875); "Shakespeare's mistaken form of the name is to be traced to confusion with Ariadne, who is also famed for her thread" (Root, 1903); "That Shakespeare may have forgotten her exact name, or may have changed it to suit his verse, is not improbable; that he confused her with Ariadne of Naxos, as has been suggested, is most improbable, as he knew his *Ovid* too well to do this" (Craig, 1905); "Since the printer himself admits that he blundered in substituting t for c, he is the logical suspect for the total error—whatever that may be and whatever his provocation may have been. F[olio] further corrected final *a* to *e*, but neglected to strike *i*" (Baldwin, 1953).[2] Daniel Seltzer, in the Signet Shakespeare edition of *Troilus and Cressida*, prints "Ariachne's," but in his notes passes over the "*i*" as though it were not there and gives in brief the story of Arachne.[3]

The force of the monological assumption, one can see, is so great that each of these learned gentlemen can entertain only the hypothesis of an either/or: *either* Ariadne *or* Arachne, not both; or, on the other hand, the hypothesis of some meaningless error on the part of Shakespeare, a copyist, or the printer. Some inadvertence introduced this absurd sound in the symphony of reason, this mere "noise" in the chain of communication.

The conflation in "Ariachne" of two myths that are and are not congruent is, however, precisely in agreement with what happens in Troilus's speech, namely, an anguished confrontation with the subversive possibility of dialogue, reason divided hopelessly against itself by submission to a "by-fould authoritie." (Most editors have preferred the

"By-fould" of the quarto to the reading of "By foule" in the folio, which I have given above.) "Portmanteau word" (Lewis Carroll's term) is not quite correct as a name for "Ariachnes," since Carroll's "slithy" (combining "slimy" and "lithe") or "chortle" (combining "chuckle" and "snort") harmoniously combine in one suitcase two compatible or more or less compatible qualities or acts, whereas "Ariachne" brings together two stories that do not fit.

The principle of identity is the basic assumption of monological metaphysics. Only if A is undividably A, or, in this case, C equal to C, does the whole structure hang together, in a chain that is described in Ulysses's famous speech on order in *Troilus and Cressida*. The order in question includes the religious, metaphysical, or cosmological links binding earth to heaven; the political or social order, which is so largely in question in *Troilus and Cressida*; the ethical, intersubjective, or performative order of the love vows between one person and another; the order of perception or of epistemology that sees and identifies things unequivocally, each as that one single thing that it is; the order of reason that makes a person or a mind one indivisible thing gathering various faculties under a unifying power or authority; the order, finally, of language, of rational discourse that posits unified entities and names them as what they are, as well as presupposing the linguistic certainties that make speech acts such as promises efficacious or what J. L. Austin in *How to Do Things with Words*[4] called "felicitous." Those certainties include the consistency and self-presence through time of the one who utters a speech act, for example, a lover's vow, as well as the endorsement of those vows by a divine guarantor who sanctifies the lover's promises and commitments. The whole shebang of Occidental metaphysics, the reader can see, is brought into question in Troilus's experience and in his speech.

Troilus's speech turns on various key words and key figures of logocentric metaphysics: the words "unity," "discourse," "cause," "authority," "vows," "sanctimony," "reason," "instance," the images of threading, folding, or tying. Threading through what Troilus says, however, is a recognition that dialogue, in the special sense of one mind's division against itself, is ultimately a matter of language or manifests itself as a subversive possibility of language. This is not to say that

Troilus has not seen with his own eyes the faithlessness of Cressida. The
consequence of that seeing, however, in its contradiction of what he had
seen, said, and heard said before, is the possibility of two simultaneous
contradictory sign systems. Each is centered on Cressida. Each ultimately
organizes everything in the cosmos around this Cressida or, alternatively,
around that Cressida. It is against reason that both of these sign systems
should be valid at once, since the they radically contradict one another. Since
these two languages are enclosed within Troilus's single mind, they double
that mind against itself. Either one of these codes alone is perfectly sane,
but both together in a single mind are madness, as he says in an interchange with Ulysses:

> *Troy.* But If I tell how thefe two did coact;
> shall I not lye, in publifhing a truth?
> Sith yet there is a credence in my heart:
> An efperance fo obftinately ftrong,
> That doth inuert that teft of eyes and eares;
> As if thofe organs had deceptio us functions,
> Created onely to calumniate.
> Was *Creffed* here?
> *Vlif.* I cannot coniure Troian.
> *Troy.* She was not fure.
> *Vlif.* Moft fure fhe was.
> *Troy.* Why my negation hath no tafte of madneffe?
> *Vlif.* Nor mine my Lord: *Creffid* was here but now. (V, ii, 140–52)

Madness is here defined as the impossibility of speaking either truly
or falsely. This is the possibility demonstrated in Gödel's theorem, the
possibility of a proposition that is derived logically from other
propositions within a system but that can neither be proved false nor
proved true. In Troilus's case, he can neither speak truly nor lie, or rather
he must inevitably do both at once. Truth is here defined as both truth of
internal agreement and truth of external correspondence. Whatever
Troilus says is true in relation to one Cressida and to one language
system deriving from that Cressida, but false in relation to the other

Cressida and to that other language system. This situation is madness. Cressida's faithlessness, the possibility that her original vows to Troilus were not grounded in a substantial, temporally continuous self that is tied to the rest of the ethical, political, and cosmic order all the way up to God, puts in question that whole order. Cressida's lying makes it possible to conceive that the story of that order, as it is told by the reasonable discourses of Western metaphysics, is itself a lie. It may be like that dangerous mimesis Plato deplores—fatherless language, language without a head, without a guarantor, without a "logos." Troilus's speech is an exploration, under the pressure of his anguish, of the disastrous implications of dialogism as a possibility intrinsic to language. Rather than being, as the word "dialogue" seems to suggest, the juxta-posing of two different minds as sources of language, dialogism is the possibility that language may be cut off from a source in any mind, human or divine. It could then generate its own coercive machine making things happen in the human world. This possibility appears when two different coherent languages struggle for domination within a single mind.

The "rule in vnitie it felfe," as the editors of the Variorum have observed, is that principle of self-identity or of noncontradiction whereby any entity is indivisibly equal to itself. This principle $(A = A)$ has been since Aristotle the basis of Western logic and Western metaphysics. The interior bonding by which a thing is ruled by its own unity and cannot be both itself and not itself at the same time, is the ground of exterior bindings leading link by link up to heaven in a series of correspondences. Only if a thing is unequivocally equal to itself can it correspond externally to other entities in an orderly series of displacements leading up to the "I am I" of God. The basis of this harmony is at once ontological and logical, or, rather, the ontological is the logical. In Western metaphysics a linguistic principle has been universalized and made the basis of the cosmic order.

The linguistic base of the cosmic model is apparent in Troilus's initial series of "ifs." These turn on the possibility of "vowing," that is, on a performative act of promising whose validity depends on its corre-spondence to the internal unity and substantiality of the self who makes the vow. "If beautie haue a foule," that is, if the external and visible sign, Cressida's beauty, corresponds to what she is unalterably within; "if foules guide vowes," if that unified subjectivity, the self-identity of Cressida, is the source of her words, of her promising to be faithful to Troilus; "if vowes are fanctimonie" (the quarto has "be fanctimonies"), that is, if such promises are sacred in the sense of being based not on the selfish and isolated self of the promisor, but on the soul's grounding on the God within it in the chain leading up to the divine "logos," which is security for all human vowing (as when one says, "I swear by Heaven to do it"); "If fanctimonie be the gods delight,"[5] that is, if this chain of signs and words is ratified by the auto-affection of the gods, taking pleasure in the return of the human word to the divine Word, in a closed circuit of linguistic equivalents; "if," finally, "there be rule in vnitie it felfe," that is, if the law of the excluded middle unalterably holds up and down this whole chain, in its specular externalization of the "I am I" of God, mirroring himself in the creation—if all these presuppositions are the case, then the Cressida Troilus has seen with his own eyes cannot be Cressida.

It is Cressida, however. With this testimony of eyes and ears the whole structure of Western culture is broken, fragmented, doubled and redoubled. This universalizing is prepared by Troilus's all-or-nothing rhetoric. He has moved throughout from part to whole and has made Cressida the type of all women. "Let it not be beleeu'd for womanhood" (V, ii, 153), he cries. The universalizing, however, is justified. If one exception to the law of self-identity can be found, then that law reveals itself to be a hypothesis, possibly no more than a theoretical fiction, a human positing, a speech act making logical thought possible but not "true," rather than an irrefutable axiom based on knowledge. Section 516 of Nietzsche's so-called *The Will to Power* turns on this contrast between knowing and positing:

We are unable to affirm and to deny one and the same thing: this is a subjective empirical law, not the expression of any "necessity" but only of an inability [nur ein Nicht-vermögen].

If, according to Aristotle, the law of contradiction [der Satz vom Widerspruch] is the most certain of all principles [Grundsätze], if it is the ultimate ground upon which every demonstrative proof rests, if the principle of every axiom lies in it; then one should consider all the more rigorously what *propositions* already lie at the bottom of it [was er im Grunde schon an Behauptungen *voraussetzt*]. Either it asserts something about actuality, about being, as if one already knew this from another source; that is, as if opposite attributes [entgegengesetzte Prädikate] *could* not be ascribed to it. Or the proposition means: opposite attributes *should* not be ascribed to it. In that case, logic would be an imperative, not to know the true, but to posit and arrange a world that shall be called true by us [sondern zur Setzung und Zurechtmachung einer Welt, *die uns wahr heiβen soll*]. [Nietzche's italics][6]

The "madneſſe" of Troilus's "diſcourſe" is the madness of his being forced by ocular testimony to break the "rule"[7] of unity, the principle of noncontradiction: "This is, and is not *Creſſid*." Shakespeare's (or the folio editors') italicizing of proper names stresses the way they are supposed to label unique unitary entities. The experience of the two Cressidas shows Troilus that the rule of unity is a positing, a "setzen," rather than a knowing, an "erkennen." The result is not only a putting in question of the external order—political, ethical, cosmological, and religious—that was dependent on assuming the law of noncontradiction to be a knowing. It is also a return of both mental and linguistic realms to warfare, disorder. If the order of logic is a hypothetical positing, if it is a fictional linguistic system of which the unity of the logically thinking self, properly named by a proper name, is not the source but a result, one element among the others, then there is no reason why a single mind should not become dialogical, divided against itself. It would then be the receptacle of two simultaneous, incompatible logical systems, each positing a different self as its base and each presupposing a different external world, a world, as Nietzsche puts it, true for *it*. This is what happens to Troilus. That "This is, and is not *Creſſid*" is internalized in a mad doubling of Troilus himself.

Dialogue seems benign enough when it names two persons conversing, however antagonistically. Such a give-and-take may presume, as it does for Jürgen Habermas, some horizon of rational agreement. When dialogue is seen as the division of a single mind against itself, it is more subversive.

When the monological becomes dialogical, the dialogical loses its "logoi" and becomes alogical. There is no Cressida in the sense of an unalterable self. She exists, Troilus is forced to believe, only as the phantasmal appearance of a self created by the baseless performatives of the vows she happens to make. These vows are sanctified by no divine correspondences. If she makes new vows, she becomes a different person. The Troilus who experiences Cressida's faithlessness is himself disintegrated. He becomes not two persons but no person, out of his mind.

If Troilus's speech is taken as a model of narrative discourse, it demonstrates the possibility of a story that is simultaneously two different incompatible stories. These can never be reduced to one by any rule of unity. They can never be simultaneously contained within any one sane mind, sane in the sense of single and orderly. Nevertheless these two stories are enclosed within the bounds of one text, one word or set of words. This makes possible the "madneſſe of diſcourſe! / That cauſe ſets vp, with, and againſt thy ſelfe." The madness of discourse is the insanity of a line of argument that is doubled. It is and is not itself. It argues both for and against itself, as in a "cause," or court case, in which the same man should, absurdly, be the lawyer for both sides. "Cause" is from Latin "causa." It is one Latin equivalent of the Greek "logos." It means cause, reason, motive, that is, rational base, as well as case, lawsuit, side, party, point in an argument. "It is the cause, it is the cause, my soul," says Othello (5.2.1). Troilus's soul has two causes, two "logoi," and is therefore subject, in Shakespeare's coinage, as the Quarto has it, to a "bi-fould authority."[8] A bifold authority is an authority doubled against itself, bifid, divided into two by a deep cleft or defile, but folded back on itself, or belonging to two enclosures or "folds."

The rest of Troilus's speech works out the consequences of this self-division. The subjection of Troilus's soul to a bifold authority means that he is like two countries at war. He is like the political situation as it is dramatized in *Troilus and Cressida* itself: Greeks and Trojans engaged in mutual destruction. As each side in the war can "fur its gloves with reason,"[9] so each part of Troilus's mind can develop its own entirely stable chain of reasoning based on its central assumption. This is, or, on the other side, this is not, Cressida. "Reaſon can," therefore, "reuolt /

Without perdition." Reason can be divided against itself like a country at civil war without the loss (perdition) of reason in outright madness, and, on the other hand, "loſſe" can "aſſume all reaſon, / Without reuolt." The loss of reason in its doubling, or the loss of Cressida in her doubling, can express itself in entirely reasonable terms without the perdition of reason in madness.

If this is, and is not, Cressid, the mind that sees and reasons about this contradiction of the law of identity is and is not mad. Troilus goes on reasoning sanely but in a way simultaneously subject to two different reasons or centers of reasoning. Troilus himself is simultaneously one and two, his soul at civil war, inseparably one mind, and yet at the same time cleft by an unbridgeable gap that is yet no gap at all, not even the tiniest hole or "orifex." "Within my ſoule," says Troilus, "there doth conduce a fight / Of this ſtrange nature, that a thing inseperate, / Diuides more wider than the skie and earth: / And yet the ſpacious bredth of this diuiſion, / Admits no Orifex for a point as ſubtle, / As *Ariachnes* broken woofe to enter." The "thing inſeperate" that is yet divided is Troilus's soul. This unity in division corresponds to the two in one of Cressida herself. She, like him, is divided irreparably. Nevertheless, one can traverse the whole surface of each without ever encountering the point of fissure, the place of folding, just as sky and earth are manifestly opposite realms even though one can never reach that horizon where there is a space or fold dividing them.[10]

Troilus's mind is divided by two "instances." Each is an indubitable fact and each stands in for a chain of reasoning binding together a series of propositions. These make two entirely different narrative lines out of Troilus's world. Each instance firmly implies its particular totality, as a synecdochic part urgently solicits its whole. "Inſtance" is from the Latin "instantia," presence, perseverance, urgency; from "instans," instant, present participle of "instare," to stand upon, be present, persist, "in," upon, + "stare," to stand. The word is used by Shakespeare with its whole range of then current English meanings: a case or example; a legal proceeding or process; suit (cp. "cauſe"); prompting, request; urgent solicitation (now archaic); an impelling motive (now obsolete): "Inſtance, O inſtance! ſtrong as *Plutoes* gates: / *Creſſid* is mine, tied with the bonds of heauen." This is the instance that presupposes the metaphysical order, chain of reasoning, or cosmological story line.

On the other hand there is the equally indubitable instance of the other Cressida. This implies not so much an alternative system of thought or an alternative story line as the suspension and fragmentation of the heavenly order that Cressida's vows to Troilus implied. Out of these fragments a new nonsystem, made of fragments that remain fragments, is created. It is not an alternative system in the sense of another coherent order, but a heap, a "bricolage" at best. It can only be described in oxymoron. It is a system of fragmentation made of knotted segments that do not belong together. It is the nonsystem made of the remnants of an act of deconstruction, like a meal of distasteful leftovers, or like a knot made of bits of used string spliced piecemeal together. The remnants are the scraps of Cressida's faith. These stand by synecdoche, according to the logic of the "inftance," for the whole line or rope: "Inftance, O inftance, ftrong as heauen it felfe: / The bonds of heauen are flipt, diffolu'd, and loos'd, / And with another knot fiue finger tied, / The fractions of her faith, orts of her loue: / The fragments, fcraps, the bits, and greazie reliques / Of her ore-eaten faith, are bound to *Diomed*." The mixture of metaphors here, the linear series of synonyms in apposition, the incoherence of the syntax (how does tying a knot fit with giving food?), enact the fragmentation, the suspension of logical order, that is named. "Five finger tied" is a powerful coinage. It suggests the dispersal of unity in an awkward multiplicity of digits, like trying to tie a knot with one hand. It suggests as well the way Cressida's "faith" to Diomedes was sealed not with the performative words of vows, but with the performative gestures of hand-holdings, embraces, sexual manipulations, digitations. A broken faith is no faith. It is no faith in the sense that Cressida's vows to Troilus should have been sanctimony bound in a puissant chain to heaven. Her faith to Diomedes is a purely human bond, five-finger-tied, based on a baseless tautology like that in Matthew Arnold's "Dover Beach": "I promise to be true to you, but since my promise is based only on my own saying, it can be suspended at any time."[11]

Such a promise is like a counterfeit note with no base in solid gold, or like those wandering fatherless written words that Socrates, in the wandering written words of the *Phaedrus,* says he so dislikes. In the nonsystem of fragmentation an instance is not part of a unified chain, affirming the chain. It is only another fragment, a leftover that does not fit. Each instance reaffirms the fractioning. The bits and pieces of which this non-order are made, moreover, are not even untied bits of line. They are "dissolved" as line in their unknotting, in Shakespeare's pun on the etymological and chemical meanings of "dissolve." The whole line, therefore, even its leftover remnants, is suspended or annihilated as line, as if it had been digested and vomited up again, which is one possible "overmeaning" for "ore-eaten."

What is the role of "Ariachnes" in this powerful sequence of reasoning about the possible dissolution of reasoning? The conflation of two myths, that of Ariadne, that of Arachne, in a single word, Ariachnes, mimes the mode of relationship between two different similar but not identical myths that exist side by side in a culture. The word, moreover, fits perfectly in Troilus's speech. It is a small-scale version of the madness of a discourse that submits simultaneously to two "causes," is subject to a bifold authority, and so tells two stories at once, absurdly, the dialogical becoming alogical. "Ariachnes" is a word that is no word. It is made of bits of two words stuck together or conflated. Another example is Sancho's coinage, "baciyelmo," in *Don Quixote,* to name Mambrino's helmet that is also a washbasin. Ariachnes fits as well the larger context of Shakespeare's play. *Troilus and Cressida* has sometimes been accused of being an incoherent string of episodes. "Ariachnes" also fits the wider context of Occidental discourse as a whole, in which the coherence of the monological has all along been undermined by the presence within it, inextricably intertwined in any of its expressions, of that other nonsystem, the "instance" of fragmentation and the absence of unifying authority. The form of relationship between these ever smaller or larger contexts, each repeating the structure of the others on a different scale, is that *mise en abîme* or fractal design present, for example, in the way a rope is made of braided or intertwined smaller cords, each of which in turn is made of smaller threads enwound, and so on down to the smallest filaments twisted to form the smallest thread.

In the case of "Ariachnes" the structure in question is that of anacoluthon. "Ariachnes" is an anacoluthon in miniature. It starts off on one path of letters toward Ariadne and switches direction in the middle to complete itself, illogically, as Arachne. This clash of incompatibles grates, twists, or bifurcates the mind, just as does Troilus's confrontation of a Cressida who is and is not Cressida. The word "anacoluthon" means, etymologically, "against following," that is, not following a consistent path or track. Anacoluthon names a syntactical pattern in which there is a shift in tense, number, or person in the midst of a sentence, so that the words do not hang together grammatically. An anacoluthon is not governed by a single logos, in the sense this time of a unified meaning.

If the word "Ariachnes" is an anacoluthon in miniature, a similar structure is repeated in the syntactical and figurative incoherence of Troilus's speech. This happens in the mixture of bond images and eating images, or in the simultaneously active and passive meanings of the word "diuides," or in the simultaneous reference of "thing" to Cressida and to Troilus's soul. These double syntactical possibilities have divided critics over the centuries in the hopeless attempt to reduce the sentence containing "diuides" and "thing" to a single path of meaning: "Within my foule, there doth conduce a fight / Of this ftrange nature, that a thing infeperate, / Diuides more wider than the skie and earth." The effort of the mind to keep this rope of words from vibrating until it disappears and no longer functions as the tightrope supporting a single line of thought is like the effort to make sense of "Ariachnes." The grammatical anacoluthon parallels also the anacoluthon of Troilus's divided mind, the narrative discontinuity of the entire play, and so on up to the immense anacoluthon of Western literature, philosophy, and history as a whole that does not make a whole.

The appropriateness or keeping of "Ariachnes" in its nonkeeping, however, goes beyond its being one more example of two words that do not fit into the same suitcase. Why Ariadne? Why Arachne? The attempt to follow out the relation between the two myths and their joint relation to Troilus's situation repeats again the mind-twisting experience of anacoluthon. "And yet the fpacious bredth of this diuifion [the division of Troilus's mind, the division between the two Cressidas who are yet one Cressida] / Admits no Orifex for a point as subtle, / As *Ariachnes* broken woofe to enter." The passage is odd, for one thing, in the mixture of both sexes' attributes. This is, to be sure, congruent with the superimposition of the two sexes in the "thing infeperate" that is subdivided, both Troilus's soul and at the same time Cressida's self. Troilus's phrasing is, however, peculiar in further ways. This bifold surface is wide open and yet has no aperture large enough even for that minuscule phallus made of the torn filament of Arachne's spiderweb or of a broken bit of Ariadne's labyrinth-retracing thread to penetrate. The web, the thread, or the woof, feminine images par excellence, images of veiling or weaving, are transformed into the instruments of a male forced entry. Ariachne's broken woof, figure of a torn or deflowered virginity, becomes, in a mind-twisting reversal of the sexes, itself a "point" that might tear, though it can find in this case no orifex to penetrate, even with its refined subtlety. (Orifex: "obs. erron. form of Orifice" [*OED*].) Tearer and torn here change places. Ariachne's broken woof both is and is not male, and is and is not female, just as the stories of Ariadne and Arachne are both alike and different, and each both alike and different from the story of Troilus and Cressida. The motifs of vows and of faithlessness; of the ambiguous relations of the sexes; of weaving or threading that does not hold; of the penetration or nonpenetration of a labyrinthine interior that is both male and female; of despair at broken vows; even the motif of hanging—all these return in each of the three stories but in a different order or structure. This makes the three stories clash as well as chime. It is impossible to resolve all three into versions of a single archetype.

"Woof" means "the threads that run crosswise in a woven fabric, at right angles to the warp threads. . . . (Variant [influenced by WARP] of Middle English *oof*, Old English *ōwef*: *ō-*, from *on*, ON + *wefan*, to weave; Root: *webb-*)" (*American Heritage Dictionary*). The woof is added to the vertical warp lines already there when the weaving begins. The woof was torn by Athene when in her envious rage she cut Arachne's web from top to bottom. The torn web of Arachne becomes the broken thread of Ariadne, woven through the warp of the labyrinth. Ariadne is, according to one version of her story, supposed to have hanged herself with her own thread in despair after Theseus abandoned her, just as Arachne hanged herself after her humiliation by Athene. Arachne was then turned into a spider, as Ariadne was turned into a constellation of stars in a ring. The broken woof of Arachne, the perjured thread of Ariadne become in Shakespeare's play the broken bonds of the vows between Troilus and Cressida. This happens in a crisscross or chiasmus changing the sex of betrayer and betrayed from the implicit mother-daughter relation in Arachne's story to the faithless seducer of the forlorn Ariadne in Theseus, and then to the betrayed lover in Troilus. The meaning of "Ariachnes" in its context lies in the labyrinth of branching incongruous relations it sets up. These are vibrating resonances that can never be stilled in a single monological narrative line. These resonances reduce the reader to the same state of exasperated dialogical madness of discourse that tears Troilus in two, that makes him both be and not be himself.

If Ariadne and Arachne are superimposed in this way, the reader might finally ask, why should the reader not also remember other Greek stories involving weaving? These stories have the same relation of ana-morphosis to the stories of Ariadne and Arachne as they do to one another. Examples are the story of Penelope and the story of Philomela. Ulysses is after all Troilus's interlocutor when Troilus makes his reference to Ariachne. Penelope was no doubt already engaged in her diurnal process of weaving and unweaving. The dark story of the tongueless Philomela weaving the words or pictograms that reveal her violation— woven cloth, woman's work, becoming a strange prosthesis for the absent tongue—contains again in a different form, making a clanging disson-ance, elements that enter into the story of Troilus, the story of Arachne, the story of Ariadne, the story of Penelope, the story of Cressida. What, to shift to another culture, about the Lady of Shalott? How can one stop the widening circle of contextual echoes with a difference? These are like so many bent and bending mirrors reflecting back distorted and yet recognizable images.

Did Shakespeare, in writing Troilus's speech, "intend" all that I have found in it? Is it only the imagined speech of an imagined character, or does it express something of Shakespeare's own views? What is the relation between Troilus's speech and the rest of the play, the rest of

Shakespeare's plays, the context of Renaissance literature, of English literature, of Western literature generally? What we so blithely name the "context" for a given text, its controlling ambience, can never be fully identified or fully controlled.[12] One certainty that dissolves with the undecidability of context is the concept of authorizing authorship, or indeed of selfhood generally in the sense of an ultimate generative source for any act of language. What we name "Shakespeare" is an effect of the text. That effect depersonalizes and disunifies. The same can be said of the texts published under the name of any other author, for example, the novels of Thomas Hardy or the poems of Wallace Stevens. The works of Shakespeare are a comprehensive and profound exploration of the possibilities inherent in the English language as it inherits the concepts, figures, and stories of Occidental culture. It seems those works must have been written by a committee of geniuses—a committee, moreover, with a wonderful repertoire of materials with which to work.

Those materials, as this reading of one passage in *Troilus and Cressida* suggests, are fundamentally heterogeneous. They contain both logocentric metaphysics and its subversion. This subversion is wrought into the conceptual words, the figures, and the myths of the Occident as the shadow in its light. Any running discourse, any story or narrative exploiting the resources of that tradition, will be dialogical not monological. It will be dialogical in the sense that it will be impossible to reduce it to a single story line organized around one originating and guiding transcendent mind.

"Deconstruction," as in one of its manifold aspects it addresses the reading of canonical texts, is not simply a teasing out of that dialogical heterogeneity's traces. The danger of heterogeneity has been traditionally recognized. Plato, for example, understood and attempted to reduce the threat posed by the Sophists. Deconstruction rather attempts to reverse the implicit hierarchy within the terms in which the dialogical has been defined. It attempts to define the monological, the logocentric, as a derived effect of the dialogical rather than as the noble affirmation of which the dialogical is a disturbance, a secondary shadow in the originating light. Deconstruction, in one of its strands, attempts a crisscross substitution of early and late and a consequent vibratory displacement of the whole system of Western metaphysics.

That this attempt always fails, so that it has to be performed again and again, interminably, is indicated by the way my terms, or any other terms I might have used, for example, the figure of shadow and light, imperturbably reaffirm the system that I am using them to challenge. In a similar way, Shakespeare's *Troilus and Cressida* is simultaneously open to the reading I have proposed and to a logocentric one that encompasses Troilus's speech as an aberration that the play, in the end, monologically surrounds, as a host might finally consume its irritating parasite. The strange logic or alogic of parasite and host in their interrelation, however, is another version of that interference of the dialogical or polylogical in the monological that weaves and reweaves Ariachne's broken woof.[13] This chapter has shown one case of that in a striking example of what Bakhtin called "microdialogue." This is the doubling in a single word that breaks the unity of a diegesis.

ELEVEN

R.?

Can anything more be said about whether these vibrations of the middle are intentional or just happen? To the question, "Did Shakespeare mean all this complexity? Did he write 'Ariachnes'?" the proper answer might be that given by "R." to a similar question in the admirable dialogue on the novel that forms the second preface to Rousseau's *La Nouvelle Héloïse*. The question is whether he has made up the letters that form *La Nouvelle Héloïse* or whether they are genuine letters that he has only gathered and edited:

N. When I ask you if you are the author of these letters, why then do you avoid my question?

R. Because I don't want to tell a lie.

N. But you also refuse to tell the truth?

R. It is still to do it honor to declare that one wants to keep silent about it. You would have a better bargain with a man who wished to lie. Moreover, do people of taste deceive themselves about the distinctive traits of authors [sur la plume des Auteurs]? How can you dare ask a question which it is up to you to resolve?[^1]

It would seem that R., or at any rate Rousseau himself, must know whether or not he has made up the letters. Nevertheless, R. claims that he does not know for sure about this. He cannot, he says, answer either yes or no to the question of authorship without taking the risk of lying, however unintentionally. Whereof one cannot speak the truth certainly one should certainly keep silent, out of a desire to honor the truth. In any case, the question of authorship, as Rousseau, or R., here recognizes, is not a matter for the "author" to decide. Authorship, like paternity, is not something that is experienced certainly, "from inside," by the authoring father as he contemplates his offspring. It is a wise father who knows his own child. Authorship, like paternity, is rather a collective fiction, the attribution by readers of a certain text to a putative fathering source, the projection of a certain unified self as the origin of a given text. Authorship, like paternity, is social and conventional through and through, not a matter for the separate self to decide. As authors (as opposed to private persons) Shakespeare, Rousseau, Pater, Elizabeth Gaskell, and the rest never existed as the subjective experience of any "I," but only came to exist as a he or a she, third-person creations projected by those who interpret the works published under the names Shakespeare, Rousseau, Pater, or Gaskell.

The most explicit statement by R. of his own possible ignorance of authorship has to do with one of the forms of doubling language with which I began this discussion of the narrative line's vibration, multi-plying, and ultimate vanishing: the epigraph. Who is the speaker or citer of a given epigraph in a novel? The author of the novel? The narrator? The author of the epigraph? The printer or editor? One of the characters? The impersonal voice of tradition? There is no way to tell for sure. An epigraph hangs there in the air surrounded by blank paper, cut off, without ascertainable bloodlines to the rest of the text. The question of who speaks an epigraph is like the question of how that prosthetic "i" got into "Ariachnes." "Goodness," says N., "you may do whatever you like, people will see through you in spite of what you do. Don't you see that your epigraph alone tells all?" (2:29). The epigraph is from Petrarch's sonnet 338, "Lasciato ài, Morte, senza sole il mondo": "Non la conobbe il mondo, mentre l'ebbe: / Connobill'io ch'a pianger qui rimasi [The world knew her not, though it possessed her; / I knew her and remain below weeping her loss]." Is this piece of language, torn from its context, to be heard as spoken by Petrarch, by Rousseau, by the printer or editor, by the reader, by some anonymous author of *La Nouvelle Héloïse*, by one of the characters or letter writers in the novel, or perhaps by John of Patmos, since a passage in John's Gospel[2] is explicitly echoed by the speaker or writer of the passage from "Petrarch," whoever at any moment he or she may be? "I see that the epigraph says nothing about the fact in question," rejoins R., "for who can know if I have found this epigraph in the manuscript, or if it is I who has put it there? Who can say if I am not at all in the same doubt as you are? If all this air of mystery [tout cet air de miſtere] is not perhaps a feint to hide from you my own ignorance concerning what you want to know?" (2:29).

Who can say? "Rousseau's" preface, the reader will have noted, is itself in the form of a dialogue. It is a dialogue, moreover, in which, as it progresses, the interlocutors change places bewilderingly. Neither R. nor N. can be unambiguously identified with the man Jean-Jacques Rousseau, citizen of Geneva. The dialogue in its form mimes the impossibility of certainly identifying the selfhood behind any speech or the authorship behind any text. Rousseau's preface, moreover, like Shakespeare's *Troilus and Cressida* and like the Ariadne story, involves lying and broken promises. All three dramatize the possible doubling of a story line in an anacoluthon that dissolves its unity as monological narrative.

TWELVE

THE ANACOLUTHONIC LIE

All the elements that relate the uncertainty of the middle to disunities in the narrative's emitting source are given in concentrated form in an admirable paragraph of Proust's *À la recherche du temps perdu*. This will bring the line of discussion back to the novel proper, after the detour through Plato, Shakespeare, and Rousseau. The passage from Proust will also facilitate a bringing together of all I have said about the presence, within the tradition of monological narrative, of the possibility not so much of "dialogue" as of what might be called "polylogology," the implicit multiplying of the authorizing source of a story. This duplicity is mimed in doubling of "logos" within my neologism. Polylogology, as I shall argue, becomes, or already is, "alogism," the absence of any ascertainable logos and the dissolution of the reader's instinctive understanding of narrative according to categories of unitary consciousness. Another name for "alogism" is the permanent parabasis of irony, about which I shall say more later. The passage in Proust has to do with storytelling (in the double sense of lying and of narration), with memory as a precarious support of narrative continuity, and with anacoluthon's function in both storytelling and lying. Anacoluthon doubles the story line and so makes the story probably a lie. A chief evidence for the middle's perturbation is small-scale details of language. This means that closereading is essential to reading narrative:

To tell the truth, I knew nothing that Albertine had done since I had come to know her, or even before. But in her conversation (she might, had I mentioned it to her, have replied that I had misunderstood her) there were certain contradictions, certain embellishments which seemed to me as decisive as catching her red-handed [qui me semblaient aussi décisives qu'un flagrant délit], but less usable against Albertine who, often caught out like a child, had invariably, by dint of sudden, strategic changes of front, stultified my cruel attacks and retrieved the situation. Cruel, most of all, to myself. She employed, not by way of stylistic refinement, but in order to correct her imprudences, abrupt breaches of syntax not unlike that figure which the grammarians call anacoluthon or some such name [de ces brusques sautes de syntaxe ressemblant un peu à ce que les grammairiens appellent anacoluthe ou je ne sais comment]. Having allowed herself, while discussing women, to say: "I remember, the other day, I . . .," she would suddenly, after a "semi-quaver rest," change the "I" to "she": it was something that she had witnessed as an innocent spectator, not a thing that she herself had done. It was not she who was the subject of the action [Ce n'était pas elle qui était le sujet de l'action]. I should have liked to recall exactly how the sentence had begun, in order to decide for myself, since she had broken off in the middle [puisqu'elle lâchait pied: literally "since she had lost her footing"], what the conclusion would have been. But since I had been awaiting that conclusion, I found it hard to remember the beginning, from which perhaps my air of interest had made her deviate, and was left still anxious to know her real thoughts, the actual truth of her recollection. The beginnings of a lie on the part of one's mistress are like the beginnings of one's own love, or of a vocation. They take shape, accumulate [se conglomèrent], pass unnoticed by oneself. When one wants to remember in what manner one began to love a woman, one is already in love with her; day-dreaming about her beforehand, one did not say to oneself: "This is the prelude to love; be careful!" [c'est le prélude d'un amour, faisons attention]—and one's day-dreams advanced unobtrusively, scarcely noticed by oneself. In the same way, save in a few comparatively rare cases, it is only for narrative convenience [pour la commodité du récit] that I have frequently in these pages confronted one of Albertine's false statements with her previous assertion on the same subject. This previous assertion, as often as not, since I could not read the future and did not at the time guess what contradictory affirmation was to form a pendant to it, had slipped past unperceived, heard it is true by my ears, but without my isolating it from the continuous flow of Albertine's speech. Later on, faced with the self-evident lie, or seized by an anxious doubt, I would endeavor to recall it; but in vain; my memory had not been warned in time; it had thought it unnecessary to keep a copy [ma mémoire n'avait pas été prévenue à temps; elle avait cru inutile de garder copie]. (French, 3:658–59; English, 3:149–50)'

A passage of an admirably graceful subtlety! The anacoluthon, or failure to follow a single syntactical track, for example in the shift from first to third person in the middle of a sentence, creates a narrative line that does not hang together. That shows, to anyone who notices it, that the story is—may be—a lie, a fiction. How could the same story apply at once to the teller and to someone else? The difficulty is in noticing the discrepancy, since memory, for Proust, far from being total and continuous, is intermittent and discontinuous. Our memories are out of our control. We remember only what our memories, acting on their own, happen to think it worthwhile to save. Lying and fiction, as Albertine's anacoluthons show, come to the same thing since both are forms of language that cannot be returned to a single paternal, patronizing logos or speaking source.

Proust, like Plato, may seem to ascribe a special adeptness in lying to women. Woman may be the mother of lies because she could never in any case be spoken of as a "paternal source," according to that differentiation in authority between the sexes that seems to be traditional to this line of thought. "Albertine," however, as the reader may have noticed, is an androgynous name or one that is sexually ambiguous. It starts masculine and ends feminine, in a miniature anacoluthon. Who is the liar here, Albertine as the example of the eternal feminine, evasive and unpossessable, in this case perhaps betraying Marcel in covert lesbian liaisons? Or is the prime liar Marcel Proust himself, who has displaced into a misogynist fiction his own experience of betrayal in a "real life" homosexual liaison?

A lie, in any case, is a piece of language that does not correspond truly to the mind that seems to have generated it. In an analogous way, a work of fiction, however much it seems to have been authored by a single mind, to be safely anchored there, may be no more than a free-floating sequence of words that creates the phantasmal illusion of some mind, that of the narrator, that of the author, that of this character or that, though none of these stands apart from language as an independent preexisting entity. This baselessness, it may be, is the mode of existence of any lie or of any work of fiction. This may be hidden in a lie or in that hypothetical but never actually existing work of fiction that would be a seamless web of consistent language, like the *Iliad* rewritten by Plato so that Homer does all the telling. An anacoluthon in its self-contradiction cannot be taken as spoken by a single unitary mind. If we could only remember both beginning and end we should be able to convict its speaker of lying at either beginning or ending, since both cannot be true. An anacoluthon may exist at different scales: from the single word "Ariachnes" or "Albertine" through Albertine's sentence with a change in the middle from "I" to "she" up to large-scale non sequiturs like the indirect discourse of *The Warden* or of *Cranford*, or like the interpolated tales in *Pickwick Papers* in their incongruity with the main narrative, or like the shift in narrators in *Lord Jim*. The anacoluthon in any of these modes brings into the open, by existing as a piece of language that must have two minds at least as its sources, the way the assumption of a single generating mind for any given text may be no more than a convention. It may be an illusion generated by the assumption that consciousness has priority over language. Language may be a mindless machine that has as one of its effects the generation of a false appearance of some mind as source.

In struggling unsuccessfully to reduce an anacoluthon to grammatical and logical unity the reader discovers his or her subjection to the habit of mechanically projecting a single mental center as the necessary source of emission for any piece of language. For Proust too the dialogical, instrument for deconstructing the monological, in the end deconstructs also itself and gives way to the alogical, that is, to a recognition that language may function without verifiable grounding in any mind or minds. The possibility of the lie or of fiction, storytelling in both senses, puts in question the assumption that consciousness precedes language and is necessary to its operation. How can one be sure that it is ever possible to tell the truth in the sense of mimetically copying a preexisting state of mind? The state of mind, it may be, is made or altered by language. This possibility appears in all those forms of language, pervasive in novels, that cannot be made to correspond to any single unified consciousness. All storytellers, both liars and narrators, in one way or another make the depersonifying shift of Albertine's anacoluthonic substitution of "elle" for "je": "Ce n'etait pas elle qui était le sujet de l'action [It was not she who was the subject of the action]."

The connection of anacoluthon with undermining the illusory coherence of any narrative and the relation of this to the way any narrative must unfold in time are worked out in the remainder of Proust's paragraph. The unity of narrative, whether it is as short as a single sentence or as long as *À la recherche du temps perdu*, is a construction of the mind projecting linear coherence on a discrete series of signs with gaps between presenting themselves one by one over time. The mind at any one moment of this process of reading is at the mercy of its memory of the earlier signs, the signs already past. Memory may either fail or falsify by distorting the earlier interpretation of the now past signs to make them fit the unity it is now in the process of factitiously creating. So inveterate is the penchant of the mind toward making a story, a narrative line that hangs together and makes a single sense, that it will make coherence out of the most incoherent of data. Only when something that does not quite fit calls attention to itself, when there is in one way or another an anacoluthon, a failure of keeping, or a misstep, some inassimilable detail, does the mind become aware of its incorrigible tendency to lie to itself in this way, to tell itself stories.

The beginning of a narrative sequence, a new start in one's life, is rarely experienced at the time as a beginning. It is lost when it happens in the flow of experiences that follow one another in time and are one by one abandoned forever, failing to leave copies of themselves imprinted in our memories. "We are condemned," as Henry James says, ". . . whether we will or no, to abandon and outlive, to forget and disown and hand over to desolation, many vital or social performances—if only because the traces, records, connexions, the very memorials we would fain preserve, are practically impossible to rescue for that purpose from the general mixture."[2] Only in retrospect, that is by a fictional projection backward, by a false or illusory memory (but is any memory other than illusory in this sense?), created by a constructive act, to make a story out of it, "pour la commodité du récit," do certain events become singled out as the beginning of a story line. They receive thereby a significance they never had at the moment they were experienced, as opposed to the significance they have as the first link in a chain of lies we tell ourselves to make sense of that segment of our lives in relation to the present. Lying, storytelling, the course of a love affair, the course of a vocation—all fit into this paradigm of an anacoluthon that cannot be seen clearly as what it is, even if it is detected by the mind (as happens rarely, for example, when Albertine "loses her footing [lâche pied]" in the midst of a sentence). Though we can notice that something has gone wrong with the narrative sequence, we can no longer remember the beginning well enough to see for certain the incoherence of the story and so perhaps discover the truth hidden behind the lie.

I say "perhaps" because for Proust it is impossible ever to be sure whether or not someone is lying. This is because, contrary to what seems common sense, a lie is a performative, not a constative, form of language. Or, rather, it mixes inextricably constative and performative language. A lie is a form of bearing witness. It always explicitly or implicitly contains a speech act: "I swear to you I am telling the truth." This speech-act aspect of a lie is not a matter of truth or falsehood. It is a way of doing something with words. Its functioning depends on faith or the lack of faith in the one who hears it, not on referential veracity. If a lie is believed it is as "felicitous" as a truth in making something happen. Marcel's painful discovery of this sad truth about lies is narrated in his endless unsuccessful attempt, prolonged even after Albertine's death, to discover whether or not she has been lying to him when she swears she does not have lesbian lovers. The passage about her anacoluthons is one link in a long chain of such passages. These express in different ways the impossibility of catching someone out in a lie, especially if one is in love with that someone, that is, predisposed to have faith in what she says.

One more thing must be said about lies in Proust. If a lie is performatively effective, it has power to create or discover the world it mendaciously names, just as a work of poetry, painting, or music, for Proust, reveals a hitherto unknown world that corresponds uniquely to that work. An example is the way Albertine's "art charmant . . . de mentir avec simplicité [charming skill in lying naturally]" (French, 3:694;

English, 3:187) keeps the writer Bergotte, in Marcel's mind at least, alive for a day after he has died. She persuades Marcel that she had a conversation with Bergotte at a time when he was actually already dead. In one extraordinary passage Marcel argues that lies give us a chance to apprehend worlds we should otherwise never have known. The passage is itself anacoluthonic. It begins in the third person and then shifts, in the sentences I am about to quote, to the first person plural:

The lie, the perfect lie [Le mensonge, le mensonge parfait], about people we know, about the relations we have had with them, about our motive [notre mobile] for some action, formulated by us in totally different terms, the lie as to what we are, whom we love, what we feel with regard to people who love us and believe that they have fashioned us in their own image [nous avoir façonnés semblables à lui] because they keep on kissing us morning, noon, and night— that lie is one of the few things in the world that can open windows for us on to what is new and unknown, that can awaken in us sleeping senses for the contemplation of universes that otherwise we should never have known [puisse nous ouvrir des perspectives sur du nouveau, sur de l'inconnu, puisse ouvrir en nous des sens endormis pour la contemplation d'univers que nous n'aurions jamais connus]. (French, 3:721; English, 3:213, trans. slightly altered)

The passage about Albertine's anacoluthons shows how stories that get written down offer chances to catch the mind at its inveterate work of reshaping things in the memory to make a consistent story out of them. This reshaping reveals (or creates) universes we should otherwise not have known. An oral anacoluthon most often slips by without being recognized, since we forget the beginning of the sentence by the time we hear its end. If the anacoluthonic sequence is written down, however, a careful reader may notice it. In Anthony Trollope's *Ayala's Angel* (1881), for example, Ayala, when she finally avows her love for Jonathan Stubbs, tells him she fell in love with him the first time she met him. The reader searches in vain, in the narrator's much earlier account of that meeting, for anything other than evidence of dislike and distaste on Ayala's part for Stubbs. Has Ayala forgotten? Has the narrator? Has Trollope? It is impossible to tell, since the anacoluthon is not signalled as such in the text.

The beginning, the moment of falling in love, is not presented by Trollope when it occurs, just as, according to Marcel, we do not experience the first moment of a love as the beginning of a new love: "When one wants to remember in what manner one began to love a woman, one is already in love with her." That first moment does not, apparently, exist as something that could be presented, since it was not present when it was present. It only exists after the fact, like a childhood or adult trauma that only becomes traumatic later on, after the fact, through what Freud calls "Nachträglichkeit." The condition of our sanity is our ability to tell lies to ourselves, to create splendid fictions of narrative coherence out of data that are not connected story lines, but dispersed and heterogeneous fragments. We can protect ourselves from the polylogical, from the intrinsic possibility that what happens to us can be simultaneously organized according to many different contradictory narrative centers, only by creating what I am calling the alogical, that is, something sustained only by its fictional pseudocoherence. The alogical is a precarious unity supported by no base in the logos in either of its two chief senses, neither by reason, nor by a mind that remains continuous with itself over time. The alogical, however, always contains within itself the traces of its miscellaneous origin, for example, in one form or another of anacoluthon. These traces are, one might say, a train of gunpowder that may cause the sequence to blow up if a single spark is applied. This liability shows that the sequence is no coherent line, but a series of juxtaposed points glued together by the power of a lie.[1]

Irony, what Friedrich Schlegel called "permanent parabasis," the permanent suspension of the narrative line, its breaking up into little disconnected pieces, is the rhetorical name for this explosion. Irony is the "final step" in the sequence I have followed from the monological to the polylogical to the alogical. Irony, however, is not at all a final step. It is a permanent possibility of disaster inherent in any narrative line and in the reader's interpretation of it. Irony names a disarticulation that has always already happened or is always happening or will happen. It exists all along the line, from the first step on. Irony exists as a vibration in each part of the narrative line making it so uncertain in meaning that it will not stay still long enough even to be appropriated as the instrument of a rhetorical deconstruction of the narrative line according to that neat narrative of progressive decomposition I have constructed here. If irony is the basic trope of narrative, as it is, then all narrative is suspended at every moment over its own impossibility. The possibility of being taken as ironical, therefore as unresolvable or unstillable in meaning, must be extended not to selected passages in the narrative text but to any passage whatsoever.

If irony is the impossibility of narrative, it also signals the impossibility of criticism in the sense of a demonstrable hermeneutic decoding of meaning. Or, to put this another way, the irony intrinsic to narrative means that criticism of narrative, like narrative itself, is suspended always on a vibrating tightrope over the abyss of its own impossibility. Far from progressing toward a full clarification, criticism, once it has encountered the pervasive presence of irony as permanent parabasis, remains itself suspended over the abyss of its inability to interpret satisfactorily. This is so, that is, if interpreting satisfactorily means referring the interpretation back to a single logos or even to identifiable multiple logoi, for example, back to any passage with a solid unequivocal ascertainable meaning, even a complex one, that criticism might take as a starting place for its journey of reading.

THIRTEEN

INDIRECT DISCOURSES AND IRONY

I turn now to indirect discourse, one of the major resources of story-telling in novels and one of the most important sources of disquieting perturbations in narrative middles. This chapter, which also will focus more closely on irony in narrative, is the penultimate essay before the extended discussion of works by Pater and Gaskell that makes up the final chapter in *Reading Narrative*. I take as examples three innocent-looking passages of indirect discourse, one from Anthony Trollope's *The Warden*, one from Elizabeth Gaskell's *Cranford*, one from the opening of Dickens's *Pickwick Papers*. It is necessary to cite each at some length in order to give the full flavor of the vibrating meaning generated by the play between different superimposed languages. I ask the reader to read each with patient attention to the different quality of irony in each:

In the meantime the warden sat alone, leaning on the arm of his chair; he had poured out a glass of wine, but had done so merely from habit, for he left it untouched; there he sat gazing at the open window, and thinking, if he can be said to have thought, of the happiness of his past life. All manner of past delights came before his mind, which at the time he had enjoyed without considering them; his easy days, his absence of all kind of hard work, his pleasant shady home, those twelve old neighbours whose welfare till now had been the source of so much pleasant care, the excellence of his children, the friendship of the dear old bishop, the solemn grandeur of those vaulted aisles, through which he loved to hear his own voice pealing; and then that friend of friends, that choice ally that had never deserted him, that eloquent companion that would always, when asked, discourse such pleasant music, that violoncello of his—ah, how happy he had been! but it was over now; his easy days and absence of work had been the crime which brought on him his tribulation; his shady home was pleasant no longer; maybe it was no longer his; the old neighbours, whose welfare had been so desired by him, were his enemies; his daughter was as wretched as himself; and even the bishop was made miserable by his position. He could never again lift up his voice boldly as he had hitherto done among his brethren, for he felt that he was disgraced; and he feared even to touch his bow, for he knew how grievous a sound of wailing, how piteous a lamentation, it would produce.[1]

Cranford had so long piqued itself on being an honest and moral town, that it had grown to fancy itself too genteel and well-bred to be otherwise, and felt the stain upon its character at this time doubly. But we comforted ourselves with the assurance which we gave to each other, that the robberies could never have been committed by any Cranford person; it must have been a stranger or strangers who brought this disgrace upon the town, and occasioned as many precautions as if we were living among the Red Indians or the French.

This last comparison of our nightly state of defence and fortification was made by Mrs. Forrester, whose father had served under General Burgoyne in the American war, and whose husband had fought the French in Spain. She indeed inclined to the idea that, in some way, the French were connected with the small thefts, which were ascertained facts, and the burglaries and highway robberies, which were rumours. She had been deeply impressed with the idea of French spies, at some time in her life; and the notion could never be fairly eradicated, but sprung up again from time to time. And now her theory was this: the Cranford people respected themselves too much, and were too grateful to the aristocracy who were so kind as to live near the town, ever to disgrace their bringing up by being dishonest or immoral; therefore, we must believe that the robbers were strangers—if strangers, why not foreigners?—if foreigners, who so likely as the French? Signor Brunoni spoke broken English like a Frenchman, and, though he wore a turban like a Turk, Mrs. Forrester had seen a print of Madame de Staël with a turban on, and another of Mr. Denon in just such a dress as that in which the conjurer had made his appearance; showing clearly that the French, as well as the Turks, wore turbans: there could be no doubt Signor Brunoni was a Frenchman—a French spy, come to discover the weak and undefended places of England; and, doubtless, he had his accomplices; for her part, she, Mrs. Forrester, had always had her own opinion of Miss Pole's adventure at the George Inn—seeing two men where only one was believed to be: French people had ways and means, which she was thankful to say, the English knew nothing about; and she had never felt quite easy in her mind about going to see that conjuror; it was rather too much like a forbidden thing, though the Rector was there. In short, Mrs. Forrester grew more excited than we had ever known her before; and, being an officer's daughter and widow, we looked up to her opinion, of course.

Really, I do not know how much was true or false in the reports which flew about like wildfire just at this time; but it seemed to me then that there was every reason to believe that at Mardon (a small town about eight miles from Cranford) houses and shops were entered by holes made in the walls, the bricks being silently carried away in the dead of night, and all done so quietly that no sound was heard either in or out of the house. Miss Matty gave it up in despair when she heard of this. "What was the use," said she, "of locks and bolts, and bells to the windows, and going round the house every night? That last trick was fit for a conjuror. Now she did believe that Signor Brunoni was at the bottom of it."[2]

The first ray of light which illumines the gloom, and converts into a dazzling brilliancy that obscurity in which the earlier history of the public career of the immortal Pickwick would appear to be involved, is derived from the perusal of the following entry in the Transactions of the Pickwick Club, which the editor of these papers feels the highest pleasure in laying before his readers, as a proof of the careful attention, indefatigable assiduity, and nice discrimination, with which his search among the multifarious documents confided to him has been conducted.

"May 12, 1827. Joseph Smiggers, Esq., P.V.P.M.P.C.,* presiding. The following resolutions unanimously agreed to:—

"That this Association has heard read, with feelings of unmingled satisfaction, and unqualified approval, the paper communicated by Samuel Pickwick, Esq., G.C.M.P.C.,† entitled "Speculations on the Source of the

* Perpetual Vice-President—Member Pickwick Club.
† General Chairman—Member Pickwick Club.

Hampstead Ponds, with some Observations on the Theory of Tittlebats"; and that this Association does hereby return its warmest thanks to the said Samuel Pickwick, Esq., G.C.M.P.C., for the same. . . ."

A casual observer, adds the secretary, to whose notes we are indebted for the following account—a casual observer might possibly have remarked nothing extraordinary in the bald head, and circular spectacles, which were intently turned towards his (the secretary's) face, during the reading of the above resolutions: to those who knew that the gigantic brain of Pickwick was working beneath that forehead, and that the beaming eyes of Pickwick were twinkling behind those glasses, the sight was indeed an interesting one. There sat the man who had traced to their source the mighty ponds of Hampstead, and agitated the scientific world with his Theory of Tittlebats, as calm and unmoved as the deep waters of the one on a frosty day, or as a solitary specimen of the other in the inmost recesses of an earthen jar. And how much more interesting did the spectacle become, when starting into full life and animation, as a simultaneous call for "Pickwick" burst from his followers, that illustrious man slowly mounted into the Windsor chair, on which he had been previously seated, and addressed the club he himself had founded. What a study for an artist did that exciting scene present! The eloquent Pickwick, with one hand gracefully concealed behind his coat tails, and the other waving in air, to assist his glowing declamation; his elevated position revealing those tights and gaiters, which, had they clothed an ordinary man, might have passed without observation, but which, when Pickwick clothed them—if we may use the expression—inspired involuntary awe and respect; surrounded by the men who had volunteered to share the perils of his travels, and who were destined to participate in the glories of his discoveries..³

Passages, *topoi*, places, *lieux de passage*, crossings, examples, samples, each cut from its context and cited here, sewn into a new context, like a prosthetic limb or organ to repair, replace, or stand in for something that might otherwise be missing in my own argument. At this point that argument cannot pass from here to there without the help of these quotations. This happens according to the law of each text's dependence on other texts that Jacques Derrida formulates: "Every thesis is (bands erect) a prosthesis; what affords reading affords reading by citations (necessarily truncated, clippings, repetitions, suctions, sections, suspensions, selections, stitchings, scarrings, grafts, postiches, organs without their own proper body, proper body covered with cuts. . . ."[4]

Would not the passages I have cited cease to be problematic if they were reinserted in their originating contexts and related back to the authorizing sources that first wrote them, the minds that generated them and were their places of emission? Would not each context determine a stable, monological program according to which the passage in question should be read? Does not citation perhaps always do violence to what it cites, always quote too little or too much, or too little and too much at once, so that the passage is neither completely free of its paternal or maternal source nor sufficiently provided with it? These are just the questions here, questions that lead to other questions. Do the passages cohere with their contexts, the whole narrative lines of which they are segments? What happens in repetition or citation? When I cite these passages here I do something oddly violent to them, or allow them to do something odd and violent to me by citing them. The act of citation changes them radically, if only by putting implicit "scare quotes" around them. They are themselves, however, already, in part at least, citations, already therefore themselves acts of violence, like the ironic undermining that is performed by repeating exactly, with the same intonation, what someone has just said to you. My citations repeat in indirect discourse, with a change of person and tense, previous states of mind or acts of language that are imagined as having already occurred for the characters. These are at a later time iterated by the narrator. This form makes possible my reiteration of them later still, here in my own text, where the passages are grafted or tipped in to help me out as examples.

The critic of a given work must begin somewhere. He or she must establish some passage or other, not necessarily the first in the text in question, as a firm foundation, open to being solidly and unequivocally interpreted. On the basis of that the movement forward on the spirals of the hermeneutical corkscrew may proceed. This positing of a beginning can, however, never securely happen, neither in a reading that keeps the founding passage fully attached to its surrounding context, if that could ever happen, nor in a reading, like mine here, that detaches citations from their original places and sews them together in juxtaposed incongruity within a critical or theoretical text, making something like Robinson Crusoe's patched garment of many skins.

The name for the oscillation of meaning in the passages quoted above is irony. All the passages vibrate with one form or another of radical irony. Since irony is a form of endless looping or feedback, this instability suggests that the interpreter can never go beyond any passage she or he takes as a starting place, if the problem of interpreting it is taken as a serious task. The interpreter remains, rather, suspended interminably in an impossible attempt to still the passage's internal movement so that it can be used as a firm stepping-off place for a more complete journey of interpretation.

There is no apparent difficulty in understanding any of these passages. Each is pellucidly clear. Each of the first two conveys the strong illusion of two personalities in particular "life situations," that of the character, that of the narrator recreating at a later time the character's words or inner state. Word and inner state seem each the perfect match, mirror, or vehicle of the other. In the passage from *Cranford* Mary Smith reports, for the understanding of her urban readers, who do not know provincial village life, Mrs. Forrester's words and the way her mind works. In the passage from Trollope the anonymous narrator of *The Warden* records not so much Mr. Harding's words as his state of mind at a certain moment of his ordeal. The opening of *Pickwick Papers* establishes the narrator as only an editor, a transparent medium through which is transmitted the words (whether formal minutes or informal notes) of the secretary of the Pickwick Club. The narrator's opening words, however, are his own, and, within a few paragraphs, the "editor" is not quoting but reporting what the characters said in the same odd form of language, indirect discourse, that is used in the other two passages.

In spite of these complications, the reader has no difficulty following in all three citations the shifts from person to person. The reading is aided by changes in person, number, and tense, and by quotation marks. It is only when the reader begins to ask questions of the passages' language, rather than taking for granted the phantasmal illusions of the personalities created by language, that the words start to become problematic. This happens according to that law Paul Valéry formulates by the example of an innocent little word like "time." The word "time" functions splendidly as a plank-walk over an abyss so long as you do not begin to jump up and down on the plank, interrogating it, testing it, in this case by asking, as Saint Augustine did long ago, "What is time?" Then the plank breaks, and you fall.[5]

Such risky questions might include the following: In the passages I have quoted, who is speaking, from what place, and to whom? Whose language or idiom is the reader given, that of the character, that of the narrator, or a mixture of the two? How can one tell, in a given sentence, where the language of the character stops and that of the narrator begins? The two languages must be constantly superimposed, the reader supposes, not so much in an anacoluthon, or switching in the middle, as in a constant doubling or displacement in which the language of the character is said over again in a shift from "I" or "we" to "he," "she," or "they" and in a shift from present tense to past tense: "He could never again lift up his voice boldly as he had hitherto done among his brethren." "[F]or her part, she, Mrs. Forrester, had always had her own opinion of Miss Pole's adventures at the George Inn . . . : French people had ways and means, which she was thankful to say, the English knew nothing about." "The bald head, and circular spectacles, which were intently turned towards his (the secretary's) face. . . ." Such language would be spoken by no one in any conceivable "real life" situation, unless in the situation of oral storytelling that is, it may be, the origin of all narrative. Indirect discourse is primarily a convention of printed narrative, though it may be borrowed from the habits of oral narrative. In either oral or written forms indirect discourse is an artifice of language. It is always at a remove from speech used in its own immediate context.

What exactly, however, is the significance of the shift from "we" to "she" to "I" in the passage from *Cranford*? Why is the indirect discourse reporting Miss Matty's speech put in quotation marks ("Now she did believe that Signor Brunoni was at the bottom of it"), whereas the same kind of indirect discourse used for Mrs. Forrester is not put inside quotation marks? What is the significance of the phrase "thinking, if he can be said to have thought," in the passage in *The Warden*? In the opening of *Pickwick Papers*, what is the basic idiom from which the others are comic deviations? Let me try to answer these question or at least show why they cannot be answered.

In the passage from *Cranford*, the speaker, Mary Smith, the narrator of the whole novel, unmarried, a little over thirty years old by the end of the novel, occasional visitor to Cranford from the large neighboring city of Drumble, speaks at first as a collective "we" for all the Cranford ladies. She then uses, apparently almost by accident, a comparison that has been made by one of those ladies, Mrs. Forrester: "as if we were living among the Red Indians or the French." The narrator's memory of this ("This last comparison . . . was made by Mrs. Forrester") leads to a sequence in which the "we" of the narrator allows a single voice, a single idiom, a single way of speaking to emerge from the group of Cranford ladies. This is mimed in the third person past tense by that narrative we (or is it a narrative I?): "French people had ways and means, which she was thankful to say, the English knew nothing about." At the end of this sequence there is a shift back to the first person plural, that is, a plunge back into the surrounding collective consciousness of the Cranford ladies as a group: "[she] being an officer's daughter and widow, we looked up to her opinion, of course." Then the present "I" of the narrator, drily skeptical now, though caught up then in the collective "panic,"[6] separates itself out: "Really I do not know how much was true or false in the reports . . .; but it seemed to me then. . . ." Finally this "I" reports, oddly within quotation marks, Miss Matty's words, but transposes them again to the third person past tense. "Now I do believe" (which is what Miss Matty presumably said) is changed to "Now she did believe." Do these quotation marks function to grant Miss Matty's mind and her idiom greater respect than Mrs. Forrester's "thoughts"? The latter are Mrs. Forrester's own or at any rate they are the unique form a powerful ideology takes within her mind. These thoughts are then swallowed up in the collective mind of the panicked "all." They are, moreover, not supposed to be cited from a single continuous speech but to be a summary of the sort of thing Mrs. Forrester said over and over at that time. The passage moves from "we" to "she" to "we" to "I" to another "she," widening and narrowing its focus constantly. The narrative line bends, stretches, vibrates to an invisible blur, divides itself into two, into three, into a multitude that is yet one, comes together again into an unequivocal or univocal one, breaks, begins again, after a brief, almost imperceptible hiatus between paragraphs, and so on throughout the novel.

What is the original line of continuous consciousness (in the sense of the constant presence to itself of a self expressed in a single idiom, an idiolect, a proper language) that is the "source" of all these doublings and redoublings, and to which the line would safely return if its oscillations were allowed to die down or could be damped? The author? The narrator? The author's memory of her younger self and its language? The characters, one by one? The "consciousness of the community," the collective "we"? What attitude does Elizabeth Gaskell have, or does the text have, or are we as readers supposed to have, of judgment, sympathy, understanding, or condescending laughter toward these various imaginary persons? No verifiable answer can be given to these questions. The irony intrinsic to indirect discourse suspends or fragments the narrative line, making it irreducible to any unitary trajectory.

The passage from *The Warden* does not quite work in the same way. In *Cranford* a multiplicity of minds are matched to a multiplicity of different idiolects. In the passage from *The Warden*, there are only two lines, that of the narrator and that of Mr. Harding. Or perhaps there is only one language, the narrator's, since the warden, we are told, may not even be thinking. The narrator may be giving language to Harding's wordless revery. Trollope apparently means, by questioning whether or not the warden was thinking, that he may not have been articulating his wordless global state of mind in distinct language. The warden, says the narrator, sat "thinking, if he can be said to have thought, of the happiness of his past life." Nevertheless, the language that ensues, as it follows the various images that are said to pass through Mr. Harding's mind, appears to be much more the warden's language, ironized by being mimed with slight hyperbole in the third person past tense by the narrator, than it is the narrator's or Trollope's. At any rate, the passage, as it progresses, rapidly comes to seem Harding's language or its corresponding consciousness transposed into the sort of language we know from elsewhere in the novel he habitually uses: "—ah, how happy he had been! but it was over now . . ." This is a translation of: "—ah, how happy I have been! but it is over now."

The difficulty comes when the reader tries to separate out the two sources of the language line, the language-producing foyer that is the narrator, the language-producing foyer that is the character. The relation between the two is elided, elliptical, specular, but in an equivocal way. Something is always missing that would make it possible to make a firm distinction and say, "This is the narrator's language; that is the warden's." The line of language is produced in the manner of a strange ellipse, a closed circuit with two foci or centers of gravity, like a planet that moves both around the sun as focus and around another focus in empty space. In the case of the passage from *The Warden*, however, each focus, when you go to seek it out, is absent, virtual, empty, an imaginary locus that seems to be generated by the substantiality of the other one. The other one, however, is missing too when you seek it out. Harding has at this point no language but that ascribed to him by the narrator, but the narrator can speak or write only language that ironically mimes language Harding would have used. Each language source is the mirror image of the other, but which is the shadow, which the substance, which the real thing, which the simulacrum or mimesis, is impossible to tell. The language of the narrator is no stable base. It is an anonymous, neutral, collective power of representing the language of the characters by miming them ironically in indirect discourse. The character, however, has, in this case at least, no language of his own, only a wordless state of mind to which language is ascribed by the narrator. This speech act conjures that state of mind into existence for the reader by waving the magic wand of a performative language that says in effect, "Let there be the Reverend Septimus Harding, and let his wordless mind be granted speech." The narrator depends on the character for his existence, the character depends on the narrator, in a constant oscillation that is characteristic both of what I am calling—in a deliberately self-doubling word—dialogology and also of the subversion of dialogue's apparent stability by irony. This doubling is an odd mirroring. It is a specular or speculative relationship in which, as one might say, the mirror is empty when I seek my face in the glass, or in which, perhaps, the face I see is more original than my own and so depersonalizes me when I copy it in order to achieve or affirm my own substance. That is what happens in Thomas Hardy's poem "The Pedigree."[7] To cite another parallel, an insight similar to Hardy's is expressed in Shakespeare's brilliant play on the double sense of "speculation"—as mirroring and as self-affirming doubling dialectical thought, thought that must go out from itself in order to become itself. The wordplay occurs in the speech of Ulysses to Achilles in *Troilus and Cressida*:

> For speculation turns not to itself
> Till it hath traveled and is married[8] there
> Where it may see itself. (3.3.109–11).

Speculum, speculation, narcissism, dialogue, ellipsis—each of these models involves a doubling that can become ultimately an annihilation. The search for a substance of the self outside the self leads to the absurdity of a bifold authority, as in the two Cressidas, each the source of the other and yet each nothing without the other. The passage I have cited from *The Warden* contains a parable for this annihilating bifurcation in the relation between Septimus Harding and his cello. This relation functions throughout the novel as an emblem for the doubling within the warden between his "consciousness" and his "conscience": "and then that friend of friends, that choice ally that had never deserted him, that eloquent companion that would always, when asked, discourse such pleasant music, that violoncello of his. . . ." The violoncello is a faithful friend, ally, and eloquent speaker, but not one that exists independent, as a power of speaking, of *its* friend, ally, and player, Harding himself. The cello "discourses" only "when asked." Mr. Harding calls its language into being by a performative request or demand. The cello's language, in return, answers and reaffirms the asking language of Mr. Harding, in a reciprocal, specular, or narcissistic relation. It is narcissistic because the cello is of course no more alive than Narcissus's reflection in the pool. Harding gives the cello life by personifying it. The echoing of Harding by his cello is not a true "marriage" or "mirroring" of two separate beings. It is an attempt at self-generation by auto-affection. In this act twoness, oneness, and nothingness are mixed. Each language has its origin in the other language source. Mr. Harding can only speak from his conscience by way of his cello, but the cello can only speak when asked by Mr. Harding. The intimate relation between Mr. Harding and his cello matches parabolically the relation of the narrator's language to that of the character in all three of the passages quoted here. It matches also the relation between the language of the author and that of the narrator. It matches, finally, the relation of the language of criticism to that of the text criticized. In each case a supplementary ironizing displacement redoubles an already acentered and duplicitous language.

The latter two relations, that between author and narrator, that between text and critic, are articulated with special clarity in the passage from *Pickwick Papers*. In *Pickwick*, moreover, the way all three examples exploit properties more salient in written, not spoken, language is made explicit. The narrator of *Pickwick Papers* is not a speaker but an editor of written documents. This follows a convention that has a long history in seventeenth- and eighteenth-century novels. Dickens's use of this convention is one of the "archaic" aspects of *Pickwick Papers*, as opposed to the use of an omniscient narrator in, say, *Middlemarch* or *Our Mutual Friend*. Nevertheless, the device of having a novel described as a manuscript found in a bottle or in an old trunk has of course continued to our own day. Dickens, however, employs this already old convention by ironically parodying it. The "editor" of *The Posthumous Papers of the Pickwick Club* at first asserts that he is entirely dependent on the manuscripts in his possession for his reconstruction of Pickwick's adventures. This pretense is then rapidly forgotten. The novel becomes straightforward narrative with a narrator not unlike the storyteller in Dickens's later novels. What matters for my purposes here is the process whereby that narrative voice gets started and established. It begins as the fiction of a citation from the minutes of a meeting of the Pickwick Club. The editor, speaking of himself in the third person, claims to be quoting these verbatim, "as a proof of the careful attention, indefatigable assiduity, and nice discrimination, with which his search among the multifarious documents confided to him has been conducted." The next section, after the extended formal citation, is in a curious kind of indirect discourse. One written document, that of the editor, paraphrases another written document, the notes of the recording secretary at the meeting: "A casual observer, adds the secretary, to whose notes we are indebted for the following account—a casual observer might possibly have remarked nothing extraordinary in the bald head, and circular spectacles. . . ." The editor's language is dependent on the language of his documents, in the same way as the language of the narrator in *Cranford* or of *The Warden* is dependent on the language or on the "thoughts" of Mrs. Forrester or of Septimus Harding. Who is the "we," however, who speaks toward the end of my citation: "which, when Pickwick clothed them—if we may use the expression . . ." Is this the "we" of the secretary who is mimed by the editor, or is it the "we" of the editor already interpolating his language into the language of the secretary's notes, or is it the language of the irrepressible Boz, that is, of Dickens himself, bursting through the parody of a pompous editor like a sun penetrating the clouds? Boz's own heteroglossic, hyperbolic, linguistic high jinks, in *Pickwick Papers*, come rapidly to efface the simple one-dimensional parody of editorial language, for example, in Jingle's elliptical wildly exuberant lying stories or in Sam Weller's fecundity in inventing "Wellerisms," to which I shall return. There is no ascertainable answer to the question whose language this is. The "we" is all these voices at once and so no one particular identifiable voice. It is several superimposed idioms at once, in ironic proliferating multiplicity.

What, then, about the first language the reader encounters in *Pickwick Papers*? Whose language is it that opens the novel, at the very beginning, before the first citation? "The first ray of light which illumines the gloom, and converts into a dazzling brilliancy that obscurity in which the earlier history of the public career of the immortal Pickwick would appear to be involved, is derived from the perusal of the following entry in the Transactions of the Pickwick Club. . . ." Is this Dickens's own idiom, or that of Boz, his invented persona, or that of the "editor," or what? Since, as Steven Marcus has recognized,[9] this sentence is virtually the moment of Boz's birth, the answer is of some importance. I say "virtually," since *Pickwick Papers* was preceded by the *Sketches by Boz*. The

Sketches, however, for all their interest, hardly belong to world literature in the way *Pickwick Papers* does. The moment of Dickens's appearance as a great creative writer happens in a pseudoperformative fiat or "let there be light." The opening sentence, with its pompous hyperbole and awkward syntax, is not Dickens himself speaking or writing. It parodies the style of adulatory biography. Dickens adopts this style in order to ridicule it: "The first ray of light which illumines the gloom"!

Dickens begins his career as a writer by pretending to be a pedantic editor who is in turn dependent on the language of the documents "confided to him" in order to be able to tell his story. Those documents themselves parody the language of parliamentary reporting. Dickens got his start as an extraordinarily facile parliamentary reporter. He was a genius at shorthand. *Pickwick Papers* is another example of a dialogical doubling. The reader can nowhere identify language that has straightforwardly emerged, without irony, from an emitting source in a "real" consciousness. Each distinguishable voice is ironically undermined. Nowhere in *Pickwick Papers* is an unironic language to be found against which other language may be measured. Even when Dickens seems most to be speaking in "his own voice," as in the political or moralizing asides by the narrator later on in *Pickwick*, or even in the direct interventions by Dickens himself, speaking in the first person, as in the farewell to his readers at the end of the novel, the wary reader suspects that this may be just another assumed voice. There is no way to be sure that this is not the case. This uncertainty happens according to a law that says any piece of language may be taken as literature, that is, as fictional, as "nonserious." This makes Wellerisms possible. I shall return to this point about literature later.

The reader is presented throughout *Pickwick Papers* with parodies of alternative ways to write, to speak, or to tell a story: picaresque language, journalistic, scientific, political, sentimental, sensational, Carlylean language, the language of travel literature, and so on. There is no personal idiom of Dickens as such, any more than there is a personal idiom in the fictional writings by Thackeray or Trollope or George Eliot. Becoming a novelist means inventing a narrative voice. Far from being a secure performative affirmation of one's hitherto precarious selfhood, this speech act is depersonalizing, in that, however hard one tries, one cannot speak in one's own voice. To put this another way, remembering the root metaphor in the word "person" (it comes from the Latin "persona," mask[10]), to become a storyteller is personalizing as if one were covering whatever personality was already there with a mask. Innumerable other masks may be superimposed over that first mask, according to a propensity for duplicitous multiplying intrinsic to signs. This is like Miss Matty's two hats simultaneously worn, one on top of another, in *Cranford*, to which I shall return in the last chapter.

The linguistic structure of all three of the cited passages is similar. In each case, though in a different way each time, the author goes outside himself or herself, doubles himself or herself, in order to affirm the self through a language that will be mirrored in the eyes of others, recognized by them, mirrored or married there where it may see itself. Elizabeth Gaskell, née Stevenson, became "Mrs. Gaskell," the well-known author of *Mary Barton, North and South, Cranford*, et cetera, by the act of inventing the language of narration in these works. The mute youth Anthony Trollope ("with all a stupid boy's slowness, I said nothing"[11]), guilty of the secret vice of daydreaming ("There can, I imagine," he said in his autobiography, "hardly be a more dangerous mental practice" [*Autobiography*, 33]), became himself through the invention of the narrative voice that speaks in those forty-seven novels and through their recognition by the reading public. Charles Dickens transcended the depersonalizing experience of the blacking-factory episode of his life[12] and had his selfhood spectacularly affirmed by hundreds of thousands of readers through the detour of his externalization of himself. He traveled out of himself into the language of Boz. In each case, however, this doubling, by an unavoidable law, became a redoubling to infinity, a multiplication of images of the self. Such a multiplication ultimately undermines the notion of fixed selfhood, even of double or triple selfhood. The self becomes vibrating, ambiguous, unstable, ironic. Such a self is not a single language-emitting consciousness or ego. The detour outside the self becomes an endless wandering, the permanent suspension of any single narratable life line.

One name we give to this wandering or suspension is "literature." Literature depends on the possibility of detaching language from its firm embeddedness in a social or biographical context and allowing it to play freely as fiction. A Wellerism is a joke that depends on the way a given utterance can have radically different meanings in different contexts. Wellerisms brilliantly identify the propensity of any utterance to become literature or to become ironic by a simple displacement into a fictional context. Wellerisms are thus related to the ironic suspension that is performed by indirect discourse. A example is what Sam Weller's father says when he hears that Sam is to be married: "'Nev'r mind, Sammy,' replied Mr Weller, 'it'll be a wery agonizin' trial to me at my time of life, but I'm pretty tough, that's vun consolation, as the wery old turkey remarked wen the farmer said he wos afeerd he should be obliged to kill him for the London market.'"[13]

I say literature is "the possibility of detaching language" from its pragmatic context in order to stress that no piece of language in itself is either literature or not literature. It depends on how you take it. That we take the three novels from which I have quoted as literary works is the result of a complex historical happening that began at a certain time in Europe. On the one hand, any piece of language can be "taken as literature." On the other hand, the so-called novels I have cited could be taken as nonliterature. No distinctive marks identify a given piece of language as literature, nor do different features allow us to say of another piece of language that it is not literature, that it is a serious use of language to refer to things as they are or to make something happen through a felicitous speech act surrounded by an enabling context in "the real world." One could imagine an imaginary telephone book, complete with Yellow Pages. It would look just like a real one, that is, like an effectively referential telephone book. We might be beguiled into taking it as such. Defoe has the preliminary "editor" of *Moll Flanders* use the same sort of language attesting to the authenticity of Moll's autobiographical account (altered, says the editor, only to make it "modester") as the editor of a genuine autobiography would use. Even if I say, "The following is fictional," I may be lying to hide the reality of the account.

Much work in literary study as a university-based institutionalized endeavor, including so-called cultural studies, has been an attempt to treat what could be taken as literary works as though they were historical, social, or autobiographical documents, that is, as though they were not literature. The institution of literary study, including of course most journalistic reviewing, is, paradoxically, a vigorous and multifaceted attempt to suppress, efface, cover over, ignore, and forget the properly literary in literature, that is, what is improper about literary language or about any language when it is taken as literature. By "improper" I mean detached from its proper referential or performative use.

Dialogue, in Bakhtin's sense, is a powerful tool for putting in question the deeply rooted ideological assumption that a literary text should be thought of as emerging monologically from a single consciousness. If the work were monological then it could be returned to its author and to the subject position of the author as a person of a certain gender, race, and class in a certain country at a certain moment in history. Dialogue has been my instrument of analysis in this section on indirect discourse, as well as in what I said earlier about citations, letters, epigraphs, interpolations—all those doublings of the narrative line. "Dialogue," however, when applied to a text, is a metaphor. It still presupposes the guiding principle of monologism: selfhood, consciousness, logos in the sense of mind. Dialogue substitutes two voices or consciousnesses for one, the ellipse for the circle. When the meaning of "dialogue" shifts from mind to word, however, as it does for Bakhtin, it deconstructs dialogism as double consciousness in the same act in which it deconstructs monologue. The assumption that "dialogue" means two minds interacting, exchanging words, nevertheless constantly reasserts itself, since that is the primary sense of the word. When dialogue comes to mean two forms of language, however, and one of those becomes a neutral, anonymous power of narration, speaking as who knows who from who knows where, then one focus of the ellipse of dialogue vanishes. The ellipse becomes hyperbolic, "thrown beyond" itself, or, in the geometric meaning of "hyperbole," an ellipse turned inside out. Hyperbole names in this case the ironic excess with which one voice mimes the other. The specular look of one consciousness at another in dialogue in its usual sense becomes a look not at the other, but at an absence.

Hyperbole in turn then becomes parable or parabola ("thrown beside," as, in a geometric parabola, the curve is "thrown beside" the line that controls it). In parable the figure of dialogue, even with one of its focii hyperbolically at infinity, is replaced by the figure of one voice or language that is controlled by an absent or allegorical meaning, at an unapproachable distance from the narrative line of language whose literal meaning functions as a visible center. This may be figured in the way a comet of parabolic orbit swings around the sun and sweeps out again to disappear forever, whereas a comet of elliptical orbit returns periodically, for example, Halley's comet.

Parable, finally, gives way in its turn to irony. Irony is the suspension of both line and any center or centers of meaning, even at infinity. Irony cannot be expressed by any geometric figure. Both subjectivity and intersubjectivity are abolished by irony. Irony belongs to no voice or voices, neither to two nor to one. Ironic language functions mechanically in detachment from any controlling center or centers, just as indirect discourse, which is irony as an operative principle of narration, can no longer be certainly identified as spoken or written by anyone in particular. Irony suspends any possible ordering according to some sequence controlled by a governing principle of meaning. Even the neat narrative sequence I have established here, from circle to ellipse to hyperbole to parable to irony as permanent parabasis is undermined from beginning to end by the possibility of being taken ironically. Rather than being a culmination or guiding telos, irony is present at the beginning, middle, and end of any narrative line. Irony can only be stabilized by an arbitrary act of the interpreter stilling the unstillable and ignoring other possibilities of meaning. No passage in a narrative, short or long, partial or complete, will stay motionless long enough, unless killed by the critic, in her or his rage for certainty, to form the stable base for a further journey or line of interpretation.

My investigation of the narrative line has constantly approached and receded from the recognition of irony as a pervasive element of undecidability making both narrative and the analysis of narrative in principle impossible, if verifiable certainty of meaning is demanded. This does not keep both narrative and the interpretation of narrative from continuing imperturbably, in defiance of this impossibility. I, Anthony Trollope, or Elizabeth Gaskell, or Charles Dickens, driven by some sense of lack or deprivation, double myself. I invent another voice, a narrator, and then other voices, "characters," beyond that, for the first speaker to repeat in indirect discourse or in citation of spoken words. I double or split my tongue to give myself, in my muteness, a tongue, but in this act I deprive myself of any tongue, idiom, voice, logos proper to me. I depersonalize myself. As Rousseau says in the second preface to *La Nouvelle Héloïse*, "Wishing to be what one is not, one comes to believe oneself to be other than one is, and that is how one goes mad."[4] The doubling of storytelling becomes madness, as Friedrich Schlegel said irony is.[5]

If one associates univocal sense-making with some masculine principle of authority, which Derrida has dubbed "phallogocentrism," then irony can be defined as a species of castration. This happens according to the Freudian law that says the doubling of the phallus signifies its absence, the vanishing of phallocentrism along with logocentrism. Phallus goes when logos goes. If it seems absurd to ascribe phallogocentrism to Elizabeth Gaskell, Jacques Lacan, in "Le Séminaire sur 'la Lettre volée,'" and Jacques Derrida, on Lacan on Poe, in "Le Facteur de la vérité," in their quite different outlinings of the rules for the game of "phallus, phallus, who's got the phallus," have identified the mother in one way or another as the phallus's keeper or, what comes to the same thing, as keeping the secret of its eternal absence. The card game of "Old Maid" is a version of that interplay.[6]

The metaphor of dialogue destroys that of monologue, and destroys the unity of the narrative line by doubling it, but it destroys itself at the same time. It destroys the phenomenological implications, the references to consciousness, of its own model. This leaves only the invisible blur of the vibrations of irony, language as a machine working without the control of any logos, the mirror empty of any face. Plato (that is, Socrates) was right. Mimesis, in the sense of double diegesis, is an extreme danger to single diegesis and to the phallogocentric idea behind diegesis. "Or can you think of anything more frightful," asks the "Or" of Kierkegaard's *Either/Or*, "than that it might end with your nature being resolved into a multiplicity, that you really might become many, become, like those unhappy demoniacs, a legion, and you thus would have lost the inmost and holiest thing of all in man, the unifying power of personality?"[7]

Unity becomes duplicity becomes a multiplicity that is legion, demoniac, alogical. That dissolves ultimately not only any concept of a stable authoring mind but also dissolves the mind, the self-possession, of any reader who yields himself or herself fully to the corrosive irony implicit in any storytelling or narrative line, however strait or straight it tries to be. It is the fascination of this danger that makes even the simplest story or narrative fragment seem inexhaustible, fathomless in its power and perfection, as Franz Kafka discovered in 1911:

The special nature of my inspiration in which I, the most fortunate and unfortunate of men, now go to sleep at 2 A.M. (perhaps, if I can only bear the thought of it, it will remain, for it is loftier than all before [denn sie ist höher als alle früheren]), is such that I can do everything, and not only what is directed to a definite piece of work [ist die, daβ ich alles kann, nicht nur auf eine bestimmte Arbeit hin]. When I arbitrarily write a single sentence, for instance, "He looked out of the window," it already has perfection. [Wenn ich wahllos einen Satz hinschreibe, zum Beispiel "Er schaute aus dem Fenster," so ist er schon vollkommen.]"[18]

This exploration by way of selected "segments," beginnings, middles, and ends in the narrative line has constantly encountered impasses, interruptions, doublings, suspensions. Starting, continuing, and concluding all occur, but they are constantly, from beginning to end, suspended over the abyss of their own impossibility. The most inclusive name for this impossibility is "irony." Irony is in one way or another the pervasive trope of narrative. Irony is another name for literature as a constant possibility of the fictional within language. The difficulty in analyzing the narrative line is the difficulty, or rather the impossibility, of mastering the unmasterable, the trope that is no trope, the figure not figurable as a turning, crossing, displacement, detour, or as any other line, the trope-no-trope of irony. I shall, in the concluding chapter, exemplify this impossibility and the way it is does not prevent interpretation from occurring by a more complete reading of two narratives.

FOURTEEN

APOLLYON IN CRANFORD

I can testify to a magnificent family red silk umbrella, under which a gentle little spinster, left alone of many brothers and sisters, used to patter to church on rainy days. Have you any red silk umbrellas in London? We had a tradition of the first that had ever been seen in Cranford; and the little boys mobbed it, and called it "a stick in petticoats." It might have been the very red silk one I have described, held by a strong father over a troop of little ones; the poor little lady—the survivor of all—could scarcely carry it.

—Elizabeth Gaskell, *Cranford*

"À entrées multiples, avec des fils d'Ariane entrelacés [With multiple entry points, with interlaced Ariadne threads]."

—Jacques Derrida, *La Vérité en peinture*

This chapter gathers all the problems in reading narrative identified and exemplified in previous chapters in a more extended intertwined reading of two works, Elizabeth Gaskell's *Cranford* and Walter Pater's "Apollo in Picardy." Having made my way through many corridors of narrative theory's labyrinth[1] I have found no center, no Minotaur, and no Ariadne at the other end of the thread[2] either, no literal grounding for the turns of the fictions I have discussed, and no escape into the sunlight of love and life. I am lost, halted, without an effort to break through, because I have already broken through. I have crossed the pass, have stepped over the line into a disorienting openness.[3] Wherever I turn, on whatever point on the line of narrative theory I stand, I continually encounter the monster, irony, ruination of my search for a solid theoretical ground on the basis of which, theory becoming application, I could read with a sense of secure mastery one novel or another. After all my search I am back where I started from, still confronting the initial examples of line

imagery in the novel cited at the beginning of *Ariadne's Thread*: the passage
about string and rubber bands from *Cranford*, the passage about the Prior
Saint-Jean's unbindable book from Pater's "Apollo in Picardy." Here are
those passages again, still waiting to be explicated:

String is my foible. My pockets get full of little hanks of it, picked up and
twisted together, ready for uses that never come up. I am seriously annoyed if
any one cuts the string of a parcel, instead of patiently and faithfully undoing
it fold by fold. How people can bring themselves to use India-rubber rings,
which are a sort of deification of string, as lightly as they do, I cannot imagine.
To me an India-rubber ring is a precious treasure. I have one which is not new;
one that I picked up off the floor, nearly six years ago. I have really tried to use
it; but my heart failed me, and I could not commit the extravagance.[4]

Devilry, devil's work:—traces of such you might fancy were to be found in a
certain manuscript volume taken from an old monastic library in France at the
revolution. It presented a strange example of a cold and very reasonable spirit
disturbed suddenly, thrown off its balance, as by a violent beam, a blaze of new
light, revealing, as it glanced here and there, a hundred truths unguessed at
before, yet a curse, as it turned out, to its receiver, in dividing hopelessly against
itself the well-ordered kingdom of his thought. Twelfth volume of a dry
enough treatise on mathematics, applied, still with no relaxation of strict
method, to astronomy and music, it should have concluded that work, and
therewith the second period of the life of its author, by drawing tight together
the threads of a long and intricate argument. In effect however, it began, or, in
perturbed manner, and as with throes of childbirth, seemed the preparation for,
an argument of an entirely new and disparate species, such as would demand a
new period of life also, if it might be, for its due expansion.

But with what confusion, what baffling inequalities! How afflicting to the
mind's eye! It was a veritable "solar storm"—this illumination, which had burst
at the last moment upon the strenuous, self-possessed, much-honoured
monastic student, as he sat down peacefully to write the last formal chapters of
his work ere he betook himself to its well-earned practical reward as superior,
with lordship and mitre and ring, of the abbey whose music and calendar his
mathematical knowledge had qualified him to reform. The very shape of

Volume Twelve, pieced together of quite irregularly formed pages, was a solecism. It could never be bound. In truth, the man himself, and what passed with him in one particular space of time, had invaded a matter, which is nothing if not entirely abstract and impersonal. Indirectly the volume was the record of an episode, an interlude, an interpolated page of life. And whereas in the earlier volumes you found by way of illustration no more than the simplest indispensible diagrams, the scribe's hand had strayed here into mazy borders, long spaces of hieroglyph, and as it were veritable pictures of the theoretic elements of his subject. Soft wintry auroras seemed to play behind whole pages of crabbed textual writing, line and figure bending, breathing, flaming, into lovely "arrangements" that were like music made visible; till writing and writer changed suddenly, "to one thing constant never," after the known manner of madmen in such work. Finally, the whole matter broke off with an unfinished word, as a later hand testified, adding the date of the author's death, "deliquio animi."[5]

My long line of exploration, with all its tangled knots of explanation and intrication following through this or that example, has all been spun out from those initial citations, or has been for the sake of returning to untie them at last at the journey's end, or, it may be, to be lost in their tangles. Any one of the nine modes of analyzing narrative I identified at the beginning of *Ariadne's Thread*[6] could be applied to each of these passages or to each of the stories from which they are cited. One could imagine a multistranded reading that would be an application of all these modes at once, as though nine fingers or fids were working to unravel the same knots at once. Would this turn them straight at last? Undoubtedly not, since, as my books on narrative have attempted in one way or another to show, all these kinds of reading reach in the end an inextricable knot. All lead to a confrontation of the thing that can never be "confronted" in the sense of theoretically dominated. This thing is what I have called an "x ignotum" or "the others." It or they remain, after all efforts of reading, still as much tangled in nets of catachresis as ever.

What, it may be asked, is the exact status and function of these examples? Is mine not a long web to weave by attachment to such fragile and marginal loom beams? The beams are themselves no more than lines, threads, bits of yarn. The question of how so much can be strung out from so little is like the question of how a gentle little spinster can carry the great red family umbrella, the stick in petticoats. The whole weight of Western tradition, nevertheless, is carried, in a different way in each case, by these two stories, or even by the two bits I have extracted from them. Each passage may be thought of as a momentary node of elements on which converge lines of force extending, first, out into the immediate context of the work from which it is extracted. From there the context expands to include the rest of each author's work and then to encompass the enormous body of nineteenth-century writing in English and other Western languages, and so out to all of Western writing back to Plato, the Bible, and beyond. To trace the lines in each knot and untie all its implications would be to show it as the repetition of other knots extending back along those networked fibers—an interminable process. This might even lead to the recognition of a tenth way to analyze narrative: a way that would ground the meaning of a given work on its relation to previous works, that is, on the various anxieties and sub-limities of influence.

Moreover, to untie the knot of one passage is to tie up the other one, or to allow it to unravel and fly to the winds. One would need to be four-handed to move rapidly enough from one to the other. As one is being done, the other knot undoes itself or is undone. They do not match one another squarely, as symmetrical knots. I have said that one could explicate each story according to each of my nine modes. An "economic," or, even more strictly, "Marxist," reading of Cranford would, for example, be of great interest. It would repay the doing. On the other hand, there would be much to say about "illustration" in "Apollo in Picardy," as of the not wholly harmonious relation between picture and word in Pater's work generally. The idea for "Apollo in Picardy" is said to have come to Pater from the engraving of a painting showing Apollo and Hyacinth by Il Domenichino (1581–1641). The story, moreover, is one of Pater's "imaginary portraits." It is a story that is called a picture. All the other modes of narrative analysis I have explored could also be used to read the two passages in their contexts. Eighteen "readings" altogether of the two stories would be possible. They might possibly all come to similar impasses, or perhaps not, but the interest would be in the different route followed each time, in the details of the knots as they are untied.

Example is catachresis. The example is not an example *of* something that could be given in a different way, conceptually, or in a congruent way in alternative examples. What the example gives can only be given in that example. What the example exemplifies is itself. It is always inadequate to that other thing that it covers over in the act of giving it a figurative name, bringing a term over from another place to the place where no proper name exists. No possibility exists, however, of substituting a better example, a more adequate, or more "exemplary" one. The example is the gentle spinster, spinner of thread, weaver of fabric, carrying the huge umbrella, phallic stick and feminine petticoats together, strong father and maternal productrice in one. The spinster supports, with difficulty, the great family of meaning she must maintain and keep in the open, to keep up appearances. The example is the unproductive survivor, the end of the line, who nevertheless carries on, carries "it" on.

Not eighteen more readings, to be sure, but something more may now be said of my two citations in the light of what I have said in earlier chapters about narrative complications and about irony.

In her quiet way, Elizabeth Gaskell, the clergyman's wife from Manchester, is a more subversive writer than Walter Pater, the putative immoralist of Brasenose College. She undoes, by ironically questioning them, millennia of male domination in literature and in family life. Published originally in irregularly spaced installments in Charles Dickens's journal, *Household Words*, between December 13, 1851, and May 21, 1853, and then brought out as a single volume in 1853, *Cranford* is like a series of bits of string, untied, stretched out, saved up, and pieced together in a row to make ultimately a narrative line telling a single story. Unlike the Prior Saint-Jean's lamentable twelfth volume in Pater's "Apollo in Picardy," the series of discrete episodes making up *Cranford* is not a "solecism," not an ungrammatical sequence like an anacoluthon. *Cranford* can be bound, stitched together within the covers of a single book, given boundaries and a bound, a goal, like a package neatly tied up with string and sent on its way. Nevertheless, the open-endedness of *Cranford* is indicated by the way it was extended ten years later, in "The Cage at Cranford" (published in Dickens' *All the Year Round* in 1863). "The Cage at Cranford" is another story about gender difference and about cloth as decent covering and as enclosure. The cloth in this case is not the red silk of the family umbrella with its central stick, but a great petticoat, the covering of a Parisian hoopskirt. This article of the latest fashion is mistakenly seen by the innocent provincial ladies of Cranford as a covered cage for some enormous parrot or cockatoo, though they cannot see how it will work, since it has no bottom. If *Cranford* is made of bits of string laid end to end and tied together in seemly knots to make a long rope, it is by no means ever to be likened to that deification of string, a rubber band or India rubber ring. Its knotted segments never pull tight the final ring as a rubber band might. Breaks and loose ends remain, as the story starts again and stops, starts again with another episode, and so on. *Cranford* seems determined to exploit to the full the multiplication of plots and episodes, the narrative discontinuity, permitted by the conventions of the Victorian novel.

"Apollo in Picardy," on the other hand, marches straightforwardly toward its goal. That end is the madness and death of the Prior Saint-Jean, sunstruck by a cold northern solar energy, the Hyperborean Apollo. Pater's well-knit story, however, is, as always with Pater, the narration of an interruption, a destructive interpolation in a closed society. This break occurs when something ancient comes back, repeats itself, is reborn out of its time. This rebirth causes a permanent rupture in those lines of development that seem to make up cultural history in the dialectical or Hegelian view of it that so influenced Pater. A "renaissance" is, in Pater's view, by no means a benign historical event, It is a dangerous break in history. That break often has something to do with a surreptitious coming out of the closet. If *Cranford*, in its quiet way, is a powerful feminist work, Pater's "Apollo in Picardy," like the rest of his work, as many recent critics have recognized, is an important part of that closeted gay literature of the late Victorian period. Homosexuality is given by Pater a historical dimension. It is a periodic disruption of "straight" society that has repeated itself over and over from Greek times to the present.

If lines for Pater, when they come together in a text or in a person, are "but the concurrence, renewed from moment to moment, of forces parting sooner or later on their ways,"[7] lines for Gaskell are letters in the epistolary sense, bits of paper written over and saved up as memorials, in this case the letters between Miss Matty's parents along with other family letters. Mary Smith, the narrator of *Cranford*, a young unmarried woman from the big city of Drumble, can then recover the past by reading these letters, with Miss Matty's help. She strings them together to make a narrative sequence, while at the same time destroying each one as it is reread. This episode follows just after the passage about string and rubber bands:

I never knew what sad work the reading of old letters was before that evening, though I could hardly tell why. The letters were as happy as letters could be—at least those early letters were. There was in them a vivid and intense sense of the present time, which seemed so strong and full, as if it could never pass away, and as if the warm, living hearts that so expressed themselves could never die, and be as nothing to the sunny earth. I should have felt less melancholy, I believe, if the letters had been more so. . . .

"We must burn them, I think," said Miss Matty, looking doubtfully at me. "No one will care for them when I am gone." And one by one she dropped them into the middle of the fire; watching each blaze up, die out, and rise away, in faint, white, ghostly semblance, up the chimney, before she gave another the same fate. (*C*, 5: 64, 66)

Admirable emblem for the writing of *Cranford*! John Ruskin, in *Ariadne Florentina*, his book about Florentine engraving, associates Ariadne with Penelope and with Arachne.[8] The drawing or incising of a line in engraving is, for Ruskin, like the unrolling of Ariadne's thread from that bobbin at her waist some old pictures show her carrying. Or it is like Penelope's endless work of weaving and unweaving that shroud. Or it is like Arachne's extrusion and spinning of her web. All three make a labyrinthine design. In that design articulate letters, signs, become arabesques, patterns traced out or embroidered. Designs in turn become again signs, letters, words, articulate sentences, legends, narratives that

may be read. This happens through an uneasy and by no means harmonious shuttling back and forth between lines as engraved pictures and lines
as letters making written language. The one function of lines effaces or
contradicts the other. On the one hand, lines as illustrations call
attention to a physical substratum in engraved or printed marks that can
never be wholly effaced by the meaning they carry. On the other hand,
the purely visual function of engraving is contradicted by the tendency
of even the most abstract design or even the most "realistic" picture to
be seen as making a sign. A picture may make a letter or word, as
happens with an illuminated capital, a hieroglyph, an ideogram, or a
rebus. In a somewhat similar way, Mary's tracing over by retelling them of
everyday events in Cranford gradually makes or uncovers a large design,
hitherto hidden. This design is like an allegorical emblem or like a coat
of arms made of a subtly repeating pattern that becomes visible through
its repetition.

The narrator of *Cranford* is such an Ariadne-Arachne-Penelope as
Ruskin describes. She is even a Procne, fabricator of a fabric that may
tell a tale. This weaving is a covering over that is at the same time an
uncovering. It makes a covering cloth that is also the picture of a crime.
That crime is a version of the endlessly repeated family story hiding
domestic violence as domestic discipline or homely propriety. *Cranford*
tells a story of the "unheimlich" violence men and women perpetrate on
one another at home in the names of love and decency. Mary recovers
the labyrinthine corridors of Cranford's past by retracing them with her
own thread, the thread of ink that flows from her pen.

This movement of recovery and decent covering over is exactly mimed
in the scene just cited in which the narrator tells how she and Miss
Matty read over the letters of Miss Matty's dead parents, elder sister, and
long-disappeared brother, consigning each to the fire after reading it,
though Mary Smith preserves it by writing it down again in the
narration. Mary violates the secrets of which the episode reports the
keeping. She makes public what should remain private by repeating it for
all to read. She violates the secrecy even more by putting the bits of old
string unostentatiously together to make a pattern, while seeming to do
no more than to display them. This act reveals what is behind the letters,

while covering it over, according to the quiet movement of Gaskellian irony. This irony never openly says what it means. It never cuts the string of any knot. It only patiently unties each knot, line by line, by retracing it in narration. Gaskell's irony lays bare what has been kept secret. It does this through the distancing duplicitous power that lies in duplication. This is like the supreme ironic insolence of repeating exactly, in exactly the same tone, what another person has said. Elizabeth Gaskell has no need of the Dickensian rubber band of masculine style. That style is in various ways parodied and subverted in *Cranford*. Gaskell's bits of string, nevertheless, in the end make a noose that is no less constricting, though she does without the "deification" of the big Dickensian rubber band.

To express this in a different figure, the narrator of *Cranford* is like an anthropologist who enters a native culture and reveals the secret workings of that culture. These workings the natives both know and yet must not know if the culture is to go on functioning. All her life Mary Smith has "vibrated . . . between Drumble and Cranford" (*C*, 16:233). She has the perspective of the thriving industrial city on provincial Cranford and speaks of its inhabitants as "they." She also has an insider's experience of Cranford and speaks of their collective opinions and views as those of a "we" in which she participates. Her laying bare of the threads of Cranford life is performed not so much by a power of abstract analysis as by a gathering, recording, and arrangement of the materials that brings out, for any eye to see, latent structural similarities and recurrent patterns. This identification of the community's hidden laws both celebrates and praises that community by lovingly describing it and, at the same time, inevitably, destroys it by bringing something fragile, that can only go on working in the darkness, too much into the light.

In this work of recovery and uncovering, the narrator of *Cranford* is like the narrator of Pater's "Apollo in Picardy," with a difference. As I have said, the inspiration for "Apollo in Picardy" was Il Domenichino's "Apollo and Hyacinth." In that painting the Greek myth is painted in early Renaissance guise as though its events had been reborn in the later Christian style and time. The narrative of "Apollo in Picardy," however, makes no reference to Il Domenichino's painting. It is presented, rather, as a commentary on "a certain manuscript volume taken from an old monastic library in France at the Revolution" (*IP*, 186). The manuscript is brought out into the daylight from the medieval darkness of the library. Its revelation is an example of the way all things were exposed by the Revolution. The narrator then brings to light the hidden meaning of what has been exposed. Pater's imaginary portrait is the unfolding of the narrative latent in the manuscript or presupposed by it, just as his "Denys l'Auxerrois," another of the imaginary portraits, is presented as the gradual and laborious deciphering of a strange fragment of stained glass picturing Dionysus. The latter has been found by the narrator in a bric-a-brac shop in Auxerre. By extrapolation from this fragment, aided by other adjacent evidence, "the story shaped itself at last" (*IP*, 168). All Pater's "imaginary portraits" trace the outlines of one or another untoward irruption of the past into an incompatible present. Old lines of force unpredictably come together again in a reenactment of the story of Apollo and Hyacinth or the story of the rending of Dionysus. Each retracing of those traces by Pater's narrators is, however, another repetition or "renaissance" in the Victorian period. The lines Pater writes down on paper as "traits" of his portrait are the repetition of a repetition. Those traits are reinhabited once more by the lines of force that sweep indifferently through nature, through history, and through each human being, body and spirit, periodically coming back together as a renaissance. What, however, can be said of the word "imaginary" in the phrase, "imaginary portraits"? I shall return later to that question.

Cranford too is the deciphering of a latent story, in this case the story latent in those bundles of old letters and in the other supporting evidence the narrator encounters in present-day Cranford. For both Gaskell and Pater narrative is a kind of detective story, a work of crypt-analysis, an effort of deciphering. Each narrative is a diegesis that is the exegesis of a prior document or set of documents or of an artifact. The difference is that Pater's two narratives are single and straightforward stories hurrying to their foreordained ends as one or another of the Greek myths is reenacted in medieval France and moves inexorably to its violent climax, the rending of Denys or the murder of Hyacinthus. In Gaskell's case, the recovered narrative is rather a series of parallel stories and anecdotes. The meaning lies in never overtly stated similarities among these, as each quietly becomes, through its echoes of the others, before and after, another parable of life in Cranford. The meaning of each episode is deferred until a later episode shows in retrospect what secret significance it had. Gaskell's storytelling, that is to say, operates through what Freud calls "Nachträglichkeit," a deferred carrying over and revelation of meaning.

What are the stories told in each case? *Cranford* is a story of the dissolution and reknitting of a community. "Apollo in Picardy" is the story of a disruptive repetition, a repetition out of time, out of phase, out of place. Such an event as that in "Apollo in Picardy" is by no means like the benign recurrences envisioned in some concepts of the eternal return. Though Pater's story may seem more radical, a mythologizing of realistic fiction's conventions, this return involves, or seems to involve, conservative metaphysical presuppositions. Elizabeth Gaskell's quiet irony, however, is a devastating subversion both of the conventions of realistic fiction and of the masculine claims to authority that underlie those conventions. In Gaskell's work what Jacques Derrida calls "phallogocentrism" is uncentered.

To begin with *Cranford*, the question implicitly posed at its beginning is the question of beginning. How did things come to be the way they are in Cranford? Why is Cranford a society of old maids, all suspicious of men or afraid of them? Cranford is a town in which there is no marrying or giving in marriage. All the family lines seem to be in danger of being cut off or of coming to an end, petering out. The frail spinster is left all alone to carry the huge red silk family umbrella. The ur-episode that has brought things to this pass is the Oedipal murder in reverse, the self-destructive tyranny of Miss Matty's father. This paternal cruelty is gradually revealed as Mary unties knot after knot of the "tangled web" of the past. Rather than being murdered by his son, this Laius cuts off his line by driving his son Peter from his house. He also makes the conditions for the marriage of his daughters so rigorous, the laws of eligibility so strict (like that Mr. ffoukes, mentioned in the novel, who can only marry someone else with a name beginning in "ff"), that he condemns his daughters to remain old maids. In effect the father has emasculated himself by exiling his son, leaving only unmarried daughters. They spend their time knitting, sewing, crocheting, and writing letters to cover their loss. They have survived the father to maintain his habits without understanding them, serving sour wine at dinner, and carrying an umbrella far too large. The ur-episode, the origin found at the end of the patient untying, fold by fold, is a failure, absence, or forbidding of origination. This happening, however, does not exist as one single archetypal event. It is repeated in different ways in all the apparently casual and anecdotal stories Mary tells about life in Cranford.

One example of all these stories (not an "origin" but one example among many of a lack of origin) is the episode in which Peter, the rector's lively and irreverent son, dresses up in his elder sister's clothes. To mock her unproductive virginity, he paces, so dressed, up and down the front garden with a pillow cradled in his arms as if it were a baby, parading before all the neighbors. He has already fooled his father once by dressing as a lady who comes to pay homage to the Rector for the "admirable Assize Sermon" he has published. Why all this cross-dressing by the novel's most masculine character? For his second transvestism the Rector flogs Peter. He runs away from home, his mother dies of sorrow, and the lives of his father and his sisters are permanently darkened. Peter's practical joke has hit the father where it hurts most, not only by his dressing as a woman, which indicates some latent femininity in the sons of such a family, but also by bringing into the open what Deborah's destiny should be. She ought to be a wife and mother, but can never be these because her father has brought her up with such economic and psychological prohibitions against sexuality that she can never marry. Peter can become masculine and adult only by running away from home, that is, by depriving his family of any son to carry on the lineage. The Reverend Jenkyns has preserved his masculine authority only by subverting its apparent goal. In an analogous way his attempt to provide for his old-maid daughters by investing his money in the Town and County Bank leads ultimately to their impoverishment. He has wanted them to be able to live on interest of the invested capital, without ever having to lift a finger to do productive work of any kind, not even housework. That is the affair of servants, as is sexuality. "As for living—

our servants will do that for us," said Villiers de l'Isle Adam.[9] Nevertheless, Miss Matty works hard to keep her servants from having "followers."

Ultimately the Town and County Bank stops payment and Miss Matty is "ruined" (C, 13:192). This word of course had both sexual and economic meanings at that time, as in the title of an ironic poem by Thomas Hardy: "The Ruined Maid." Hardy's ruined maid is ruined sexually, but flourishes economically as a result of the first ruination. The bank failure in *Cranford* is tied to national and international economic crises, one of those periodic depressions to which capitalism was prone in the nineteenth century, and in the twentieth century too for that matter. Secluded and self-enclosed as Cranford is, this town inhabited by nothing but old maids, where there have been no marriages for the last fifteen years at least, nevertheless is part of the great world. Cranford is woven into that larger context by many threads and subject to its vicissitudes. This is one implication of the bank failure episode. It makes *Cranford* just as devastating a critique of capitalism as Gaskell's *Mary Barton* or *North and South*, perhaps more devastating. Just as Miss Matty's unhappiness and unfulfilled life as an old maid is an attack on one feature of bourgeois Protestantism's sexual attitudes, the assumption that you can increase sexual virtue by keeping it unused, so the failure of the bank calls attention to the analogy between these sexual assumptions and capitalism. The latter presupposes that money will go on increasing in interest and value when it is kept sequestered from productive work and allowed to multiply itself, like an old maid hoarding her virtue. Instead of that, capital uses itself up, in this case at least.

"I have often noticed," says Mary Smith, the narrator, "that almost every one has his own individual small economies—careful habits of saving fractions of pennies in some one peculiar direction—any disturbance of which annoys him more than spending shillings or pounds on some real extravagance" (C, 5:60–61). One proleptic example Mary gives of this is the man who is irrationally upset when a member of his family tears out pages for some other use from a now useless bank book after the failure of the bank: "this little unnecessary waste of paper (his private economy) chafed him more than all the loss of his money"

(C, 5:61). By a fetishistic transfer, the paper that stands for the money (which is lost in any case) has come to seem more valuable than the money itself, perhaps because it cannot lose value as long as it is not used. In the same way the paper on which *Cranford* is printed creates value out of nothing but paper with marks on it, and an "uncut" first edition is worth more than one that has been cut and read. All the "elegant economy" (C, 1:5) of the ladies of Cranford, however, saving bits of string, candles, butter, cloth, or sour wine, will not protect, save, or cover them (as one says one's bets are covered) from the drying up of their resources. The only way to save string (or a rubber band either) is to use it, to put it to work to extend the line further. This is just what Peter's father cannot bring himself to let his children do, just as, clergyman though he is, he invests his money in a joint-stock bank in the hope not only of saving it but of multiplying it, getting a plus value out of his frugality, making something out of nothing. Nothing, however, comes of nothing, as the old maids of Cranford show.

Or rather they show it by covering it up. The "origin" of Cranford's sad state, as I have said, is one or another failure of origination. This paradigmatic story is repeated laterally in all the anecdotes about Cranford Mary tells in the present or recovers from the past. Examples are Miss Matty's abortive romance with Mr. Holbrook, forbidden by her father; the story of Captain Brown, who is killed, Deborah Jenkyns thinks, for reading Dickens's *Pickwick Papers*; the story of Signor Brunoni and the man-fearing "panic" of the ladies at Cranford. Brunoni's name is really Samuel Brown. The identity of names calls attention to the analogy between the Brunoni episode and the episode of Captain Brown, though this analogy is never overtly asserted.

I have said these stories' meanings are covered over as well as revealed. The emblem for this in the novel is cloth and clothing, to which an inordinate amount of attention is paid. An amazing number (to a male reader at least) of different kinds of cloth and clothing are named in *Cranford*. Many of the episodes in one way or another turn on precise identification of the name, quality, value, texture, and social significance of one kind of cloth or another. Here, as in Marx's *Das Capital*, cloth speaks.[10]

The novel opens with the observation that there are no men in Cranford: "Whatever does become of the gentlemen, they are not at Cranford. What could they do if they were there?" (*C*, 1:1). By the second paragraph, the subject of clothing has been introduced: "the last gigot, the last tight and scanty petticoat in wear in England, was seen in Cranford" (*C*, 1:2). The narrator moves in the next paragraph to the story of the gentle little spinster carrying the magnificent family red silk umbrella. Soon she is telling the story of Miss Betty Barker's Alderney cow that fell in a lime pit, lost its hair, and had to be dressed in a flannel waistcoat and flannel drawers. Later Mary describes the way the Miss Jenkynses put down pieces of newspaper to protect a new drawing-room carpet from the sun: "We spread newspapers over the places, and sat down to our book or our work; and, lo! in a quarter of an hour the sun had moved, and was blazing away on a fresh spot; and down again we went on out knees to alter the position of the newspapers" (*C*, 2:20). Then there is the "white 'Paduasoy'" (*C*, 5:67) that Miss Matty's mother had been given by her husband-to-be to satisfy her girlish vanity. The same cloth then becomes a christening cloak for her first baby, Miss Matty's elder sister Deborah. Later the "large, soft, white India shawl, with just a little narrow border all around" (*C*, 6:87), which Peter sends his mother from India, becomes her shroud when she dies of grief over his running away from home. "It was just such a shawl as she wished for when she was married, and her mother did not give her," says the broken-hearted husband, "but she shall have it now" (ibid.).

So sensitive are the ladies of Cranford to subtle differences in texture and social meaning between one kind of cloth and another that Miss Jenkyns, for example, criticizes Mrs. Fitz-Adam for appearing too soon after her husband's death as a "well-to-do widow, dressed in rustling black silk": "bombazine [a cheaper cloth] would have shown a deeper sense of her loss" (*C*, 7:95). The supplementary episode, "The Cage at Cranford," is, as I have said, about a hoopskirt from Paris taken as a bird cage by the innocent ladies of Cranford. The novel itself contains a story about a cat who ate a piece of fine old lace that was being cleaned by being soaked in milk. The cat had to be given an emetic to force it to give the lace back (*C*, 8:118–19). Sometimes the novel falls into lyrical lists of articles of clothing and kinds of cloth: "bonnets, gowns, caps, and shawls, . . . merinoes and beavers, and woollen materials of all sorts (C, 12:176). *Cranford* is full of descriptions of the ladies of Cranford sewing, knitting, crocheting, buying clothes, discussing fine points of attire, and so on. When Miss Matty first gets an inkling that the bank has failed, for example, she is in Mr. Johnson's shop trying to decide what color cloth to spend her five sovereigns on for her yearly new silk dress: "if the happy sea-green could be met with, the gown was to be sea-green: if not, she inclined to maize, and I to silver grey" (C, 13:183). Later on, when Miss Matty has lost all her money and has opened a shop on her own, the narrator finds her sitting behind her counter "knitting an elaborate pair of garters" (C, 15:222).

Most of all, however, the narrator takes note of the punctilio of the Cranford ladies about caps and bonnets: "The expenditure on dress in Cranford was principally in that one article referred to. If the heads were buried in smart new caps, the ladies were like ostriches, and cared not what became of their bodies. Old gowns, white and venerable collars, any number of brooches, up and down and everywhere . . . —old brooches for a permanent ornament, and new caps to suit the fashion of the day; the ladies of Cranford always dressed with chaste elegance and propriety, as Miss Barker once prettily expressed it" (C, 8:110–11). The ladies are like ostriches, for whom the covering of the head stands by synecdoche for the covering of the body, which may take care of itself, naked or covered. The cap calls attention to itself, according to the paradox whereby a covering may reveal itself not only as covering, thereby indicating that something is hidden behind it, but also, by some obscure similarity in shape or texture, may bring into the open what it hides by being a simulacrum of it. The covering must therefore be covered in its turn, the cap capped, in a vain attempt to cover even the fact that there is a covering.

Twice in *Cranford* the odd motif of a cap over a cap comes up. This happens once when Miss Matty is flurried by an unusually early morning call. She forgets her spectacles and does not notice that she is still is wearing her private morning cap with yellow ribbons underneath the cap she has put on to receive a visitor: "I was not surprised to see her return with one cap on top of the other. She was quite unconscious of it herself, and looked at us with bland satisfaction" (*C*, 7:90). A little later there is a discussion of an odd article of clothing called a "calash": "Do you know what a calash is? It is a covering worn over caps, not unlike the heads fastened on old-fashioned gigs [a kind of covered carriage]; but sometimes it is not quite so large. This kind of head gear always made an awful impression on the children in Cranford" (*C*, 7:97). It makes an awful impression on us readers too, to think of it.

Cranford itself is a kind of cloth or covering, woven of the narrator's words and out of bits and pieces of old letters and reported conversation. The novel is a decent covering over the indecent, those unspeakable facts of sexual and gender difference, of marriage, copulation, birth, and death, of the ever-renewed psychic violence of family life, of the impingement of world economy on domestic economy. These facts are the novel's real subject throughout. They are facts about which one must keep silent, or only speak indirectly, as the caps speaks for what it hides at a double remove. The head, which does not need covering, stands for the body which does. These facts are, in a passage already quoted, like "the Queen of Spain's legs—facts which certainly existed, but the less said about the better" (*C*, 12:177). Not to speak about them by covering them with decent layers of petticoats and skirts and then to speak compulsively about those clothes is of course to speak after all of that whereof one should be silent. *Cranford*, in its own way, speaks at every turn of those facts the less said about the better. It speaks of them by not speaking of them. It hides and reveals them at once. The knowing reader, as a result, is in the situation of the guests at Mrs. Forrester's tea party, who, though they do know, must pretend that they do not know, that she has made all the preparations herself, in the practice of "elegant economy": "She knew, and we knew, and she knew that we knew, and we knew that she knew that we knew, she had been busy all the morning making tea-bread and sponge-cake" (*C*, 1:4).

Mary Smith, as a cover for Elizabeth Gaskell, performs a woman's work of elegant economy in writing *Cranford*. She weaves new fabric out of old bits of thread. She makes a decent covering for what should be kept hidden, sewing a species of shroud for old facts that had better remain dead. At the same time she exposes the facts. The covering is a displaced form of the facts, or it is the facts themselves in a desiccated form still preserving the old shape. The memorial retelling of these stories is like old flowers dried and mounted in a book of specimens. Mary Smith herself uses this figure in speaking of "correspondence, which bears much the same relation to personal intercourse that the books of dried plants I sometimes see ('Hortus Siccus,' I think they call the thing) do to the living and fresh flowers in the lanes and meadows" (C, 3:34).

Cranford is made throughout of the double line of irony intrinsic in the act of repetition or reusing. It reaffirms the male values intrinsic in the old stories and in the conventional modes of storytelling. At the same time, these are subtly undermined. Their lack of solid ground is shown. Is "Apollo in Picardy" similar or different in its duplicities or doublings? It follows again the old story of Apollo and Hyacinth, doubled in the Middle Ages or Renaissance, as in Il Domenichino's anachronistic painting, and then doubled again in Pater's telling. The Prior Saint-Jean's unbindable and unboundable twelfth volume is without internal order and without firm edges or limits as a material object. It exemplifies the interference of one principle of logic, logic without illustration, by another principle of logic. This other logic is active through picture or illustration as a "bringing to light." The Prior Saint-Jean, as his name suggests, is a late incarnation of the Christian interpretation of Christ as the Word, the Logos. Christ, in John's Gospel, is the immanent presence in the world of the divine Word that spoke the creation into being. That Word keeps the world orderly and "monological," single-based throughout all time. Though Christ describes himself as the light of the world, the Prior Saint-Jean's Logos transforms that light into the unpictured logic of reasoned discourse. Such discourse was in the Middle Ages written language governed by the trivium, literally a "meeting of three ways": grammar, rhetoric, and logic. On that basis the Prior has constructed his twelve-volume work on the quadrivium, now four meeting roads: arithmetic, geometry, astronomy, and music. Pater significantly omits from his list of the Prior's topics the most explicitly visual discipline in the quadrivium, geometry. The Logos and its codification, the trivium, gives the law to the expression of the Logos in language or other signs. On that ground the Prior Saint-Jean's "cold and very reasonable spirit" (*IP*, 186) has woven a fabric demonstrating the way this Logos extends into every corner of the creation's auditory and visible spaces. He builds arithmetic on logic, and then astronomy and music on the laws of number. The movement of sun, moon, stars, and planets, along with the orderly universe of sounds in music, are thereby returned to their ground in the cold reason of letter and digit, inaudible and invisible except as abstract signs.

The metaphor of threads for the Prior Saint-Jean's argument is used by Pater himself. This not only justifies my use of "Apollo in Picardy" as a key text for the investigation of line imagery in narrative, it also brings into the open the association of such figures with the notion of a unified story or argument. A unitary discourse, as Aristotle said, marches from rational beginning through sequential middle in an unbroken causal chain to a neat end tying all the threads in a seemly knot. The whole sequence is grounded in a principle of order that is both immanent, holding everything knitted in one web together, and transcendent, as outside ground. This pattern is one version of logocentric metaphysics, the basic paradigm for thinking and for storytelling in the West. It has been the basis also for the presumed coherence of history and of the single human life. This paradigm has ruled from Aristotle and Plato down through all the Christian centuries, ever since Augustine and the other fathers of the Church assimilated Greek and Latin thought to the Bible. "Apollo in Picardy" brings into the open once more the way that paradigm reduces time to space, making temporality a thread, a road, or a spatial design like a labyrinth. Pater's description of the Prior Saint-Jean's treatise can be taken as a model for the line of coherent and grounded narrative this book has been interrogating throughout: "Twelfth volume of a dry enough treatise on mathematics, applied, still with no relaxation of strict method, to astronomy and music, it should have concluded that work, and therewith the second period of the life of its author, by drawing tight together the threads of a long and intricate argument" (*IP*, 186).

The Prior Saint-Jean's logic is anti-visual, abstract, and impersonal. Apollyon, Hyperborean Apollo, a god in exile, driven north of the Alps, returns to reenact that saddest and most equivocal of the ancient legends about Apollo. Apollyon is a powerfully visual invasion into the Prior Saint-Jean's sedate life. As Apollo reincarnated, he is still the sun-god, even if that sun "is almost like a mock sun amid the mists" and this pale Apollo "the northern or ultra-northern sun-god" IP, 185). As the sun-god, Apollyon is the principle of illustration or bringing to light. This is evident in all the ways his coming is associated with images of light. It is also indicated in the way his ruination of the Prior Saint-Jean's treatise is effected through inspiring the Prior to illustrate his thought with pictures and diagrams. As the principle of illustration, of making visible, Brother Apollyon also stands for personality and the human body, the human form divine that comes to seduce the Prior Saint-Jean just as Gustav Aschenbach is seduced by Tadzio in Thomas Mann's "Der Tod in Venedig." This illicit fascination for the personal and bodily destroys Saint-Jean's orderly and logical treatment in his treatise of "a matter, which is nothing if not entirely abstract and impersonal" IP, 187).

"Apollo in Picardy" is an oblique allegory of the disruption of heterosexual patriarchy, as it is embodied in the Christian church, by homosexuality. The latter is here identified, as it often was, rightly enough, in late Victorian England, with Greek culture. "Apollo in Picardy" might be taken as a covert argument by Pater the classics tutor, fellow of Brasenose College, Oxford. If you base your education of the elite male youth of England on training in Greek and Latin, he might be saying, you are, no doubt inadvertently, importing a disruptive challenge to the heterosexual logocentrism of the apparently dominant Christian culture. "Apollo in Picardy" suggests that Christianity and the classics cannot be reconciled.

The Prior's lamentable volume 12 is the displaced revelation of an obscure personal drama. This is the Prior's infatuation with Apollyon: "under the glow of a lamp burning from the low rafters, Prior Saint-Jean seemed to be looking for the first time on the human form, on the old Adam fresh from his Maker's hand. . . . Could one fancy a single curve bettered in the rich, warm, white limbs; in the haughty features of the face, with the golden hair, tied in a mystic knot, fallen down across the inspired brow? And yet what gentle sweetness also in the natural movement of the bosom, the throat, the lips, of the sleeper!" (*IP*, 190) The Prior's personal story, the story of a homosexual outing, is an inassimilable break in the logical sequence of his theological argument. It is the story's secondary plot that has subverted the meaning of the main plot and can by no means be made homologous with it. As Pater puts this: "Indirectly the volume was the record of an episode, an interlude, an interpolated page of life" (*IP*, 187). Episode, interlude, interpolation: what the Prior writes when he is under Apollyon's influence has no business being there. It is an intervention out of keeping. Brother Apollyon represents an alternative logos, opposed to the Christian one, as though there should be a mocking double of the real sun in the sky. He drives the Prior mad by making his mind dialogical, subject simultaneously to two competing and contradictory "logoi." The Prior's cold and reasonable spirit is "disturbed suddenly, thrown off its balance, as by a violent beam, a blaze of new light, revealing, as it glanced here and there, a hundred truths unguessed at before, yet a curse, as it turned out, to its receiver, in dividing hopelessly against itself the well-ordered kingdom of his thought" (*IP*, 186).

The opposition between heterosexuality and homosexuality is carried in part by a contrast between verbal and visual means of expression. "Apollo in Picardy" has as one of its topics the irreconcilable opposition between picture and text." Thinking and representing by letter and digit can never be combined harmoniously with thinking and representing by illustration. In one case signs are abstract. They carry their meaning without being visible or audibly similar to it. In the other case the sign pictures its meaning, however conventionally. When the Prior goes mad, "the hard and abstract laws, or theory of the laws, of music, of the stars, of mechanical structure, in hard and abstract *formulae*," desert him, and he begins to "*see* the angle of the earth's axis with the ecliptic, the deflexions of the stars from their proper orbits with fatal results here below, and the earth—wicked, unscriptural truth!—moving round the sun" (*IP*, 200). Saint-Jean already sees, in short, under the inspiration of Apollyon, the universe of Galileo's "sed movet," recovering ancient astronomy as it anticipates modern science with the help of Apollyon's "ineffacable memory . . . of the entire world of which those languages [Greek, Latin, Arabic] had been the living speech" (*IP*, 200). Saint-Jean even *hears* the music of the spheres. Ultimately his scientific insight, wholly out of its time, echoing one element in Greek thought and anticipating modern developments, becomes Blakean anthropomorphic vision. The Prior begins painting in his manuscript "winged flowers, or stars with human limbs and faces" (*IP*, 201).

Nevertheless, the two forms of notation, "abstract" and "pictorial," can never be absolutely separated, any more than heterosexual and homosexual are fixed categories or essences. A residue of the pictorial is present in even the most abstract notation. Even the most representational hieroglyph already begins to be a conventional sign and to lose its pictorial quality. We see its meaning and not the way it is a picture of something. In this reciprocal contamination, in part, lies the subversive power of picture when juxtaposed to text. The presence of an illustration calls attention to the pictorial aspects already present in alphabetic writing and in arithmetic notation. The Prior Saint-Jean's treatise is covertly dialogical even before it becomes overtly so under Brother Apollyon's influence. Though in the earlier volumes there are "by way of illustration no more than the simplest indispensable diagrams" (*IP*, 187), these prepare the way for the excessive irruption of illustration in the twelfth volume.

Brother Apollyon's coming is accompanied by strange effects of light, the Prior's dream of "a low circlet of soundless flame" (*IP*, 188), a thunderstorm in late November, and a persistent aurora lasting all winter in the northern sky. If Saint-Jean is dazzled by a flash of light, a "beam of insight, or of inspiration" (*IP*, 201), during his madness, Pater uses the aurora image to describe the destructive intervention of illustrations into the Prior's treatise. The illustrations break the logical line of the argument, untie that line, turn it back on itself like a labyrinth or like a hieroglyphic sign. The logical line, against its nature, is made to signify something else, as though it were the visible embodiment of those musical harmonies the Prior's treatise intends to describe abstractly. In an analogous way, the great monastic barn Brother Apollyon hopes to build with his harp-playing is "a sort of music made visible" (*IP*, 193).

Northern lights are indirectly a manifestation of the sun, the result, as Pater accurately notes, of "a veritable 'solar storm'" (*IP*, 186). The aurora's sun is a cold or dark sun, however. The effect of the shimmering aurora on the ordered dim light of the night sky is uncanny, diabolical. This is Pater's forceful image of the way illustration, in that twelfth volume, begins as marginal decoration, then becomes pictures or hieroglyphs showing forth theory as visual presentation, and finally makes the lines of writing and numeration themselves waver and bend, so they become pictures too, in spite of themselves: "the scribe's hand had strayed here into mazy borders, long spaces of hieroglyph, and as it were veritable pictures of the theoretic elements of his subject. Soft wintry auroras seemed to play behind whole pages of crabbed textual writing, line and figure bending, breathing, flaming, into lovely 'arrangements' that were like music made visible" (*IP*, 187).

Apollo in his disguise as a god in exile[12] still has the doubleness he had among the Greeks, for example, in Sophocles *Oedipus the King*, as discussed at the beginning of this book. Apollo brings both disease and healing. He is both poison and remedy, "pharmakon" in both its senses. Apollo is both marvelously in tune with nature and at the same time wantonly cruel, destroying carelessly the furred and feathered creatures who come at his call. The killing of Hyacinth, among the ancient legends associated with Apollo, is the high point of this sadism. It is turned directly at humanity, at the human form divine Hyacinth represents, as well as at nature in the form of the blue flower that springs from Hyacinth's blood. The climax of Pater's story is the reenactment of this episode with a change. The new element is that the Prior is accused of the murder. Saint-Jean has become possessed. He is now the double of Apollo-Apollyon, as Apollo-Apollyon is doubled in himself, being both Greek and Biblical, and as the Prior is as guilty as Apollyon of that Greek form of love, the love that dare not speak its name. This love is hinted at throughout this story, for example, in the description of Apollyon and Hyacinth throwing the discus naked in the moonlight, like two Greek boys, and perhaps also in what is said about "some shameful price, known to the magicians of that day" which the Prior pays, in his madness, to Apollyon "to draw down the moon from the sky" (*IP*, 202).

A quadruple doubleness, equivocation, or duplicity, is present in "Apollo in Picardy": (1) the doubleness in Apollo himself, (2) the doubleness in nature that he reflects, or which the contradictory copresence of a Greek cosmos and a Christian cosmos manifests, (3) the insane doubleness of Prior Saint-Jean as he is possessed by two conflicting principles of reason, and (4) the doubleness of the text that tells this story. The text too, whether thought of as expressing the narrator's mind or Pater's mind, is dialogical in a more radical sense of doubleness than is understood by many recent appropriations of Bakhtin. The doubleness in Pater's case is an irreconcilable duplicity of grounds for language.

All four of the dialogical modes I have identified come together in the strange description of the carving and inscription in the north gable's apex of the monastic barn Apollyon assists in building. He raises it by the magic of his harp playing and singing, just as the ancient Apollo did similar works through music:

That idle singer, one might fancy, by an art beyond art, had attracted beams and stones into their fit places. And there, sure enough, he still sits, as a final decorative touch, by way of apex on the gable which looks northward, though much weather-worn, and with an ugly gap between the shoulder and the fingers on the harp,¹³ as if, literally, he had cut off his right hand and put it from him:—King David, or an angel? guesses the careless tourist. The space below has been lettered. After a little puzzling you recognize there the relics of a familiar verse from a Latin psalm: "*Nisi Dominus aedificaverit domum*," and the rest: inscribed as well as may be in Greek characters. Prior Saint-Jean caused it to be so inscribed, absurdly, during his last days there. (*IP*, 193–94)

"Wherefore if thy hand or thy foot offend thee, cut them off, and cast them from thee: it is better for thee to enter into life halt or maimed, rather than having two hands or two feet to be cast into everlasting fire. And if thine eye offend thee, pluck it out, and cast it from thee: it is better for thee to enter into life with one eye, rather than having two eyes to be cast into hell fire" (Matt. 18:8–9).¹⁴ These terrifying injunctions by Jesus to a self-maiming are recommended self-punishment for an offense that is obscure. The offense is implicitly sexual, like David's sins. David too played the harp, as did Apollo, in another doubling of Hellenic and Biblical motifs. It is some offense to the innocence of the little child who is said by Jesus a few verses earlier in *Matthew* to be the only one worthy of heaven: "Except ye be converted, and become as little children, ye shall not enter into the kingdom of heaven. . . . But whoso shall offend one of these little ones which believe in me, it were better for him that a millstone were hanged about his neck, and that he were drowned in the depth of the sea" (Matt. 18:3, 6).

The cutting off of a hand or foot, like the plucking out of an eye, is of course a displaced self-castration. In the case of the emblematic carving at the northern apex of the Prior's barn, the accidental disfiguration is a parabolic punishment of Apollyon for the seductive offenses that hand has committed, drawing all nature awry and leading astray the poor Prior, and Hyacinth too. The "gap" is an appropriate figuration for the self-division within Apollo-Apollyon. Apollyon is both Greek god, "beneficent and properly solar" (*IP*, 185), and at the same time devil or fallen angel, star dropped from the sky. The "gap" is also a fitting emblem for the fragmentation or self-division at all levels of the story. These breaks make it impossible to integrate that story except as the narrative of a disintegration. This disintegration is natural, spiritual, personal, and textual at once.

The carved harpist is angel, devil, Old Testament king, and Greek god at the same time, "absurdly." The inscription below the figure expresses once more the nonsense of a mind, a cosmos, and a language subject to two different "logoi" at once. The verses from Psalm 127 affirm the need for every domestic enclosure, every barn and dwelling, to be under the single aegis of the Lord God, to be built and maintained in one name, monotheistically: "except the Lord build the house, they labor in vain that build it" (Psalm 127:1). By causing the Latin verse to be inscribed, absurdly, in Greek letters, the Prior Saint-Jean manifests once more the way he is of two minds, two-minded, subject to two Lords. Though the New Testament was written in Greek, the Old Testament was of course written in Hebrew and most commonly read within Christianity in Hebrew or Latin, not in Greek. Latin words in Greek characters—the effect is of a grating or clashing, a failure in keeping that sets one's teeth on edge. Such an incongruity suggests some alien presence has entered the house of language to confound it. Some parasitical guest or the Lord of an enemy host has upset the priority of the Prior's Lord and has turned the Prior, it may be, into a lost soul who will henceforth belong to another house. Pater indicates this possibility in another Biblical citation (from Matt. 12:44) at the end of the story. This episode shows the mad Prior sequestered away from the Grange under suspicion of having caused the death of Hyacinth. The Prior's one desire is to return to the Grange to die. "He is like the damned spirit, think some of the brethren, saying 'I will return to the house whence I came out'" (*IP*, 205).

One final evidence that the Prior's madness is schizophrenia, a division of the mind, is the way he identifies the blue distance, into which he looks longingly, both with the blue of the hyacinths that sprang up magically on the morning after the murder of Hyacinth and, at the same time, with the blue of Mary's gown: "Gazing thither daily for many hours, he would mistake mere blue distance, when that was visible, for blue flowers, for hyacinths, and wept at the sight; though blue, as he observed, was the color of Holy Mary's gown on the illuminated page, the color of hope, of merciful omnipresent deity" (*IP*, 205). For the Prior even the sky is subject to two sovereignties, Apollo the sky-god and Mary, mother and daughter of the Christian God, mediatrix, as the sky is, of that god's presence in nature. It is this double subjection that drives the Prior mad. It *is* his madness, as the interpolative twelfth volume shows.

To return to that volume, finally, as the residual trace of the Prior's madness, the narrator's names for it—an episode, an interlude, an inter-polated page of life—seem hardly accurate. An episode, an interlude, or an interpolation properly come between two segments of a continuous sequence and suspend that sequence momentarily. The Prior's twelfth volume, on the contrary, makes a break that can never be healed. It suspends the sequence of his discourse permanently. It puts it perma-nently off the track in a mad oscillation of double meaning. The Prior's language becomes all interpolation, interpolation within interpolation, "till writing and writer changed suddenly, 'to one thing constant never,' after the known manner of madmen in such work" (*IP*, 187). The sly insertion of a mocking and unidentified citation here mimes the Prior's double mindedness once more, as does the way the narrator describes the breaking off of the manuscript.

Far from returning to the logical argument after the interpolation, the Prior breaks off altogether, in the middle of a word. He is impossibly torn between two different ways of ending his argument. He is suspended permanently, paralyzed, halted without an effort to break through, in the midst of an unfinished word. What follows is another form of doubleness, writing by another person in another hand that gives the date of the Prior's death: "Finally, the whole matter broke off with an unfinished word, as a later hand testified, adding the date of the author's death, 'deliquio animi'" (IP, 187). The Latin means "a failure of mind." The last words of the Prior's manuscript are, like the Latin words in Greek characters, a piece of written language that does not quite make logical sense as part of the text to which it is added. It makes that text almost an anacoluthon, like the one in Proust discussed earlier. The mind that has failed can never speak of its own failure. Nevertheless, it here almost seems to do so, though "in another hand." This is an absurdity, like speaking of one's own death after it has happened, or it is like what Poe's M. Valdemar says: "I am dead."[15] "Deliquio" is a noun meaning "eclipse, failure," used, for example, of the sun or of liberty. The corresponding verb is "delinquo, -liqui, -lictum." This verb means "to fail, be wanting, especially to fail in duty, to commit a crime."

I have said that the text of "Apollo in Picardy," or the mind of its narrator, as that manifests Pater's mind, is dialogical too. The text has caught the Prior's disease or commits again his crime. This is evident in the undecidability of the narrator's attitude, his unwillingness to take sides. He tells the story, but with reticent irony. He assigns moral judgments to others ("as some maintain"), and leaves it to the reader to choose for Christ or for Apollo. This doubleness of text, narrator, and author is signaled at the beginning in the way the narration starts with a long quotation about the hyperborean sun-god from "a writer of Teutonic proclivities" (IP, 185). Pater experts tell me that this quotation is not a quotation at all. It is a concocted pseudoquotation, apparently made up by Pater himself in parody of some German mythographer or perhaps of Heinrich Heine's "Gods in Exile." The text of the story is two-minded from the beginning, as befits its subject. It duplicitously assigns its own subversive notion of a mock sun and a mock sun-god to a mock prior authority, another text that does not exist or that is really an incongruent aspect of itself. This is like Latin words in Greek letters. The text is not like father and son, son speaking in the name of, or with the authority of, the father, or like a monastic order with a prior paternally in charge and brothers subject to the prior. "Apollo in Picardy" is rather like brother and brother, identical twins, or even Siamese twins, a single mind divided with itself, within itself, a monstrosity. In this it repeats from the beginning the self-division it describes.

The Prior's manuscript is said to be "traces" of "devilry, devil's work" (*IP*, 186) effected by Apollo as Apollyon. The twisted lines of the imaginary manuscript are said to be what remain as memorial traces recording the destructive intervention of Apollyon into the Prior Saint-Jean's life. In retracing those lines Pater's story repeats or incarnates the dialogical drama once more. It brings the lines of force with their double node back together again in the lines of the story, the lines on Pater's page. This happens according to the textual or linguistic mode of that compulsion to repeat that is Pater's constant subject. What has once happened leaves traces of itself, visible configurations or marks. These have an irresistible tendency eventually to repeat themselves. Any text calls forth its duplication, its reprinting, and its commentary, such as this one, which repeats the configuration once more, in its own way.

The Prior Saint-Jean's manuscript is imaginary, however. It exists only as a projection of Pater's manuscript. His portrait, moreover, is also "imaginary," a resemblance without model. It creates its own referent rather than copying it. The Prior Saint-Jean exists nowhere but in the pages of "Apollo in Picardy." The doubling in question is the phantasmal self-division of the groundlessly dialogical rather than the solidly grounded copy or reenactment of an archetype. Neither of the two logoi in this example of dialogology exists outside the text that generates it. Pater's story mimes the impossible attempt of a text to create its own model by internal bifurcation. What this attempt gives with one hand, the illusion of a prior grounding in a previous text, it takes away with the other, in the revelation that this is illusory. The reader consequently feels she or he has been cheated or tricked, for example, when one discovers the alleged citation is bogus. The recognition that the citation is false, the portrait imaginary, the writer of "Teutonic proclivities" an aspect of Pater himself, hollows out what Pater writes. It also makes it seem phantasmal. It lacks the authority of a single authoring mind, since that mind needs grounding in a prior mind or text, however illusory, of which its own activity, in this case, deprives itself.

The possibility of doubleness or of self-division at all levels—cosmic, personal, historical, natural, and linguistic—was always present in Pater's theory of repetition. Pater's theory is one version of an anti-Platonic concept of repetition that has many exemplars in the nineteenth century besides Pater. That concept, as I have elsewhere tried to define it,[16] is physical, metaphysical, and personal at once. It depends, in Pater's case, as in Nietzsche's theory of the eternal return, in part on certain nineteenth-century notions of the universe as a finite conglomeration of matter in motion driven by physical forces, with time extending infinitely in both directions. Any state of such a universe will sooner or later recur, down to the tiniest detail. Every slight variation on that state will also occur and recur, in a dizzying perspective of exact repetition along with repetition with all degrees of difference. Each human body and each human life, for Pater, are, as he says in a passage already cited from the "Conclusion" to *The Renaissance*, "but the concurrence, renewed from moment to moment, of forces parting sooner or later on their ways" (ed. cit., 234). If those lines of force sooner or later part, and the body, the life incarnating them, therefore dissolves, the lines will also sooner or later come together again, reincarnating that life in a new body. This seems to guarantee an orderly universe of perpetual rebirth or "renaissance." Such a universe would be a constant recurrence of figures from the past, each one of which is the personal incarnation, emblem, or hieroglyph of an entire culture or mode of life. Pater's "imaginary portraits," along with his portraits of historical figures, might seem to be the records of such orderly and harmonious repetitions.

Nothing, however, in the presuppositions of Pater's theory of repetition prevents the lines of force from coming together again in a context that is unsuitable for them. Nothing prevents two sets of lines of force from coming together at the same time, absurdly, so producing a conflicting double culture, double person, or double text. All Pater's stories and portraits of historical personages are dramatizations of one or another of these lamentable possibilities. Winckelmann, for example, in *The Renaissance*, is born out of his time. He is a romanticist before romanticism. Duke Carl of Rosenmold, in one of the imaginary portraits, is a fictive figure also born out of his time and so doomed to unhappiness, frustration, and failure. "Apollo in Picardy" exemplifies the even more unhappy possibility of a double simultaneous reincarnation producing a bifurcated culture. In "Apollo in Picardy" a reborn Saint John becomes a damned spirit, and a beneficent Apollonian sun-god becomes Apollyon, a devil. Apollyon is in the end the double of the Prior, the outer manifestation of a doubleness within the Prior himself.

This doubleness is anticipated by a Biblical passage that identifies Apollo with the devil, or with an unfaithful angel, a star fallen from the sky as manifestation of a division or war in heaven. The passage in question comes, appropriately enough, from the Revelation of St. John the Divine: "And the fifth angel sounded, and I saw a star fall from heaven unto the earth: and to him was given the key of the bottomless pit. . . . And they [the locusts that were like horses, men, women, lions, and scorpions] had a king over them, *which is* the angel of the bottomless pit, whose name in the Hebrew tongue is Abaddon, but in the Greek tongue hath *his* name Apollyon" (9:1, 11).[7] The next verse (9:12) introduces the motif of doubling: "One woe is past; *and*, behold, there come two woes more hereafter."

Pater's "Apollo in Picardy," one might say, is about the double woe, or the woe of doubleness. In Pater's story, Saint John, the biblical denouncer of Apollyon in Revelation, is reborn as the Prior Saint-Jean. Saint-Jean becomes in the end himself the angel of the bottomless pit, the fallen star, Apollyon. Saint-Jean belongs finally to the abyss that is no home or enclosure rather than to the house of the Lord. Or it might be better to say that his mind becomes, under the influence of Brother Apollyon, the scene of the battle in heaven between light and darkness, or between two kinds of light, God's light and the diabolical light that is, from God's point of view, darkness, insight and blindness at once:

—that astounding white light!—rising steadily in the cup, the mental receptacle, till it overflowed, and he lay faint and drowning in it. Or he rose above it, as above a great liquid surface, and hung giddily over it—light, simple, and absolute—ere he fell. Or there was a battle between light and darkness around him, with no way of escape from the baffling strokes, the lightning flashes; flashes of blindness one might rather call them. (*IP*, 201)

With this Biblical, Miltonic, melodramatic apocalypse, the modest novel (hardly a novel, more a series of anecdotes) by Elizabeth Gaskell, the clergyman's wife from Manchester, would seem to have little resonance. Moreover, the forms of the two texts differ greatly. *Cranford* is made of doublings, prostheses, graftings of one story on another, bits of narrative line saved and gathered in a hank by a confessed string-saver. *Cranford* even lacks a central body on which the others are the grafted limbs. The meaning of *Cranford* is generated by the echoing of the several stories as they follow one another in a line. No one of them is the archetype of which the others are "examples" or "repetitions." "Apollo in Picardy," on the other hand, though it crosses *Cranford* by way of the presence in both of images of lines or strings, focuses, like its brother story, "Denys l'Auxerrois," on a single violent apocalyptic episode, a single climactic interpolation. That episode, however, is doubled both in itself and in its doubling by its brother story, "Denys l'Auxerrois." Denys is set against Apollyon. Each of these is the repetition of an earlier myth, a doubling redoubled, phantasm behind phantasm in a "mise en abîme." As for Nietzsche, so for Pater, both Apollo and Dionysus are paradoxical, self-contradictory in themselves, and they tend to turn into one another.

"Dionysus speaks the language of Apollo; but Apollo, finally the language of Dionysus,"[18] says Nietzsche, in a passage in *The Birth of Tragedy* that is ignored by those who read Nietzsche's argument as affirming an unequivocal opposition between two factors joined in tragedy—Dionysian music and Apollonian sculptured image. The same elements enter into Pater's thought too. This is scarcely surprising, since Nietzsche's and Pater's sources in German Romanticism are similar. In Pater too, Apollo and Dionysus turn into one another, or speak one another's language, though the combination of the ingredients is somewhat different. Music for the Prior Saint-Jean is the triumph of applied logical and abstract form. Music is a product of the Logos as reason. It is an audible expression of the divine groundswell of creation, Logos as rhythm, proportion, ratio, measurement, harmony. Music, for Nietzsche, on the contrary, is the direct expression of "the primal unity, its pain and contradiction."[19] Music, for Nietzsche, is subversive of character, personality, distinct thinking, and distinct form. Pater's Apollo, like Nietzsche's, is a god who presides over images or pictures that are "like music made visible" (*IP*, 187). Pater's music made visible is not, however, as for Nietzsche, a beautiful aesthetic veil of form over the Dionysian abyss. It is itself the abyss, associated with the temptation of visible form, of picture, of the shapely human body that confounds the Prior's abstract logic and seduces him astray. The formulations of Pater and Nietzsche make a chiasmus. The same elements are present, but in a crisscross relation. Nevertheless, does not Nietzsche, like Pater, see the Apollonian as a force for subversion? Moreover, form is for Nietzsche too not wholly foreign to the Dionysiac. What Nietzsche calls the "originary contradiction" in Dionysian music is the presence within it already of Apollonian form along with formless pain. And does not Pater, in "Denys l'Auxerrois," also set the Dionysian pipe organ, that drives men and women to excess and madness, against the shapely harmonies of Apollo's harp, the reed against the harp? The pipe organ Denys constructed in Auxerre "was the triumph of all the various modes of the power of the pipe, tame, ruled, united. Only, on the painted shutters of the organ-case, Apollo with his lyre in his hand, as lord of the strings, seemed to look askance on the music of the reed, in all the jealousy with which he put Marsyas to death so cruelly" (*IP*, 180–81).[20]

For Pater and Nietzsche both Apollo and Dionysus are the embodiments of double antithetical concepts. These concepts tend to turn into one another or to be differentiated versions of one another rather than stark opposites. Neither can be defined as prior to the other or as the origin of the other. The Prior in his treatise assumes the priority of reason, logic, word, cipher, the logos in all its senses, over the visible and audible. By way of his encounter with Apollyon he has a devastating experience of the reversibility of this hierarchical sequence through Apollonian music and light. Light as music, music made visible, is made to seem prior and originary. Is that not after all what Nietzsche was saying in affirming that Apollo in the end stammers in the language of Dionysus?[21]

Pater's thinking about Apollo and Dionysus is not neatly embodied in the two stories drawn from those myths, any more than *The Birth of Tragedy* is all Nietzsche had to say about the two gods. For Nietzsche, one needs not only the notebooks preliminary to *The Birth of Tragedy*,[22] but also the later revisions and recantations of that first book, for example, in *Ecce Home*, down to Nietzsche's identification of himself with Dionysus, and Cosima Wagner with Ariadne, in his last period ("Ich bin dein Labyrinth," says Ariadne to Dionysus in one of Nietzsche late poems), leading finally to the last enigmatic note to Cosima in January 1889, just at the moment Nietzsche went insane: "Ariadne, ich liebe dich. Dionysus."[23]

In Pater's case, the corridor of interpretation would lead from the two stories here discussed to "A Study of Dionysus," "The Bacchanals of Euripides," to the essays on Greek sculpture in *Greek Studies*, to *Plato and Platonism*, and back then to all the portraits, imaginary and historical, in which the figures of Apollo or Dionysus are covertly or openly present. The trajectory might turn again finally to an investigation of the relation between Pater's thought and Hegel's *Vorlesungen über die Ästhetik*, which seems to have deeply influenced Pater.

This is a tempting corridor to follow, but too long to walk down here. It would lead back to the recognition of an unexpected similarity in difference, for Pater, between Apollo and Dionysus. Both are powers of order or understanding in the sense that each concentrates in a body, a person, a narrative, a complex set of ethical and religious motifs. Both figures occur and reoccur throughout history and help one to understand history. Each is a gathering of forces that are of immemorial antiquity and come together now and then in a hieroglyph of joined motifs that takes fire, in a gemlike flame generated by the proximity of forces destined sooner or later to part on their ways, just as the Mona Lisa is all the women of history embodied in a single momentary enigmatic smile. On the other hand, the forces coming together as shapely and readable form in the stories of Apollo and Dionysus, in all their reincarnations, are never, for Pater, compatible with their historical or material surroundings. They destroy those contexts, burn them up or explode them, as Denys and Apollyon both do in Pater's little stories. Dionysus and Apollo are associated always with suffering, with exquisite pain, and with death. They are a gathering or regathering, but also a dispersal. Both Dionysus and Apollo mean this, rather than being opposites, though the rending of Dionysus stresses pain suffered, while Apollo's killing of Hyacinth is pain imposed, the masochism in Denys's story set against Apollonian sadism. Freud has taught us, however, how each of these turns into the other, for example, in the sadistic pleasure of tearing Denys limb from limb.

For Pater as for Nietzsche, in their different ways, both Apollo and Dionysus impose forms that are destructive. Each breaks the lines of rationality. At the same time the shapeliness of both Pater stories covers over this breaking. Pater's stories are so neatly excised and finished, like cameos, that it is difficult to confront the violence they describe, just as Nietzsche's *The Birth of Tragedy* has been notoriously subject to reductive misreading.²⁴ Both Dionysus and Apollo bring violence. They are for Pater both emblems of violence's irruption into the calm of ecclesiastical life. They are the violence that makes form, brings form to birth in a renaissance, in one case the form of the Dionysus story, in the other case, the form of the Apollo story. Those forms both cover and reveal the violence latent in each myth. The violence of the Dionysus story's masochistic ending in the ritual rending of Denys (" . . . his body, now borne along in front of the crowd, was tossed hither and thither, torn at last limb from limb. The men stuck little shreds of his flesh, or, failing that, of his torn raiment, into their caps; the women lending their long hairpins for the purpose" [*IP*, 183]) is matched by the sadistic ending of the Apollo story in the murder of Hyacinth and the insanity of the Prior. The coming of Apollo as reason, as light, as illumination, becomes excessive, hyperbolic, and so destroys itself, turns into madness. Denys, on the other hand, represents the principle of life and growth, the sacred vine. That benign power becomes excess, drunkenness. Like a fruit or a cell proliferating in dehiscence, it bursts its skin and destroys itself. It becomes death through an excess of life.

All of this doubling is admirably concentrated in the way the material-ization of logical thought, the line of writing, in the Prior's treatise wavers, turns back on itself. It becomes knot, configuration, convoluted image, hieroglyph, the emblem of emblematization, and so destroys itself as line and as logic. The line of writing becomes a grafted element that does not fit, a page that cannot be bound, an incongruent interpolation. This break-in makes the interlude a permanent deviation.

With all this, as I have said, the quietness of *Cranford* would seem to have little to do. Apollyon, however, somewhat surprisingly, is present in *Cranford*. The last word here should, after all, be given to Elizabeth Gaskell for carrying the possibilities of doubling towards a limit of ironic openness. One incident, recovered from Miss Matty's family history in the chapter called "Old Letters," is the story of the threatened invasion of England by Bonaparte. "I know I used to wake up in the night many a time, and think I heard the tramp of the French entering Cranford" (*C*, 5:72–73), says Miss Matty. She goes on to tell how her father the rector preached at the time of the invasion scare a set of afternoon sermons "proving that Napoleon (that was another name for Bony, as we used to call him) was all the same as an Apollyon and Abaddon" (*C*, 5:73). In this novel where everything echoes in intertwining resonances, strand by strand within each link, Apollyon, the destroyer, fallen star, angel turned devil, is not, as for Pater, the subversive power of the visible and audible. He is the name for a political threat to England's national integrity. Apollyon is, however, in both cases, though in a different way in each case, the emblem of sexuality as invasion and disruption. The fear of Napoleon as Apollyon is one version of that pervasive fear all the ladies of Cranford have that men will enter their town, their houses, their persons. "A man . . . is *so* in the way in the house!" (*C*, 1:2), says one of the ladies. They are "dismayed" by the coming of Captain Brown and "moan" over "the invasion of their territory by a man and a gentleman" (*C*, 1:5). Miss Matty and Miss Jenkyns, as I have said, spend much time trying to keep their maidservant from having "followers," though Mary is sure that she has seen "a man's coat-tails whisk into the scullery once" (*C*, 3:37). This fear of invasion reaches hyperbolic proportions in the admirable chapter called "The Panic." In this chapter the coming of Signor Brunoni touches off a growing hysterical conviction in the ladies that there are thieves and footpads lurking everywhere, threatening their homes, their possessions, and their bodies. All the strange fantasies of the spinsters of Cranford, bred of fear of sex, unconscious desire of sex, come to the surface in this episode. An example is Miss Matty's charming, amusing, and pathetic confession:

. . . she owned that, ever since she had been a girl, she had dreaded being caught by her last leg, just as she was getting into bed, by some one concealed under it. She said, when she was younger and more active, she used to take a flying leap from a distance, and so bring both her legs up safely into bed at once. . . . But now the old terror would often come over her, . . . and yet it was very unpleasant to think of looking under a bed, and seeing a man concealed, with a great fierce face staring out at you; so she had bethought herself of something—perhaps I had noticed that she had told Martha to buy her a penny ball, such as children play with—and now she rolled this ball under the bed every night; if it came out on the other side, well and good; if not, she always took care to have her hand on the bell-rope, and meant to call out John and Harry, just as if she expected men-servants to answer her ring. (*C*, 10:148)

"Panic"—the word means literally "of Pan." It names the sort of fear inspired by the Greek god of fields, flocks, wild animals, and shepherds, a fear not too different from that collective Dionysiac frenzy Pater describes in "Denys l'Auxerrois." It is fear of sexuality's power, fear of the life force. The fear is an expression of the power. Pan is associated by Pater with the "intolerable noise of every kind of pipe-music" ("Denys l'Auxerrois," *IP*, 174). The phrase is echoed by Yeats in "News for the Delphic Oracle": "Down the mountain walls / From where Pan's cavern is / Intolerable music falls."[25] If panic is "a sudden unreasoning hysterical fear, often spreading quickly,"[26] the fear is an expression of what it fears. It becomes what it would hold off, as fear of contagion becomes the contagion. One striking example of this is financial panic. This is defined as "a widespread fear of the collapse of the financial system, resulting in unreasoning attempts to turn property into cash, withdraw money, etc."[27] The contagious fear of the instability of the system destroys the system, since the value of money rests on faith.

This happens in the collapse of the bank in which Miss Matty's father has invested all his money for her security. The fetishism of money, attempts to save it, capitalize it, to make it multiply and gather interest by being kept secret and untouched in a shining reservoir, are a displacement of attempts to preserve sexual power and keep it pure by not using it. A spendthrift wife or daughter may be taking revenge on her husband's or father's sexual prowess by way of an indirect depletion of it. A woman who spends her husband's money wastefully may be symbolically emasculating him. Neither the ladies of Cranford nor Mary are spendthrifts of this sort. Far from it. They are skilled in practicing "elegant economy." They have collaborated in the strategies that have hoarded them as dried flowers, hortus siccus, old maids. As part of the sexual capital owned by their fathers, they have not only been part of what he has saved. They have also in their turn learned all sorts of ways to save. Nevertheless, they have taken their revenge on men, though with the utmost discretion and indirection, as when Miss Pole speaks of Signor Brunoni's flowing beard as "that muffy sort of thing about his chin" (C, 9:131). This is a marvelous put-down. Brunoni's beard, symbol of abundant masculinity, here becomes a female article of clothing, another of those kinds of woven cloth, thread, yarn, or fur used by women to cover their nakedness. A muff is a hollow tube of cloth or fur open at both ends and used to warm the hands. It is often a female genital symbol, for example, in the opening of Kafka's "Die Verwandlung [The Metamorphosis]."[28] To call Signor Brunoni's beard a muff is obliquely to say that his beard covers no masculine prowess. It is in this like the hats, galoshes, shawls, umbrellas, and gowns of the ladies. The claim made by the race of men to have power, wisdom, and foresight, to have something women do not have, is unfounded. Miss Pole says this in so many words a little later on: "Well, Miss Matty! men will be men. Every mother's son of them wishes to be considered Samson and Solomon rolled into one—too strong ever to be beaten or discomfited—too wise ever to be outwitted. If you will notice, they have always foreseen events, though they never tell one for one's warning before the events happen; my father was a man, and I know the sex pretty well" (*C*, 10:144–45). If the ladies of Cranford are female chauvinists, their shrewd distaste for men takes the form of a suspicion that men are impotent. They have direct and indirect ways to say, "You see they are no better than we are, worse in fact. They make false claims, as we do not." Of all those who employ this strategy, Mary the narrator, Elizabeth Gaskell's spokesperson, is the most powerful. *Cranford* is a strong political and sexual indictment of men. It is more effective, it may be, than Gaskell's overtly political books like *Mary Barton* and *North and South*. *Cranford* quietly indicts the injustices of male power. It subtly demonstrates men's inauthenticity and feebleness. It also makes a sly use of men's modes against themselves. The latter happens in many ways in *Cranford*. It is most persuasively done, however, as is appropriate in a work of literature, by showing how literary and social styles are analogous. This analogy is kept insistently before the reader. I shall return to this.

First, I must recognize challenges that might be made to my affirmation that men are put in question, indicted, and dismissed in *Cranford*. It is true that the novel, in its tracing back of the reasons why Cranford is a society of old maids, blames the fathers for forbidding the daughters to marry, for saving them up like useless dried flowers or unused rubber bands. It reproaches the fathers also for symbolically emasculating the sons by repressing their energy and wit or by banishing them, as the old leader of a herd drives the young males away so he can have all the females to himself. The fathers have not recognized that the family is a realm where one saves by spending and where the impurity of exogamy is necessary to the continuation of the family line. The novel also mocks men for a parallel form of false saving: the creation of a capitalist economy of bankers and joint-stock companies that assumes money will multiply by being sequestered, kept safe and pure. This ideology has also imposed on the women a prohibition against any productive work other than housework—cooking, sewing, cleaning, perhaps with a Kierke-gaardian dust brush.[29] Such submission to an ideal of genteel sufficiency means living parasitically on the interest of invested money, getting something for nothing, living on what were called "ten per cents," that is, stocks bringing ten percent interest, a tithing in reverse. Between them, Protestantism and capitalism have brought the women of Cranford to the dead end the novel confronts at its opening. The situation becomes even worse when Miss Matty loses all her money. Though the women are shown as collaborating in what has been done to them, the villains in *Cranford* are the menfolk. The main evidence against them is the community of Cranford itself as a proleptic emblem of the goal all society will reach if men like Miss Matty's father have their way. In its reticent and oblique way *Cranford* ranks high in cogency among Victorian feminist critiques of patriarchal society. It even holds its own with more overtly feminist documents of the twentieth century like Virginia Woolf's *A Room of One's Own.*

This, however, is not a full and fair accounting of the role of men in *Cranford*, nor of the positive values of Cranford society. If the community of spinsters works despite the absence of men, this is partly through their goodwill, good humor, and charity toward one another. *Cranford* is as much a celebration of the quaint mores of the women of Cranford as an exposé of their comic or pathetic limitations. In the same way, an anthropologist may both warmly admire and coldly analyze the alien culture he or she studies. Moreover, the recurrent action of the novel is not so much the disastrous invasion of this all-female society by one or another threatening male as it is the story of the successful return of the men, the accommodation of the women to the presence of men, and their recognition that after all they need men, that they cannot "go it alone."

Cranford follows the classic narrative pattern of the threatened dissolution of a society followed by its triumphant reconstitution. The reconstitution takes place in the classic way too: as a series of marriages. Like many feminist novels of the nineteenth century, *Middlemarch*, for example, *Cranford* has the most conventional and traditional of endings: "they married and lived happily ever after." The marriages in *Cranford* occur in defiance of the social, sexual, economic, and class prohibitions that should prevent them. Mr. ffoulkes finds his Mrs. ffaringdon and marries her, in spite of everything—"a very pretty genteel woman she was—a widow with a very good fortune . . . and it was all owing to her two little ff's" (*C*, 7:96). Captain Brown makes his successful conquest of the ladies of Cranford, in the name of Dickens's style in *Pickwick Papers*, as against Miss Jenkyns's championship of the archaic style of Dr. Johnson, that style she has learned from her father to admire. Captain Brown is killed for reading Dickens, at least in Miss Jenkyns's confused memory of it. He is another victim of those avenging fathers, but before that he has conquered the ladies and has been conquered by them. He has become a tame man about the house, helping the ladies with little practical matters, such as suggesting that the hairless cow should be clothed in flannel. After his death, his daughter Miss Jessie is married when her lover suddenly returns. Miss Matty's maid is ultimately allowed to marry one of her "followers." She even has a baby, much to Miss Matty's gentle amazement, since she has not noticed the signs of Martha's pregnancy. Lady Glenmire crosses class lines to marry Mr. Hoggins, the local surgeon, just as his sister, Mary Hoggins, has risen in the world by marrying a man with the elegant and aristocratic name of Mr. Fitz-Adam. "No one, who had not some good blood in their veins, would dare to be called Fitz" (*C*, 7:96), says Mrs. Forrester, not knowing that the prefix signifies the bar sinister, as in Fitz-Roy for the illegitimate children of the king. "'Marry!' said Miss Matty once again [about one of these marriages]. 'Well! I never thought of it. Two people that we know going to be married. It's coming very near!'" (*C*, 12:173).

Finally Peter, the long lost son and brother, returns in triumph from India to rescue Miss Matty from penury and from the ignominy of running a tea shop. In the last chapter, "Peace to Cranford," he engineers a grand party, with a conjuring show by Signor Brunoni. All the community of Cranford come together in harmony at last, breaking all prejudices and barriers. The real conjurer is Peter, still up to his old tricks, animating and amazing the most aristocratic of all, the Honourable Mrs. Jamieson, by tall tales about how once high in the Himalayas he shot a cherubim: "But, Mr. Peter—shooting a cherubim—don't you think—I am afraid that was sacrilege!" (*C*, 16:241). Shooting a cherubim—it is a splendid comic emblem for the happy ending of *Cranford*. That ending has crossed all the frontiers of class and sex, broken all the prohibitions, and made it possible for Cranford to renew itself by a kind of promiscuous bringing together of different realms. The hyperbole of the emblem indicates its magical quality—the way, like all true happy endings, it takes place against all reason and likelihood, even as a species of transgression or sacrilege. Marriage across class lines, or a party bringing all social strata happily together, breaks laws or taboos that seem as impossible to cross as the barrier between earth and heaven. This "peace" has, after all, been brought to Cranford by the men, especially by the lively, irreverent, and irresponsible Peter.

Is it so sure, however, that *Cranford* has a conventional happy ending? Such an ending would reaffirm those social, sexual, ethical, and aesthetic values that have been challenged, the values of the male-dominated Protestant and capitalist society that Elizabeth Gaskell seemed most concerned to put in question. This reaffirmation would go along with a neat tying together of the thematic and imagistic strands of the novel. This would assert the aesthetic values of integrity and coherence that mirror the social and ethical values made concrete in the marriages in *Cranford* and in Peter's "entertainment" (*C*, 16:240). The random bits of string would after all be transformed into their divine form, the rubber band. The India rubber ring binds all neatly together, like that marriage ring Dionysus slips on Ariadne's finger, or like the marriage rings in *Cranford*, or like the ring of Cranford citizens from all classes in the Assembly Room watching Signor Brunoni's conjuring tricks.

This is not, however, the last word about *Cranford*. A clue to a further reading is indicated by the way "The Cage at Cranford," a decade later, opens the story back up again, beyond the apparently definitively closure of the happy ending of *Cranford* proper. "The Cage at Cranford" does this by way of a characteristically comic anecdote with covert sexual overtones raising questions about what is absent or present behind the veils of female clothing. If "The Cage at Cranford" is taken as part of *Cranford*, it is as though the "ending" had been misplaced in the series, thus calling attention to the arbitrariness, after all, of this repetitive chain's ordering links. The story of Signor Brunoni might have come before the story of Captain Brown, since the meaning of each depends on its echo of the other in theme and structure. This echo finds its overt sign in the similarity of names. *Cranford* may then not be an orderly sequence, with beginning, middle, and end, nor even a gradual revelation through a moving forward during the time of the narration, as Mary Smith makes her series of visits to Cranford. Such a progressive uncovering, so it seems, would allow a retrospective reconstruction of the ur-event supporting a sequential and causally connected putting together of all the data. This would make the ending of *Cranford* like the final chapter of triumphant revelation and ordering in a detective story, or like the moment of recognition in *Oedipus the King* as Aristotle would have us read it. Working ironically against this mode of ordering in *Cranford*, against the firm rubber band of archaeology and teleology, of understanding by way of beginnings and endings, are all those repetitive echoings of this part with that part that invite the reader to think of *Cranford* as after all bits of string gathered together in an arbitrary series. The episodes are like links in a chain without preordained order. They have a different meaning depending on how they are ordered or stressed. In this they are like the sequence of words in Quince's reading of the prologue of "Pyramus and Thisbe" in *A Midsummer Night's Dream*: "His speech was like a tangled chain; nothing impaired, but all disordered" (5.1.125–26).[10]

Series: the word comes through Latin "series" from the Greek "seirá," for chain, loop, lasso, rope, string. As in the case of a lasso or woven chain, for example, one that is made by crocheting, each loop is made of smaller threads woven together, each link of lesser links. In a similar way the local texture of Cranford, beneath the level of episode or anecdote, is made of microscopic bits of text that echo other bits before and after, though they echo the larger patterns as well. The result is a fractal design. This echoing sets up an internal vibration of meaning often working counter to the large-scale forward march of the story. If a narrative is always made in chain stitch, each link is woven of little chains, in what might be called the grain of the chain. This small-scale lace texture the critic must tease apart.

In *Cranford* the "true" events of Elizabeth Gaskell's childhood are transmuted, fictionalized, made timeless, by being turned into literature. This transformation may find its synecdoche in the creative narration of the fictional narrator, Mary Smith. The work of literature produced by this transmutation has as its secret subject the putting in question of paternal authority and the substitution for it of an ambiguous feminine authoring and authorizing power. This power cuts the work off from its actual sources. It creates something that has no fathering origin, but that draws its meaning from internal formal relations, as Brunoni echoes Brown. Such a meaning is groundless if being grounded means having a stable source of meaning outside itself. The meaning of *Cranford* is in part generated by the coming and going of similarities and repetitions between one part and another. Two antithetical forms of repetition are both at work in *Cranford*, the repetition that cuts meaning off from origins as well as the one grounded in the progressive revelation of an origin and in the representation of "solid facts" of history and culture. These two forms of ordering work in dissonant counterpart, one against the other: the classical Aristotelian ordering by beginning, middle, and end, the ironic reversible ordering by repetition backward and forward without fixed grounding in an archetype. The texts of *Cranford* and its appendage, "The Cage at Cranford," impose on the reader an uncomfortable fluctuation between these two forms of ordering and these two forms of meaning. Which, if either, should take precedence over the other?

Perhaps the most useful way to ask this question is to ask who is the author of *Cranford*, who the narrator, and by what stylistic authority does she speak? The narrator of *Cranford* is the apparently unmarried Mary Smith, who has "vibrated all her life between Cranford and Drumble." She is the persona or spokeswoman for the author, the married Elizabeth Gaskell, who had herself vibrated between Manchester and Knutsford, the real village on which Cranford is supposed to be based. That the narrator is unmarried puts her to some degree outside the social transactions and responsibilities that Elizabeth Gaskell had accepted.

By what stylistic authority, according to what stylistic models, does Mary Smith, "a well-to-do and happy young woman" (*C*, 9:133), tell her story? The question of the proper style for storytelling and for living comes up insistently in *Cranford*. Miss Deborah Jenkyns's archaic championing of Dr. Johnson as the only correct model for literature and for life is set against Captain Brown's admiration for *Pickwick Papers*. Miss

Matty's old lover, the eccentric country bachelor Mr. Holbrook, whom her father has forbidden her to marry, praises Tennyson for his truth to nature: "black as ash-buds in March. . . . Black: they are jet-black, madam" (C, 4:52). This stylistic truth is explicitly opposed to the style of Johnson's poems through the irony of Miss Matty's thinking in error they sound alike. It would seem that Elizabeth Gaskell is firmly on the side of Dickens's and Tennyson's truth to life as against the pompous abstractions of Johnson. It appears to have been a sense of etiquette and proper modesty that led Dickens to insist that Gaskell should change all the references to Dickens to allusions to Leigh Hunt for the printing of *Cranford* in *Household Words*.

The question of stylistic propriety is, however, not quite so simple in *Cranford*. It could hardly be said that Cranford models itself on *Pickwick Papers*. The two works are not much alike, either stylistically or thematically. Another way to investigate this is to ask by what authority the narrator, or the author behind that mask, writes. Is it by way of a borrowed authority, an authority drawn from one of those paternal models (Dickens perhaps, if not Johnson), or does Gaskell implicitly substitute some specifically feminine authority of narration? Is she like an Ariachne telling her own story, weaving her own web in defiance of Theseus in all his masculine strength and priggish pomposity, or like Penelope holding off her suitors by an endlessly renewed process of weaving, just as Scheherazade keeps herself alive only so long as she goes on telling stories? What might one mean by a feminine authority of writing as opposed to a masculine one? Writing is writing. It hardly seems to be sexually differentiated.

Mary Smith's narrating authority comes from her double position as both inside the community and outside it. She is like an anthropologist who has been invited into a tribe or community, but is at work on a monograph exposing all its laws and telling all its secrets.¹¹ Mary Smith is, moreover, unmarried, like the ladies at Cranford, but unlike them she has a father whose authority she respects and who gives her security. She may make fun of her father's feeble letter-writing ability, but she trusts his warning about the imminent failure of the Town and Country Bank. Though Mary is unmarried, she lacks the sexual innocence and timidity of Miss Matty and the others. She knows when Martha is pregnant. She shares the male reader's amused condescension toward the Amazon society of Cranford, while at the same time presenting it sympathetically and speaking for it in the first person plural: "In kindly pity for him, we began to say . . ." (*C*, 2:15).

This vibrating doubleness in the placement and attitude of the narrator mirrors the thematic doubleness I have identified. On the one hand, if the reader generalizes from the story of the Reverend Jenkyns and his children, *Cranford* is the story of a failure of masculine authority that banishes the sons, invests money in an attempt to save that is really spendthrift speculation, and sets up such a rigid code for marriage, establishes such an inflated price on the exchange of women, that no daughter can marry. The women are left unmarried and without revenue, each one the end of the line, a little spinster carrying a huge family umbrella. The capital is spent. Only small letters remain, little ff's, like those in the names ffoulkes and ffaringdon, the missing capital letter doubled. This recalls Freud's claim that the doubled penis or the doubling of its sign signifies castration. The problem of *Cranford* is how to avoid a society so select that it will die off entirely, like those short-lived religious sects in which the men all emasculate themselves.

On the other hand, the theme of male authority's failure in *Cranford* gradually turns into its opposite. The narrative solves the problem of how to get the men back into Cranford before it is too late. Seen from this aspect, the theme of *Cranford* is the failure of women to do without men, the failure of feminine authority. Impasses are repeatedly dissolved in *Cranford* by the entry of some intrepid male who dares the interdict laid down by the fathers, marries one or another of the remaining marriageable women, and starts the family line again. Both of these possibilities of reading are supported by the text. What *Cranford* means is not one or the other but their incompatible copresence.

What of the authority of writing itself? By whose authority does Mary tell this story of the putting in question of masculine authority and the reaffirming of it, beyond the revelation of its dubiety? The style of Dickens, that gives life, as in *A Christmas Carol* or Sam Weller's "swarry" in chapter 37 of *The Pickwick Papers* (both mentioned in *Cranford*), is set against the style of Johnson in *Rasselas* or *The Rambler*. The latter is a pompous male style that petrifies. *Cranford* itself, however, is hardly, as I have said, written in the style of *Pickwick Papers*. The caricaturing or sentimental styles of Sam's "swarry" or of the Christmas dinner in *A Christmas Carol* must be set against the careful sociological realism of Gaskell's description of Miss Betty Barker's tea party in chapter 7 of *Cranford*, "Visiting." Gaskell is implicitly showing Dickens how it ought to be done. She proposes her style as the correct authoritative alternative to both Johnson's style and Dickens's. Miss Barker's tea party in *Cranford* is not so much modeled on Sam's swarry as it is the rejection of it and the proposal of an alternative stylistic model. Sam's swarry, it will be remembered, is itself already a parody by the servants of the "soirées" of the high society of Bath. One of the latter is attended by Mr. Pickwick and described by Dickens in the chapter preceding Sam's "swarry." The high society soirée is already shown as a parody of solemnity in Phiz's illustration for it. In Sam's swarry the footman and valets of Bath high society then ape their already comic betters. This works to show how silly the "real" soirées are, just as Gaskell's oblique parody of Dickens undermines the authority and authenticity of his writing while at the same time paying him homage, according to the double power of all parody.

The relation of life-style to literary style becomes overt in a curious passage of characteristically brilliant ironic indirection in which Mary Smith reports the wandering speech of that champion of Dr. Johnson, Miss Deborah Jenkyns, as she lies near death, weakened by age in mind and body:

"Ah!" said Miss Jenkyns, "you find me changed, my dear. I can't see as I used to do. If Flora were not here to read to me, I hardly know how I should get through the day. Did you ever read the 'Rambler'? It's a wonderful book— wonderful! And the most improving book for Flora"—(which I dare say it would have been, if she could have read half the words without spelling, and could have understood the meaning of a third)—"better than that strange old book, with the queer name, poor Captain Brown was killed for reading—that book by Mr. Boz, you know—'Old Poz'; when I was a girl—but that's a long time ago—I acted Lucy in 'Old Poz.'"—She babbled on long enough for Flora to get a good long spell at the "Christmas Carol," which Miss Matty had left on the table. (*C*, 2:33)

Dickens as life-giving is here once more set against Johnson as death-dealing in his pompous incomprehensibility. Or is he? Captain Brown, says Miss Jenkyns, was killed for reading *Pickwick Papers*. "Poor, dear, infatuated man!" (*C*, 2:26), she says when she hears of his death. He was reading the latest number when he looked up, saw a train approaching, saved a child who had wandered on the track, and was himself killed. Miss Jenkyns's odd phrasing, however, suggests that there is some mortal danger involved in reading Dickens, some transgression against the mores of Cranford, a transgression punishable by death. That law-breaking is easy to identify. Dickens stands both for the sexuality that has been banished from Cranford and for the irreverence of irony, caricature, and parody. These, however, are the powers that Mary Smith in her more gentle and oblique way has also employed. She too may deserve the hemlock as a subversive invader. More than a little furtive guilt is present in her gratuitous exclamations of admiration: "dear Miss Jenkyns, how I honoured her!" (*C*, 2:18).

Miss Jenkyns in her weakness of mind confuses Boz with Poz and remembers acting Lucy in *Old Poz*. *Old Poz* is a short play for children by Maria Edgeworth in *The Parent's Assistant* (1795), in which the heroine, Lucy, saves an old man from being imprisoned for vagrancy by her father, the local magistrate.[12] Like Luciana in the tableaux vivants in Goethe's *Die Wahlverwandtschaften*,[13] Miss Jenkyns imagines herself heroically dominating her father while still remaining properly feminine. This self-image clashes ironically with her actual subservience to her father and to his standards. Far from saving Captain Brown, she condemns him for defying those paternal standards. He seems to her somehow to have been justly killed for that defiance. The transgression had already been anticipated by Boz himself, that is, by Dickens, who becomes identified in Miss Jenkyns's mind with the vagrant, Poz, in Maria Edgeworth's play.

Mary Smith, it might be said, succeeds where Miss Jenkyns fails. She succeeds in challenging male authority, both the familial authority of the fathers and the authority of male writing. She substitutes her own authority for that. Writing, like sewing or weaving, can be a form of feminine authority (or authoring), even a form of inaugural engendering. Taking up the pen is one way for women to do without men. How, exactly? By imitation, ironic parody, manipulation of men's tools against them. Gaskell has impressive mastery of the techniques of novel writing. These techniques, in spite of the many female novelists who preceded Gaskell, were developed largely by men to express a male-centered view of things, as in the convention of the masculine, God-imitating, omniscient narrator that George Eliot adopts and that Gaskell elsewhere exploits.

By shifting to a woman narrator, *Cranford* brings into the open the claims of a possible separate female authority of narration, the authority of a weaving that hides and reveals. *Cranford* wields that most powerful of feminine weapons, ironic obeisance to masculine authority. Such writing indicates the limitations of male power. Male power, it shows, is death-dealing in the guise of life-giving, a death's head in the guise of paternal life-giving, both in its creation of Protestant capitalism's socioeconomic system and in its authorizing of a certain deadly mode of writing. If Johnson's pomposities are the obvious target of *Cranford's* critique of male writing, Dickens too is covertly included among those attacked. Dickens was right to insist that he be kept out of the version of *Cranford* published serially in *Household Words*. Stealthily, with what used to be called "feminine guile," Gaskell is challenging him too, questioning his right to be the capital model of proper narrative style: "'Have you seen any numbers of "The Pickwick Papers"?' said [Captain Brown]. . . . 'Capital thing!'" (*C*, 1:12).

Elizabeth Gaskell replaces Dickens's claim to be captain with her own kind of authoritative writing. The subverting strength of female authority lies in the double bind it manipulates, tying men in a double knot. If novels can be written as well by women as by men, then novels are intrinsically antiphallogocentric. You do not need a penis to write one, only a pen. If this is not the case and only a man can be a true writer, then a woman writer is, as Dr. Johnson said of women preachers, like a dog walking on its hind legs. Female writing is destructive parody, just as the trained dog apes man. It is therefore in another way anti-phallogocentric. Female writing cuts the ground out from under men by ironically miming them, like a dog walking on its hind legs. At the same time it affirms a counter authority that might be defined as specifically feminine. This authority is life-giving as opposed to the male fathering that takes life as it gives it, like the male lion who eats his own cubs. Female authority favors procreation, family love, food, and warmth. Nevertheless, it has no illusions about the transcendent basis for these. It sees such pompous illusions as potentially death-dealing, as the society of propriety, money, and restraints on marriage, set up by the fathers with the collaboration of the womenfolk, has in Cranford become.

At the same time the female attitude, as represented by Mary Smith, exposes the necessity of illusions and of the rules and taboos they justify, which are the basis for any workable society. Mary Smith meanwhile reveals those illusions to be illusions. She ironically undermines them through her external urban perspective on Cranford at the same time as she shows their necessity. She weaves them again into her story of the triumphant return of male power to Cranford, as well as in the marriages and parties that make possible the happy ending. Cranford, as I have said, tells the story of the threatened destruction and then reconstruction of a society. Its aporia lies in the irony of its attitude toward the conventions that are so powerfully challenged and then reaffirmed in only a slightly different form. These conventions are both necessary and artificial, both good and bad, both life-giving and death-dealing.

Cranford is based on a subversive female questioning power that forbids any definitive closure. This openness keeps the story unfinished, able to be begun again beyond its nominal ending. The seriality of the series tends to exceed its closure. The best name for this subversive, questioning power is irony. The central decentering irony of Cranford is the way it shows both that women can do without men and that they cannot do without men. This ironic oscillation in attitude perplexes any careful reader and keeps him or her in uncertainty. This uncertainty keeps the story going in another way: in the impossibility of a decisive, univocal, monological commentary on it.

CODA

The function of storytelling is to keep the storytelling going. All stories are potentially interminable. They contain in themselves the seeds of their eternal rebirth or their eternal recurrence. For Pater, the story of Apollo and Hyacinth, like the story of Dionysus's dismemberment, has the power to happen over and over again. That means also the power to be told again and again. For Gaskell, the story of the assimilation and neutralization of men by the women of Cranford can also happen over and over. It happens in a potentially endless series of ironic anecdotes expressing the double bind of a simultaneous need for men and women's ability to do without men. If the function of storytelling is to prolong storytelling, as, for example, in the seemingly endless narratives each of us silently tells himself or herself from birth to death, this function is ambiguous in value. It holds off death by keeping the story going. At the same time it keeps the storyteller and the listener suspended in a state of unappeased desire. This might find its emblem in Penelope's perpetually repeated nocturnal weaving and unweaving of her web. The cloth she weaves is a shroud. Nevertheless, at the same time it functions to keep the suitors at bay until her absent husband finally returns. All the narrative of *The Odyssey*, with its potentially endless series of stories, is suspended over that action of weaving and unweaving.

The function of all narrative is not to come to an end, but to keep the line, series, or chain of repetitions going. All storytelling, in continuing interminably, wards off death. At the same time, by not ending, it deals death to male assumptions about beginning, middle, end, and underlying ground. All storytellers are therefore like Penelope, or like Scheherazade,

or like the poet in William Carlos Williams's "Asphodel, That Greeny
Flower":

> And so
>
> >   with fear in my heart
> >   I drag it out
> >   and keep on talking
> >   for I dare not stop.
> >   Listen while I talk on
> > against time.[1]

Like the poet here, all storytellers speak in the shadow of death. Their
narrations are a way of coming to terms with death, At the same time
they are thano-apotropaic. Only so long as the storyteller goes on telling
story after story or retelling versions of the same story will he keep
himself or herself and the listeners alive. The story told, however, is
always the story of death. Walter Benjamin expresses this in a celebrated
formulation: "Death is the sanction of everything the storyteller can tell.
He has borrowed his authority from death. . . . The novel is significant,
therefore, not because it presents someone else's fate to us, perhaps
didactically, but because this stranger's fate by virtue of the flame which
consumes it yields us the warmth which we never draw from our own
fate. What draws the reader to the novel is the hope of warming his
shivering life with the death he reads about."[2]

The indecisiveness intrinsic to storytelling is indicated in the way
stories keep putting off their closure. An intrinsic uncertainty prevents
even so conventional a novelist as Anthony Trollope from uttering once
and for all the formulaic closure, "They married and lived happily ever
after." Perhaps that ending is only a disguised way of saying, "They
died," since happy lives are no longer worth telling stories about. All the
stories we tell ourselves, tell others, or hear and read from others,
function as one of the main ways in which our lives, as Freud said in
Beyond the Pleasure Principle, are nothing but more or less prolonged detours
to death. That death we all secretly desire but desire to reach only in our
own way, in our own good time.[3] Fear of death, desire of death—the

irresolvable doubleness of narrative irony oscillates always between these extremes. The irony intrinsic to all storytelling is another name for the uncertainty that forbids closure and keeps the story continuing. Kierkegaard defines irony as freedom from antecedent conditions, as the possibility of making ever-new beginnings: "the outstanding feature of irony . . . is the subjective freedom which at every moment has within its power the possibility of a beginning and is not generated from previous conditions."[4] Kierkegaard might just as well have said that the great attraction of irony is that it frees us from the intolerable burden of coming to an end.

To introduce Kierkegaard here is to recognize how absurd it is to define irony as a specifically feminine way to suspend "phallogocentric" structures of beginning, end, and supporting, authorizing ground. "Apollo and Picardy" is as much an ironic text as is *Cranford*. Fear of death, desire of death, are universal. They transcend sexual difference, as well as the distinction between straight and gay, just as does irony as a mode of language. If Jane Austen or Elizabeth Gaskell are great ironists, so too are Swift, Kleist, Stendhal, and Thackeray, not to speak of Socrates. Reliance on the difference of the sexes necessary to the analysis of *Cranford* ends by abolishing itself. It abolishes itself in the recognition of a transsexual opposition and secret kinship between closed form and open form—Protestant or capitalist seriousness and Peter Jenkyns's jokes or Mary Smith's ironic mode of narration, the embrace of death and the suspension that holds off the moment of death.

I began this book with the assertion that canonical literary works in the Western tradition are stranger than we have been led to expect. All my examples come from that tradition. How it may be with narratives in other traditions, this book does not pretend to judge. I claim, however, to have shown that both in theory and in practice the assumptions about narrative continuity and homogeneity that are important ideologemes in our culture from Aristotle's *Poetics* to the present do not hold up against a reading of a wide variety of examples. The examples I have read, from Sophocles's *Oedipus the King* down to Gaskell's *Cranford* and Pater's "Apollo in Picardy," are, so it seems, strangers within the homeland of that tradition. Or perhaps we should conclude that the patrimony of a homogeneous Western tradition, unambiguous support of the values of a unified culture, does not exist. It does not exist, that is, except perhaps as the inextinguishable nostalgia for a lost and forever unattainable homeland. Such a nostalgia, for example, haunts Matthew Arnold in "The Buried Life":

> Yet still, from time to time, vague and forlorn,
> From the Soul's subterranean depth upborne
> As from an infinitely distant land,
> Come airs, and floating echoes, and convey
> A melancholy into all our day.[5]

It would be best, however, to abandon the false lure of that nostalgia and to find ways to live within the ironic openness our tradition's stories engender. That task is one feature of the call to help create the democracy to come. Such a democracy would do without the hierarchies affirmed by what I have called the phallogocentric way of thinking and storytelling. The call from the always future democracy should have more force than the one coming from the vague and forlorn nostalgia Arnold names.

NOTES

Preface

1. Just before Red Schalarch kills Lönnrot in Borges's "La muerte y la brújula" ("Death and the Compass") he says, "The next time I kill you . . . I promise you the labyrinth made of the straight line which is invisible and everlasting [una sola línea recta y que es invisible, incesante]" (Jorge Luis Borges, "La muerte y la brujula," in *Ficciones* [Madrid: Alianza Editorial, 1982]).

2. W. B. Yeats, *The Variorum Edition of the Poems*, ed. Peter Allt and Russell K. Alspach (New York: Macmillan, 1977), 630.

One: Aristotle's Oedipus Complex

1. See Sigmund Freud, *The Complete Letters . . . to Wilhelm Fliess*, trans. and ed. Jeffrey Moussaieff Masson (Cambridge, Mass.: Harvard University Press, 1985), 272, and *The Interpretation of Dreams*, in *Works*, Standard Edition, ed. James Strachey (London: Hogarth Press and Institute of Psycho-Analysis, 1953), 4:261–64; Claude Lévi-Strauss, "The Structural Study of Myth," *Structural Anthropology* (Garden City, N.Y.: Anchor-Doubleday, 1967), 202–28; Jacques Derrida, "La Mythologie blanche," *Marges de la philosophie* (Paris: Minuit, 1972), 247–324; "White Mythology," *Margins of Philosophy*, trans. Alan Bass (Chicago: University of Chicago Press, 1982), 207–71.

2. S. H. Butcher, *Aristotle's Theory of Poetry and Fine Art, with a Critical Text and Translation of The Poetics* (New York: Dover, 1951), 95, 97; 24:1460a. This is a reprint of the fourth edition (1907) of Butcher's book. Further references will be to this translation. The first numbers are the page numbers, which are followed by the chapter number and the section number in the traditional numbering. This notation will be followed subsequently. I have also consulted three other translations of the *Poetics*, those by Lane Cooper, Gerard Else, and Hamilton Fyfe. See *Aristotle on the Art of Poetry*, trans. Lane Cooper (Ithaca, N.Y.: Cornell University Press, 1947); Aristotle, *Poetics*, trans. Gerard F.

Else (Ann Arbor, Mich.: University of Michigan Press, 1970); Aristotle, *The Poetics*, trans. W. Hamilton Fyfe, Loeb Classical Library (Cambridge, Mass.: Harvard University Press, 1991).

3. For an authoritative account of the complexities of Aristotle's epistemology see Jonathan Lear, *Aristotle: The Desire to Understand* (Cambridge: Cambridge University Press, 1988), esp. chap. 4, "Man's Nature," 96–151.

4. The notion that the animal world is determined by our ability to see viable creatures in one view is exceedingly strange, if you think of it. It certainly makes man the measure of all things, as Protagoras said he is.

5. Sophocles, *Oedipus the King*, trans. and commentary by Thomas Gould (Englewood Cliffs: Prentice-Hall, 1970), 1. Further references will be to this text. Citations from *Oedipus the King* will be indicated by line number. Citations from Gould's commentary will be identified by page numbers. I have also consulted the translations by Bernard M. W. Knox, F. Storr, David Grene, and Robert Fagles. See Sophocles, *Oedipus the King*, trans. Bernard M. W. Knox (New York: Pocket Books–Simon and Schuster, 1972); Sophocles, *Oedipus the King*, in *Sophocles*, trans. F. Storr, Loeb Classical Library (Cambridge, Mass.: Harvard University Press, 1981), 1:1–139; Sophocles, *Oedipus the King*, trans. David Grene, in *Sophocles* (Chicago: University of Chicago Press, 1954), 1:9–76; Sophocles, *Oedipus the King*, in Sophocles, *The Three Theban Plays*, trans. Robert Fagles (Harmondsworth, England: Penguin, 1984), 155–251.

6. When we pray in a time of trouble we want to put the blame somewhere and then try to appease that origin of our woe or apotropaically ward it off. The chorus at the opening of *Oedipus the King* invokes all the gods. The Theban elders pray earnestly and anxiously to any gods around by all of their epithets, in the hope that somebody will answer. It is as if they were asking, "Is anybody out there? If so, please answer! We need help."

7. An enormous secondary literature of course exists on *Oedipus the King*, Sophocles, and other Greek tragedies that use the terminology employed in the *Oedipus*. Among these see Bernard M. W. Knox, *Oedipus at Thebes: Sophocles' Tragic Hero and His Time* (New Haven: Yale University Press, 1957), and *Studies in Sophoclean Tragedy* (Berkeley: University of California Press, 1964); John Jones, *On Aristotle and Greek Tragedy* (London: Chatto and Windus, 1967); André Green, *Un Oeil en trop: Le Complexe d'Oedipe dans la tragédie* (Paris: Minuit, 1969); Jean-Pierre Vernant and Pierre Vidal-Naquet, *Myth and Tragedy in Ancient Greece*, trans. Janet Lloyd (Brighton, Sussex: Harvester Press, 1981; New York: Zone Books, 1990; distributed by MIT Press). See especially Jean-Pierre Vernant's essays in that

volume, "Oedipus without the Complex," "Intimations of the Will in Greek Tragedy," and "The Historical Moment of Tragedy in Greece: Some of the Social and Psychological Conditions"; Sandor Goodheart, "Oedipus and Laius' Many Murders," *diacritics* (March 1978), 55–71; Cynthia Chase, "Oedipal Textuality: Reading Freud's Reading of *Oedipus*," in *Decomposing Figures: Rhetorical Readings in the Romantic Tradition* (Baltimore: Johns Hopkins University Press, 1986), 175–95; Frederick Ahl, *Sophocles' Oedipus: Evidence and Self-Conviction* (Ithaca: Cornell University Press, 1991); Jean-Joseph Goux, *Oedipus: Philosopher*, trans. Catherine Porter (Stanford: Stanford University Press, 1993).

8. William Faulkner, *Absalom, Absalom!* (New York: Vintage, 1972), 263.

9. Freud, *Interpretation of Dreams*, 4:264.

10. See Arthur W. H. Adkins, *Merit and Responsibility: A Study in Greek Values* (Oxford: Oxford University Press, 1960), and Jean-Pierre Vernant, "Intimations of the Will in Greek Tragedy" and "The Historical Moment of Tragedy in Greece: Some of the Social and Psychological Conditions," *Myth and Tragedy in Ancient Greece*. See also the brilliant discussion of *Oedipus at Colonus* by Sarah Winter, "Lacanian Psychoanalysis at Colonus," in her *Freud and the Institutionalization of Psychoanalytical Knowledge: Profession, Discipline, Culture*, (Stanford: Stanford University Press, 1998).

11. Gould observes in a note on l. 713 (p. 92) that in Sophocles's version no crime or sin by Laius led to the oracle's prediction. Though some other authors say his crime was the seduction and abduction of Pelops's youngest son, Chrysippus, nothing at all is said about that in Sophocles's play. The reasonable cause that explains the gods' anger in many works of Greek literature, for example in the *Iliad* or in the *Odyssey*, is conspicuously missing here.

12. Elizabeth Gaskell, *Cranford; The Cage at Cranford; The Moorland Cottage*, World's Classics (London: Oxford University Press, 1965), 177.

13. "Ode to a Nightingale," l. 34.

14. *Illuminationen* (Frankfurt am Main: Suhrkamp, 1969), 69; *Illuminations*, trans. Harry Zohn (New York: Schocken, 1969), 82. See also Philippe Lacoue-Labarthe's translation into French of Hölderlin's translation of the *Antigone*, accompanied by his brilliant and indispensable essay on Hölderlin's notes on *Oedipus* and *Antigone*, "La Césure du speculatif," in Friedrich Hölderlin, *L'Antigone de Sophocle, suivi de La Césure du speculatif par Philippe Lacoue-Labarthe* (Paris: Christian Bourgois, 1978).

15. Gould's long note to ll. 261–63 spells this out for "tychē" (luck), "paiein" (to strike), "diplos" (double), "enallesthai" (to leap on), "epenthroiskein" (to mount and penetrate) (46–48).

16. By "underthought" Hopkins meant a sequence of figures and allusions within a work, for example, in a Greek tragedy, that echoes at a distance the main action and thought of the work. The underthought is an "echo or shadow of the overthought . . . an undercurrent of thought governing the choice of images used." "In any lyric passage of the tragic poets," Hopkins says, ". . . there are—usually; I will not say always, it is not likely—two strains of thought running together and like counterpointed; the over-thought that which everybody, editors, see . . . and which might for instance be abridged or paraphrased . . . the other, the underthought, conveyed chiefly in the choice of meta-phors etc used and often only half realised by the poet himself. . . . The underthought is commonly an echo or shadow of the overthought, something like canons and repetitions in music, treated in a different manner" (letter to W. M. Baillie, January 14, 1883, *Further Letters of Gerard Manley Hopkins*, ed. C. C. Abbott [London: Oxford University Press, 1956], 252–53). Hopkins's example is the references to the story of Io as a parallel to the Danaids' flying from their cousins in the opening chorus of Aeschylus's *Suppliants*.

17. "Die Worte sich selbst oft besser verstehen, als diejenigen von denen sie gebraucht werden" (Friedrich Schlegel, "Über die Unverständlichkeit" [1800], *Kritische Schriften* [Munich: Carl Hanser, 1964], 531; "On Incomprehensibility," *German Aesthetic and Literary Criticism: The Romantic Ironists and Goethe*, ed. Kathleen Wheeler [Cambridge: Cambridge University Press, 1984], 33).

18. For Derrida's explication of the various possible meanings of this sentence, see Jacques Derrida, *Donner la mort*, in *L'Ethique du don: Jacques Derrida et la pensée du don*, ed. Jean-Michel Rabaté and Michael Wetzel (Paris: Métaillé-Transition, 1992), 79–107, esp. 79–84; *The Gift of Death*, trans. David Wills (Chicago: University of Chicago Press, 1995), 82–115, esp. 82–88.

19. See William Empson, *The Structure of Complex Words* (Cambridge, Mass.: Harvard University Press, 1989).

20. See Gould's note on l. 88, pp. 26–27. Gould lists the following lines where "tychē" means not by chance but by a god: ll. 80–81, 87–88, 102, 145–46. There are other places too.

21. See Gould's note on l. 1398: "Apollo, too, had to assault the great snake whom he found in possession of Mother Earth's 'navel' before he could re-enter and set up his oracular seat there" (156).

22. See Paul Gordon, *The Critical Double* (Tuscaloosa: University of Alabama Press, 1995), 22–24, and Jacques Derrida, "La Mythologie blanche."

23. Gordon, 23.

24. Aristotle, *The Rhetoric*, trans. Lane Cooper (New York: Appleton-Century, 1932), 189, 1405b.

25. *Poetics*, 79; 21:1457b. The reader will note that the example uses the figure of seed-sowing that I am employing to distinguish incest from adultery.

26. As Sarah Winter and other scholars have shown, *Oedipus at Colonus* has centrally to do with geographical borders and regions, the enclosures of the Greek city-state. Oedipus ultimately finds a home in Athens, or rather in its outlying "deme," or township, Colonus, where Sophocles was born. Oedipus's secret grave in the grove of the Eumenides there becomes a sacred place that protects the city of Athens. See Sarah Winter, "Lacanian Psychoanalysis at Colonus."

27. Aristotle, *Rhetoric*, 188–89, 1405b.

28. See Friedrich Schlegel, "Über die Unverständlichkeit" ("On Incomprehensibility"); Schlegel, "Fragmente," in *Kritische Schriften* (Munich: Carl Hanser, 1964); Schlegel, *Philosophical Fragments*, trans. Peter Firchow (Minneapolis: University of Minnesota Press, 1991]); Sören Kierkegaard, *The Concept of Irony*, trans. Howard V. Hong and Edna H. Hong (Princeton: Princeton University Press, 1992); Kevin Newmark, "*L'Absolu littéraire:* Friedrich Schlegel and the Myth of Irony," *MLN* 107, no. 5 (December 1992): 905–30; Georgia Albert, "Understanding Irony: Three *Essais* on Friedrich Schlegel," *MLN* 108, no. 5 (December 1993): 825–48; Paul de Man, "The Rhetoric of Temporality, II: Irony," in *Blindness and Insight*, 2nd ed. (Minneapolis: University of Minnesota Press, 1983), 208–28; Paul de Man, "The Concept of Irony," in *Aesthetic Ideology*, ed. Andrzej Warminski (Minneapolis: University of Minnesota Press, 1996), 163–84.

29. See de Man's discussion of this, "Rhetoric of Temporality, II: Irony," 215–16. "Irony," says de Man, paraphrasing Baudelaire, "is unrelieved *vertige*, dizziness to the point of madness" (ibid., 215).

30. De Man, "Rhetoric of Temporality," 218; "Excuses (*Confessions*)," in his *Allegories of Reading* (henceforth AR), (New Haven: Yale University Press, 1979), 300–301; and de Man, "Concept of Irony," 179.

31. "Concept of Irony," 179.

32. For de Man's most forceful statements on the madness of irony, see "The Concept of Irony," esp. 180–81, as well as the last sentences of *Allegories of Reading*. The latter conclude de Man's discussion of Rousseau: "This isolated textual event, as the reading of the *Fourth Rêverie* shows, is disseminated throughout the entire text and the anacoluthon is extended over all the points of the figural line or allegory; in a slight extension of Friedrich Schlegel's formulation, it becomes the permanent parabasis of an

allegory (of figure), that is to say, irony. Irony is no longer a trope but the undoing of the deconstructive allegory of all tropological cognitions, the systematic undoing, in other words, of understanding. As such, far from closing off the tropological system, irony reinforces the repetition of its aberration," 300–301.

33. That is what "anagnōrisis" means: "ana" (against) plus "agnōrisis" (ignorance).

34. "Die *Verständlichkeit* des Ganzen beruhet vorzüglich darauf, dass man die Scene ins Auge fasst, wo Oedipus den Orakelspruch *zu unendlich deutet, zum nefas* versucht wird" ("The *understanding* of the whole rests especially on this: that one hold fast before one's eyes the scene in which Oedipus *interprets* the oracle's words *too infinitely*, is tempted *towards nefas* [that is, a criminal impiety]"), Friedrich Hölderlin, *Remarques sur Oedipe/Remarques sur Antigone*, a bilingual edition in German and French, trans. François Fédier (Paris: Bibliothèque 10/18, 1965), 53, my translation.

35. "Der König Oedipus hat ein Auge zuviel vieleicht" (Friedrich Hölderlin, "In Lieblicher Bläue . . . / In Lovely Blueness . . . ," *Poems and Fragments*, a bilingual edition, trans. Michael Hamburger [Cambridge: Cambridge University Press, 1980], 602–3).

36. See Goodheart, "Oedipus and Laius' Many Murderers," and Chase, "Oedipal Textuality: Reading Freud's Reading of *Oedipus*."

37. "Diese Leiden dieses Mannes, sie scheinen unbeschreiblich, unaussprechlich, unausdrücklich [*sic*]" (Hölderlin, "In Lieblicher Bläue . . .," 602–3).

38. Hölderlin, *Remarques sur Oedipe/Remarques sur Antigone*, 51.

39. Paul de Man, *AR*, 205.

40. Even W. B. Yeats, a poet not given to turning away from dark insights, falsified the last lines of *Oedipus the King* in his translation of the final chorus. To say "Call no man fortunate that is not dead. / The dead are free from pain" is not at all the same thing as to say, in Gould's more literal translation, "Here is the truth of each man's life: we must wait, and see his end, / scrutinize his dying day, and refuse to call him happy / till he has crossed the border of his life without pain" (ll. 1528–30). For Yeats's adaptation see W. B. Yeats, *The Poems*, ed. Richard J. Finneran (New York: Macmillan, 1983), 566.

41. In Henry Sussman, *The Aesthetic Contract: Statutes of Art and Intellectual Work in Modernity* (Stanford: Stanford University Press, 1997).

Two: Narrative Lines

1. Henry James, *The Complete Tales*, ed. Leon Edel (Philadelphia: J. B. Lippincott, 1964), 9:317.

2. See chap. 1 of *Ariadne's Thread* (New Haven: Yale University Press, 1992), 1–27.

3. Gérard Genette, "Discours du récit," *Figures III* (Paris: Seuil, 1972), 65–273; Gérard Genette, *Narrative Discourse*, trans. Jane E. Lewin (Ithaca: Cornell University Press, 1980).

4. For this characterization see my "Stevens' Rock and Criticism as Cure: II," *Georgia Review* (1976) 30:330–48, reprinted in *Theory Now and Then* (New York: Harvester Wheatsheaf, 1991), 117–31.

5. See Sigmund Freud, "The Uncanny," trans. Alix Strachey, *Collected Papers* (New York: Basic Books, 1959), 4:368–407.

Three: The End of the Line

1. My title pays homage to Neil Hertz's fine book, *The End of the Line* (New York: Columbia University Press, 1985).

2. The Greek words "dēsis" and "lysis" mean "tying" and "loosing," respectively. "Lysis" is the root of such English words as "analysis" and "paralysis."

3. Anthony Trollope, *The Warden*, World's Classics (London: Oxford University Press, 1963), 259.

4. My reference, of course, is to Frank Kermode's book on narrative closure, *The Sense of an Ending* (New York: Oxford University Press, 1967).

5. George Eliot, "Finale," *Middlemarch* (Harmondsworth, England: Penguin, 1974), 890.

6. *Macbeth*, 2.ii.36.

Four: Beginnings

1. Edward W. Said, *Beginnings* (New York: Basic Books, 1975); Jacques Derrida, "Hors livre: Préfaces," *La Dissémination* (Paris: Seuil, 1972), 7–67.

2. Paul Valéry, "Introduction à la méthode de Léonard de Vinci," *Oeuvres*, Pléiade ed. (Paris: Gallimard, 1957), 1:1153–99.

3. Anthony Trollope, *Is He Popenjoy?* World's Classics (London: Oxford University Press, 1944), 1–2. Trollope uses the word "unravelling" in these opening paragraphs: "This is quite as much as anybody ought to want to know previous to the unravelling of the tragedy of the Jones's" (ibid., 1).

4. Søren Kierkegaard, *Either/Or*, trans. David F. Swenson and Lillian Marvin Swenson (Princeton: Princeton University Press, 1971), 1:38.

5. *Either/Or*, 1:37.

6. Samuel Weber, in a brilliant unpublished essay entitled "Benjamin's 'Task of the Translator,'" has discussed the way Sterne in *Tristram Shandy* breaks this line of connection by asserting that it goes only one way. The child is related to the parents, but not the parents to the child: "'Tis a ground and principle in the law, said Triptolemus, that things do not ascend, but descend in it; and I make no doubt 'tis for this cause, that however true it is, that the child may be the blood or seed of its parents—that the parents, nevertheless, are not of the blood and seed of it; inasmuch as the parents are not begot by the child, but the child by the parents" (Laurence Sterne, *The Life and Times of Tristram Shandy* [Harmondsworth, England: Penguin, 1967], 326). Weber uses this figure to identify the curious relation between translation and original in Walter Benjamin's essay. The translation is related to the original, but the original has no filiation to the translation. I shall return to *Tristram Shandy* later, in my discussion of middles, using there Howard Anderson's Norton Critical Edition of *Tristram Shandy* rather than the Penguin edition cited by Weber.

Five: Middles

1. *Either/Or*, ed. cit., 1:35.

2. Anthony Trollope, *An Autobiography*, ed. David Skilton (London: Penguin, 1996), 153.

3. See Martin Price, "The Irrelevant Detail and the Emergence of Form," *Aspects of Narrative* (New York: Columbia University Press, 1971), 69–91, and Roland Barthes, "L'Effet du réel," *Communications*, no. 11 (1968), 84–89.

4. Anthony Trollope, *The Last Chronicle of Barset*, World's Classics (London: Oxford University Press, 1961), pt. 1, 74.

5. For the citations from Emerson, Stevens, and Ammons, see Ralph Waldo Emerson, "Circles," *Essays: First Series, Collected Works*, ed. Joseph Slater et al. (Cambridge, Mass.: Belknap Press of Harvard University Press, 1979), 2:186; Wallace Stevens, *Collected Poems* (New York: Vintage, 1990), 71; A. R. Ammons, *Collected Poems: 1951–1971* (New York: Norton, 1972), 105.

6. I am following here Ronald Paulson, *Hogarth's Graphic Works*, 2 vols. (New Haven and London: Yale University Press, 1970). The first plate of the *Analysis of Beauty* is plate 210 in Paulson. *Tailpiece, or The Bathos* is plate 240 (reproduced here from the collection of Ronald Paulson), both in vol. 2. The translations are given on 1:259.

7. Seeds of cucumber, pumpkin, gourds, and the like were thought to restrain passions and cool the blood.

8. Laurence Sterne, *Tristram Shandy*, ed. Howard Anderson, Norton Critical Edition (New York: Norton, 1980), vol. 6, chap. 40, 333–34. Further citations will indicate volume and chapter numbers, as well as page numbers from this edition.

9. For a fuller discussion of Friedrich Schlegel from a different perspective, see my "Catachreses for Chaos: Irony and Myth in Friedrich Schlegel," in Michael Clark, ed., *Revenge of the Aesthetic* (Berkeley and Los Angeles: University of California Press, forthcoming). See also Werner Hamacher, "Position Exposed: Friedrich Schlegel's Poetological Transposition of Fichte's Absolute Proposition," *Premises*, trans. Peter Fenves (Cambridge,Mass.: Harvard University Press, 1996), 222–60.

10. Friedrich Schlegel, "Brief über den Roman," in *Gespräch über die Poesie, Kritische Schriften* (Munich: Carl Hanser Verlag, 1964), 515; "Letter about the Novel," *Dialogue on Poetry and Literary Aphorisms*, trans. Ernst Behler and Roman Struc (University Park: Pennsylvania State University Press, 1968), 101. For the arabesque in Friedrich Schlegel, see Karl Konrad Polheim, *Die Arabesque: Ansichten und Ideen aus Friedrich Schlegels Poetik* (Munich: F. Schöningh, 1966), and Wolfgang Kaiser, *The Grotesque*, trans. Ulrich Weisstein (Gloucester, Mass.: Peter Smith, 1968), 48–54. Kaiser observes that the terms "grotesque" and "arabesque" were used more or less interchangeably in Germany in Friedrich Schlegel's epoch. Kaiser (49) also suggests that Schlegel was probably influenced in his association of the arabesque with Raphael's decorations for the Logge in the Vatican by Goethe's essay of 1789, "Von Arabesken [Concerning Arabesques]." Goethe's essay ends with a praise for Raphael's Vatican "arabesques." For the opposition between spirit and letter in Friedrich Schlegel's theory of language, see Heinrich Nüsse, *Die Sprachtheorie Friedrich Schlegels* (Heidelberg: Carl Winter, Universitätsverlag, 1962), chaps. 6–8, pp. 68–97.

11. Schlegel, *Dialogue on Poetry and Literary Aphorisms*, 89–90, trans. slightly altered; *Kritische Schriften*, 505.

12. Schlegel, *Kritische Schriften*, 382, my trans.

13. De Man, *AR*, 205.

14. See Paul de Man's discussion of this in "The Concept of Irony," 181–84.

15. "Mit der Ironie ist durchaus nicht zu scherzen. Sie kann unglaublich lange nachwirken" (Schlegel, "Über die Unverständlichkeit," 370; "On Incomprehensibility," 37).

Six: Balzac's Serpent

1. In the first (1831) edition of *La Peau de chagrin* this figure was cited as coming from chap. 322 of *Tristram Shandy*, which is an error. Maurice Allem, the editor of the modern

edition of *La Peau de chagrin* I have used, says it is in chap. 312. This must be a reference drawn from a French translation of Sterne's novel. Corporal Trim's flourish is actually in vol. 9, chap. 4, in the usual English numbering, or chap. 284 if one counts consecutively from the beginning in English editions.

2. See Gérard Genette, *Palimpsestes* (Paris: Seuil, 1982).

3. Cited in Honoré de Balzac, *La Peau de chagrin*, ed. Maurice Allem (Paris: Garnier, 1950), 304, my trans. Allem also reproduces the successive permutations of the epigraph. I have taken them from his reproductions, thereby compounding the distance and difference from the "originals."

4. For a superb book about *La Peau de chagrin*, see Samuel Weber, *Unwrapping Balzac: A Reading of La Peau de chagrin* (Toronto: University of Toronto Press, 1979).

5. Felix Davin, Preface to Honoré de Balzac, *Etudes philosophiques, La comédie humaine* (Paris: Seuil, 1966) 6:704, my trans.

Seven: "The Figure in the Carpet"

1. Walter Pater, "Conclusion," *The Renaissance: Studies in Art and Poetry* (1893 text), ed. Donald L. Hill (Berkeley: University of California Press, 1980), 186–87.

2. Johann Wolfgang von Goethe, *Elective Affinities*, trans. James Anthony Froude and R. Dillon Boylan (New York: Frederick Ungar, 1962), 139; *Die Wahlverwandtschaften* (Munich: Deutscher Taschenbuch Verlag, 1975), 115.

3. Gerard Manley Hopkins, *Sermons and Devotional Writings*, ed. Christopher Devlin (London: Oxford University Press, 1959), 100.

4. Gerard Manley Hopkins, "The Wreck of the Deutschland," *The Poems*, ed. W. H. Gardner and N. H. MacKenzie, 4th ed. (London: Oxford University Press, 1967), 58.

5. I have discussed *Die Wahlverwandtschaften* in *Ariadne's Thread* (New Haven: Yale University Press, 1992), 164–222.

6. See Hubert Damisch, "La Danse de Thésée," *Tel Quel* no. 26 (Summer 1966): 60–68, and *Ariadne's Thread*, 12–13.

7. Cited by Victor Erlich, *Russian Formalism: History-Doctrine*, 4th ed. (The Hague: Mouton, 1980), 241. Tolstoi was attacking critics who attempted to reduce *Anna Karenina* to a brief formula. Critics rather, he said, should inquire into "the laws governing that *labyrinth of linkages* [labirint sceplenij] which is literary art."

8. Henry James, "Preface" to *Roderick Hudson*, New York Edition of 1907–9 (reprint, New York: Augustus M. Kelley, 1971), 1:vi–vii. Further references to Henry James's work will be identified by volume and page numbers in this edition.

9. I have discussed James's remarkable account of reading again his own work in "Re-Reading Re-Vision: James and Benjamin," *The Ethics of Reading* (New York: Columbia University Press, 1987), 101–22.

10. This is the traditional definition of catachresis, which means, etymologically, "against usage."

11. See Alan Friedman, *The Turn of the Novel* (New York: Oxford University Press, 1966); Peter K. Garrett, *Scene and Symbol from George Eliot to James Joyce: Studies in Changing Fictional Mode* (New Haven: Yale University Press, 1969); Robert Alter, *Partial Magic: The Novel as a Self-conscious Genre* (Berkeley: University of California Press, 1975).

12. Shlomith Rimmon-Kenan, *The Concept of Ambiguity: The Example of Henry James* (Chicago: University of Chicago Press, 1977). In my view, Rimmon-Kenan's concept of ambiguity is too much a (laudable) attempt to reduce the indeterminacy of "The Figure in the Carpet" to a logical scheme. The multiple possible ambiguous readings of James's fictions are not merely alternative possibilities. They are intertwined with one another in a system of unreadability, each possibility generating the others. See Rimmon-Kenan's response to an earlier version of this analysis of "The Figure in the Carpet," and my reply to her: Shlomith Rimmon-Kenan, "Deconstructive Reflections on Deconstruction," *Poetics Today* 2 (Winter 1980–81): 185-88; J. Hillis Miller, "A Guest in the House: Reply to Shlomith Rimmon-Kenan's Reply," *Poetics Today* 2 (Winter 1980/81): 189–91. Two other valuable discussions of James's story may be mentioned. One is Tsvetan Todorov, "The Structural Analysis of Literature: The Tales of Henry James," in *Structuralism: An Introduction*, ed. David Robey (Oxford: Clarendon Press of Oxford University Press, 1973), 73–103. Though this essay does not discuss "The Figure in the Carpet" in detail, but rather attempts to find a common theme in all James's tales, the figure in *James's* carpet, so to speak, Todorov's formulation is close to my own: "James's tales are based on the quest for an absolute and absent cause. . . . The secret of James's tales is, therefore, precisely this existence of an essential secret, of something which is not named, of an absent, overwhelming force which puts the whole machinery of the narrative into motion." I differ from Todorov in arguing that James allows also for the possibility that the "cause" may be not only absent but nonexistent, a phantom projection. Another discussion of "The Figure in the Carpet" (Wolfgang Iser, *The Act of Reading: A Theory of Aesthetic Response* [London: Routledge and Kegan Paul, 1978], 3–10), uses James's story as an opening illustration of the way readers have expected narratives to have kernel meanings which, once reached, will allow the reader to throw away the husk, so to speak, dismiss the surface details as superficial, as mere means of access to the

deeper significance. Once that is found, the story can be dispensed with as the vehicle of a separable meaning. Iser argues that the meaning is in the details, but this assumption too, as I shall argue, is part of the metaphysical paradigm.

13. All citations from "The Figure in the Carpet" are from this volume of the New York Edition reprint, ed. cit., identified by page number.

14. The citation is from the *Aeneid*, 1:405. It describes the Aeneas's recognition of his divine mother, Venus.

15. The Greek word "istos" means ship's mast; weaver's yarn beam; loom; warp; web; tissue; spider's web; honeycomb; wand, rod, shaft, shank; penis.

Eight: Multiplications of the Line

1. See this chapter's epigraph from Jacques Derrida, *Glas* (Paris: Editions Galilée, 1974), 116; trans. John P. Leavey, Jr., and Richard Rand (Lincoln: University of Nebraska Press, 1986), 100.

2. George Eliot, *Middlemarch*, ed. cit., 38, 789.

3. Anthony Trollope, *The Warden*, ed. cit., 163.

4. Robert Browning, "The Glove," *The Complete Poetical Works* (Boston: Houghton Mifflin, 1895), 256.

5. *The Warden*, 235–37.

6. George Eliot, *Daniel Deronda* (Harmondsworth, England: Penguin, 1967), 704–9.

7. See Cynthia Chase, "The Decomposition of the Elephants: Double-Reading *Daniel Deronda*," *Decomposing Figures: Rhetorical Readings in the Romantic Tradition* (Baltimore: Johns Hopkins University Press, 1986), 157–74.

8. Thomas Hardy, *The Life and Death of the Mayor of Casterbridge* (London: Macmillan, 1975), 331.

9. J. Hillis Miller, *Ariadne's Thread*, ed. cit., 210–13.

10. Charles Dickens, *Little Dorrit* (London: Oxford University Press, 1953), 662–63.

11. See my *Illustration* (Cambridge: Harvard University Press, 1992) for an analysis of illustrations for Dickens's and Henry James's novels and of the problematic of graphic/verbal relations generally.

12. Eliot, *Middlemarch*, 896.

13. Marcel Proust, *À la recherche du temps perdu*, ed. Jean-Yves Tadié, Pléiade ed. (Paris: Gallimard, 1989), 4:424; *Remembrance of Things Past*, trans. C. K. Scott Moncrieff, Terence Kilmartin, and Andreas Mayor (New York: Vintage, 1982), 3:876 (henceforth French and English in parenthetical references, followed by the volume and page numbers).

14. Thomas Hardy, *The Return of the Native*, New Wessex paperback (London: Macmillan, 1974), 413.

15. D. H. Lawrence, *Women in Love* (New York: Modern Library, n.d.), x, 7. The striking juxtaposition of foreword and opening words exists only in the old and unauthoritative Modern Library edition of *Women in Love*. The more authoritative Penguin edition (Harmondsworth, England, 1995), ed. David Farmer, Lindeth Vasey, and John Worthen, with introduction and notes by Mark Kinkead-Weekes, reprints, with new editorial matter, the scholarly Cambridge University Press edition (Cambridge, 1987). The Penguin edition, like the Cambridge one, relegates the "Foreword" to an appendix (485–86) just following the text of the novel. That appendix explains that the foreword was originally printed separately as an advertising leaflet. The beginning now becomes the end; the word before the first word, or "foreword," is an "appendix" that might be removed supposedly without harm to the living body of the novel. The reader of the Penguin edition must wade through thirty-six pages of chronology, introduction, and a note on the text before reaching the first words of the novel proper. Seventy-six pages of appendices, notes, and a bibliography of "further reading" follow the end of the novel. Much might be said of this sandwiching of the novel between the cacophonous voices of various editors and commentators. All these additions make a veritable polylogue in which Lawrence's voice is just one among many. I am more interested here, however, in the shift in the Modern Library edition among Lawrence's own voices, between the "I" of the foreword, speaking urgently in the present tense, to the more impersonal past-tense narrator of the novel proper, who speaks of the characters in the third person.

16. I am appropriating here the figure used by Freud at the end of the twenty-third lecture of *A General Introduction to Psycho-Analysis*, trans. Joan Riviere (New York: Liveright, 1935), 327–38. "There is, in fact," says Freud, "a path from fantasy back again to reality, and that is—art." Art is a fantasy substitute for pleasures ("honor, power, riches, fame, and the love of women") the artist cannot get in real life. If he can get others to share in his fantasies, however, he becomes a successful artist. He is then rewarded with that for which his art compensated the lack: "then he has won—through his fastasy—what before he could only win in fantasy: honor, power, and the love of women." Against this happy return from a detour to the main road may be set the darker image of a perpetual detour in *Jenseits des Lustprinzips* (*Beyond the Pleasure Principle*): ". . . it is the difference in amount between the pleasure of satisfaction which is *demanded* and that which is actually *achieved* [zwischen der gefundenen und der geforderten Befriedigungslust] that provides the driving factor which will permit of no halting at any position attained, but, in the

poet's words, 'ungebändigt immer vorwärts dringt' ['presses ever forward unsubdued': Mephistopheles in Goethe's *Faust*, pt. 1, sc. 4, l. 1857]. The backward path [der Weg nach rückwärts] that leads to complete satisfaction is as a rule obstructed by the resistances which maintain the repressions. So there is no alternative but to advance in the direction in which growth is still free [noch freien Entwicklungsrichtung fortzuschreiten]— though with no prospect of bringing the process to a conclusion or of being able to reach the goal" (Freud-Studienausgabe [Frankfurt am Main: Fischer, 1989]), 3:251–52; trans. James Strachey [New York: Bantam, 1967], 77).

17. Charles Dickens, *Oliver Twist*, ed. Kathleen Tillotson (Oxford: Clarendon Press of Oxford University Press, 1966), 383.

18. *Oliver Twist*, 384.

19. *Oliver Twist*, lxv.

20. Mikhail Bakhtin, *Problems of Dostoevsky's Poetics*, trans. Caryl Emerson (Minneapolis: University of Minnesota Press, 1984), 181–269; and Bakhtin, *The Dialogic Imagination*, trans. Caryl Emerson and Michael Holquist (Austin: University of Texas Press, 1981), 259–422.

21. "The excerpt we cited from Raskolnikov's dialogized interior monologue is a splendid model of the *microdialogue*; all words in it are double-voiced, and in each of them a conflict of voices takes place"; "Thus dialogic relationships can permeate inside the utterance, even inside the individual word, as long as two voices collide within it dialogically (microdialogue, of which we spoke earlier)" (Bakhtin, *Problems of Dostoevsky's Poetics*, 74, 184).

22. For persuasive radical readings of Bakhtin and Voloshinov that go against the grain of much received scholarly opinion, see Tom Cohen, "*Othello*, Bakhtin, and the Death(s) of Dialogue," *Anti-Mimesis from Plato to Hitchcock* (Cambridge: Cambridge University Press, 1994), 11–44; Cohen, "'Well!': Voloshinov's Double-Talk," *Sub-Stance* 21 (Fall 1992), no. 2: 91–101; Cohen, "The Ideology of Dialogue: The Bakhtin/De Man (Dis)Connection," *Cultural Critique* 33 (Spring 1996): 41–86. A revised version of the latter is incorporated as a chapter in Cohen's *Ideology and Inscription: Cultural Critique after Benjamin, De Man, and Bakhtin* (Cambridge: Cambridge University Press, 1998). See also Paul de Man, "Dialogue and Dialogism," *The Resistance to Theory* (Minneapolis: University of Minnesota Press, 1986), 106–14.

Nine: Plato's Double Diegesis

1. The implications of this passage for narrative theory have been discussed by Gérard Genette in "Frontières du récit," *Figures II* (Paris: Seuil, 1969), 49–69; and by

Philippe Lacoue-Labarthe, "Typographie," in S. Agacinski et al., *Mimesis des articulations* (Paris: Aubier-Flammarion, 1975), 167–270, translated as "Typography," in Philippe Lacoue-Labarthe, *Typography: Mimesis, Philosophy, Politics* (Cambridge, Mass.: Harvard University Press, 1989), 43–138.

2. Plato, *Republic*, trans. Paul Shorey, *The Collected Dialogues*, ed. Edith Hamilton and Huntington Cairns, Bollingen Series (Princeton: Princeton University Press, 1961), 629–30; 382d, e. Further references to Plato are to this edition (which places in the margins the pagination and page subdivisions of the 1578 edition of Plato by Henri Estienne [Stephanus]) and are indicated parenthetically in the text, with the page number in the Bollingen edition followed by the pages in the Estienne edition.

3. James Joyce, *Ulysses* (Harmondsworth, England: Penguin, 1971), 123.

4. James Joyce, *Finnegans Wake* (New York: Viking, 1947), 3.

5. Friedrich Nietzsche, *Die Geburt der Tragödie*, *Sämtliche Werke*, Kritische Studienausgabe, ed. Giorgio Colli and Mazzino Montiinari (Munich and Berlin: Deutscher Taschenbuch Verlag, and De Gruyter, 1988), 1:93–94; *The Birth of Tragedy* and *The Case of Wagner*, trans. Walter Kaufmann (New York: Vintage, 1967), 90–91.

6. Or is it intentional irony? It is impossible to be sure. It would be unwise to assume that anything is beyond Plato either stylistically or conceptually.

Ten: Ariachne's Broken Woof

1. William Shakespeare, *Troilus and Cressida*, New Variorium edition by H. V. Hillebrand and T. W. Baldwin (Philadelphia: Lippincott, 1953), 275–80. Meredith Skura many years ago called this passage to my attention. All citations from *Troilus and Cressida* will be from this edition. I retain the seventeenth-century orthography to keep before the reader that it is a question here of what Shakespeare wrote, or at least of what his compositors set from something he may have written or something that may have been copied from something he wrote. Readers are welcome to refer to a modernized text such as the Signet edition referred to in a footnote below. It should be remembered, however, that a modernized text is likely to cover over just the sort of problem I am trying to identify. This is the problem for meaning that is generated at the level of the materiality of the letter, or even at the level of marks of punctuation, usually much changed in modernized versions. In the case I am discussing here it is the little "i" in "Ariachnes." This "i" does not seem to belong where it is and so stands out as a species of surd, something that is irrational and perhaps ought not to be voiced.

2. Variorum edition, 279–80.

3. William Shakespeare, *Troilus and Cressida*, ed. Daniel Seltzer, *The Complete Signet Classic Shakespeare* (New York: Harcourt Brace Jovanovich, 1972), 1044.

4. J. L. Austin, *How to Do Things with Words* (Oxford: Oxford University Press, 1980).

5. The word is "sanctimony" or "sanctimonies," not "sanctifying," not the act of vowing but the act become a thing, substantive, the act as thing, vow as sanctimony.

6. I say "so-called" because *The Will to Power* was assembled by Nietzsche's sister after his death from notebooks whose entries are not at all in the order the posthumous book presents them. It is a concocted book. Recent editions return to the chronological order of entries in Nietzsche's notebooks. For this citation see Friedrich Nietzsche, *Sämtliche Werke*, ed. cit., 12:389, from fall 1887; Nietsche, *The Will to Power*, trans. Walter Kaufmann and R. J. Hollingdale (New York: Vintage, 1968), 279.

7. The word "rule" means "measure," "norm." It would be one translation of "logos."

8. The *OED* gives *Troilus and Cressida* as the first instance of the word "bifold."

9. "You furre your gloues with reafon," says Troilus to his brother Helenus as the Trojans argue about whether or not to return Helen to the Greeks (II, ii, 39). On the Trojan side the war gradually becomes an internal or intrafamily quarrel, as it does on the other side too. The immediate context of Troilus's reproach, like the drama as a whole, plays on the word "reason" and on the feminine (but also masculine) image of the glove or sleeve.

10. Compare Martin Heidegger's use of the figure of the "Riß" (rift) in "Der Ursprung des Kunstwerkes," *Holzwege* (Frankfurt am Main: Klostermann, 1972), 7–68; "The Origin of the Work of Art," *Poetry, Language, Thought*, trans. Albert Hofstadter (New York: Harper and Row, 1971), 15–87; and his use of the fourfold unity in difference of earth and sky, divinities and mortals, in "Das Ding," *Vorträge und Aufsätze* (Pfullingen: Neske, 1954), 37–59; "The Thing," *Poetry, Language, Thought*, 163–86. I have discussed these mappings in "Slipping Vaulting Crossing: Heidegger," *Topographies* (Stanford: Stanford University Press, 1995), 216–54.

11. "Ah, love, let us be true / To one another! for the world, which seems / To lie before us like a land of dreams, / So various, so beautiful, so new, / Hath really neither joy, nor love, nor light, / Nor certitude, nor peace, nor help for pain" (Matthew Arnold, "Dover Beach," ll. 29–34, *Poems*, ed. Kenneth Allott [London: Longmans, 1965], 242).

12. Jacques Derrida has put in question J. L. Austin's assumption that a "felicitous" speech act must have a proper context. The surrounding circumstances, for Austin, determine, for example, whether a minister's "I pronounce you man and wife" is the real

thing or only a practice ceremony. For Derrida, however, the context can never be, as he puts it, "saturée," saturated. See J. L. Austin, *How To Do Things With Words*, and Jacques Derrida, "Signature événement contexte," *Marges de la philosophie* (Paris: Minuit, 1972); Derrida, *Limited Inc.* (Evanston, Ill.: Northwestern University Press, 1988), 365–93. For "saturée" see *Marges*, 369, and *Limited Inc.* (Evanston, Ill., 1988), 3: "a context is never absolutely determinable, or . . . its determination can never be entirely certain or saturated [saturée]."

13. See my "The Critic as Host," *Theory Now and Then* (Hemel Hempstead, England: Harvester Wheatsheaf, 1991), 143–70.

Eleven: R.?

1. Jean-Jacques Rousseau, *Oeuvres complètes*, Pléiade ed., ed. Bernard Gagnebin and Marcel Raymond, 4 vols. (Paris: Gallimard, 1964), 2:27–28, my trans. Further references will be to this edition.

2. John 1:10: "He was in the world, and the world was made by him, and the world knew him not" (King James Version).

Twelve: The Anacoluthonic Lie

1. Paul de Man long ago called my attention to this admirable passage, as well as to the passages in Rousseau cited and discussed above. For a brief discussion of anacoluthon in Proust, see de Man's "The Concept of Irony," *Aesthetic Ideology*, 178. See also Paul de Man, *AR*, 289–90 and 300–301, including fns. 12 and 21.

2. Henry James, "Preface" to *The Golden Bowl*, New York Edition, 23:xxv.

3. I have written in more detail elsewhere about these issues as they arise in both Proust's *À la recherche du temps perdu* and Trollope's *Ayala's Angel*. See "'Le Mensonge, le mensonge parfait': Théories du mensonge chez Proust et Derrida," trans. Yasmine Van den Wijngaert, aided by Chantal Zabus and Cécile Hayez, *Passions de la littérature*, ed. Michel Lisse (Paris: Galilée, 1996), 405–20, and *Black Holes* (Stanford: Stanford University Press, 1999).

Thirteen: Indirect Discourses and Irony

1. Anthony Trollope, *The Warden*, ed. cit., 123.

2. Elizabeth Gaskell, *Cranford; The Cage at Cranford; The Moorland Cottage*, ed. cit., 135–37.

3. Charles Dickens, *The Posthumous Papers of the Pickwick Club* (Harmondsworth, England: Penguin, 1972), 67, 68–69.

4. Jacques Derrida, *Glas*, trans. cit., 168; "toute thèse est (bande) une prothèse; ce qui se donne à lire se donne à lire par citations (nécessairement tronquées, coupures, répétitions, succions, sections, suspensions, sélections, coutures, greffes, postiches, organes sans corps propre, corps propre couvert de coups . . .)" (Jacques Derrida, *Glas*, ed. cit., 189).

5. If I just use the word "time" in a sentence, says Valéry, I have no problem with it, but as soon as I detach the word from its familiar linguistic surroundings and ask what it means, then "il se change en énigme, en abîme, en tourment de la pensée [it changes into an enigma, an abyss, a torment of thought]" (Paul Valéry, "Poésie et pensée abstraite," *Oeuvres*, ed. Jean Hytier, Pléiade ed. [Paris: Gallimard, 1957], 1:1314–37, my trans.). In a celebrated passage in book 11 of *The Confessions*, Saint Augustine asks, "What then is time? [quid est enim tempus?]" (*The Confessions*, trans. Edward B. Pusey [New York: Pocket Books, 1952], 224). The whole of Augustine's chapter 11 is one of the great meditations on time in the Western tradition. For a full discussion of it in the context of narrative theory, see Paul Ricoeur, *Temps et récit* (Paris: Seuil, 1983), 1:19–53; Ricoeur, *Time and Narrative*, trans. Kathleen McLaughlin and David Pellauer (Chicago: University of Chicago Press, 1984), 5–30.

6. The chapter is entitled "The Panic."

7. Thomas Hardy, *Complete Poems*, ed. James Gibson (London: Macmillan, 1976), 460–61. See my discussion of this poem in "Prosopopoeia in Hardy and Stevens," *Tropes, Parables, Performatives* (New York: Harvester Wheatsheaf, 1990), 248–54.

8. Other texts have "mirror'd" in place of "married," which seems more plausible, though both words work to generate meaning. "Mirror'd" and "married" are like the two words in "Ariachnes," divided in this case into two versions of the text. I have cited the version of *Troilus and Cressida*, ed. Daniel Seltzer, in *The Complete Signet Classic Shakespeare*. For the most part this version follows the quarto.

9. Steven Marcus, *Dickens: From Pickwick to Dombey* (New York: Basic Books, 1965).

10. "Persona" meant, more specifically, the mask worn by the actors in Greek and Latin drama, or the part, character, or person represented by the actor, or the character that someone sustains before the world.

11. Anthony Trollope, *An Autobiography*, 10.

12. "No words can express the secret agony of my soul as I sunk into this companionship; compared these every day associates with those of my happier childhood; and felt my early hopes of growing up to be a learned and distinguished man, crushed in my breast. The deep remembrance of the sense I had of being utterly neglected and

hopeless; of the shame I felt in my position; of the misery it was to my young heart to believe that, day by day, what I had learned, and thought, and delighted in, and raised my fancy and my emulation up by, was passing away from me, never to be brought back any more; cannot be written." Quoted in John Forster, *The Life of Charles Dickens*, 3 vols. (London: Chapman and Hall, 1872), 1:33.

13. *Pickwick Papers*, 539.

14. My trans.: "Voulant être ce qu'on n'est pas, on parvient à se croire autre chose que ce qu'on est, et voilà comment on devient fou" (Rousseau, *Oeuvres complètes*, 2:21).

15. Discussing irony in Cervantes and Shakespeare, Schlegel speaks of the "Schein des Verkehrten und Verrückten oder des Einfältigen und Dummen [the semblance of the absurd and of madness, of simplicity and foolishness]" in irony (Friedrich Schlegel, "Rede über die Mythologie," *Gespräch über die Poesie, Kritische Schriften*, 501–502; "Talk on Mythology," *Dialogue on Poetry and Literary Aphorisms*, 86).

16. Jacques Lacan, *Ecrits* (Paris: Seuil, 1966), 11–61; Jacques Derrida, *La Carte postale* (Paris: Aubier-Flammarion, 1980), 439–524. Translations of both essays are conveniently collected in *The Purloined Poe: Lacan, Derrida, and Psychoanalytic Reading*, ed. John P. Muller and William J. Richardson (Baltimore: Johns Hopkins University Press, 1988), 28–54, 173–212.

17. Sören Kierkegaard, *Either/Or*, ed. cit., 2:164.

18. Franz Kafka, *Tagebücher 1910–23*, ed. Max Brod (Frankfurt am Main: S. Fischer, 1986), 29; *The Diaries . . . 1910–1913*, ed. Max Brod, trans. Joseph Kresh (London: Secker and Warburg, 1948), 45. "Vollkommen" means complete, entire, finished, full, as well as perfect. Kafka's first great story, "The Judgment," which he finished in a single burst of inspiration during one long night in 1912, opens showing the protagonist "with his elbows propped on the writing table . . . gazing out of the window at the river, the bridge and the hills on the farther bank with their tender green" (Franz Kafka, "The Judgment," *Selected Short Stories*, trans. Willa and Edwin Muir [New York: Modern Library, 1952], 3). Kafka's "arbitrarily" chosen examplary sentence is by no means fortuitous, nor is the fact that the protagonist of "The Judgment" sits with his elbows propped on the writing table. Writing opens a window to a magical land on the other shore, a land that can be reached only through just those words, each sentence of which contains the whole, in perfection and completeness: "Er schaute aus dem Fenster."

Fourteen: Apollyon in Cranford

1. The reference is not only to this book but to three previous books about narrative, all originally part of the same project: *Ariadne's Thread*, ed. cit.; *Illustration*, ed.

cit.; and *Topographies* (Stanford: Stanford University Press, 1995). See the preface for a discussion of the project now completed.

2. My epigraph is in Jacques Derrida, *La Vérité en peinture* (Paris: Flammarion, 1978), 280; Derrida, *The Truth in Painting*, trans. Geoff Bennington and Ian McLeod (Chicago: University of Chicago Press, 1987), 244.

3. The reference is to the Simplon Pass episode in Wordsworth's *The Prelude*. See William Wordsworth, *The Prelude*, ed. Ernest de Selincourt, 2nd ed., rev. by Helen Darbishire (Oxford: Clarendon Press, 1959), 209: "I was lost; / Halted without an effort to break through" (6:596–57, 1850 version)

4. Elizabeth Gaskell, *Cranford; The Cage at Cranford; The Moorland Cottage*, ed. cit., 5:61–62. All further references to *Cranford* will be to that edition, indicated in the text as *C*, followed by the chapter and page numbers. The chapter epigraph is in *Cranford*, 1:2–3.

5. Walter Pater, "Apollo in Picardy," *Imaginary Portraits*, ed. Eugene J. Brzenk (New York: Harper and Row, 1964), 186–87. All further references to *Imaginary Portraits* will be indicated in the text by *IP* and the page number.

6. The nine modes of linear terminology (which correspond to nine ways of analyzing narratives) are: (1) the physical aspects of letters and books; (2) narrative sequence or diegesis (explored in this present book); (3) character; (4) interpersonal relations; (5) economics; (6) topography; (7) illustrations; (8) figurative language; (9) mimesis. See *Ariadne's Thread*, 19–21.

7. Walter Pater, "Conclusion," *The Renaissance: Studies in Art and Poetry* (1893 text), ed. cit., 187.

8. See John Ruskin, *Ariadne Florentina* (1873–76), *Works*, Library Edition, ed. E. T. Cook and Alexander Wedderburn, 39 vols. (London: George Allen, 1903–12), 22:280–490. The Library Edition with all its illustrations and editorial apparatus is now also available in a CD-ROM version (Cambridge: Cambridge University Press, 1996).

9. W. B. Yeats cites this aphorism apropos of his visits to Lionel Johnson's house around 1888 or 1889: "talking there by candlelight it never seemed difficult to murmur Villiers de L'Isle Adam's [*sic*] proud words, 'As for living—our servants will do that for us'" ("The Tragic Generation," *Autobiography* [Garden City: New York: Doubleday Anchor, 1958], 203). The words are said by Axël towards the end of Villiers de l'Isle-Adam's play, *Axël*: "Vivre? les serviteurs feront cela pour nous" (*Axël* [Paris: Maison Quantin, 1890], 283). For a more literal translation see Philippe Auguste Villiers de l'Isle-Adam, *Axel*, trans. June Guicharnaud (Englewood Cliffs, N.J.: Prentice-Hall, 1970), 183: "Live? Our servants will do that for us."

10. See Karl Marx, *Capital*, trans. Samuel Moore and Edward Aveling (New York: International Publishers, 1974), 1:52. For a brilliant discussion of the way cloth speaks in Marx, see Werner Hamacher, "*Lingua Amissa*: The Messianism of Commodity-Language and Derrida's *Specters of Marx*," *Ghostly Demarcations: A Symposium on Jacques Derrida's Specters of Marx*, ed. Michael Sprinker (London and New York: Verso, 1998).

11. In *Illustration*, ed. cit., I discuss by way of various examples the relation of picture and text.

12. As scholars have asserted, Pater was in "Apollo in Picardy" influenced by Heinrich Heine's "Die Götter im Exil [The Gods in Exile]," *Sämtliche Schriften* (Munich: Hanser, 1975), vol. 5, pt. 1.

13. Pater's footnote reads: "or sundial as some maintain, though turned from the south" (*IP*, 194). The footnote itself is a form of dialogue, as all footnotes are. It is a species of interlude or interpolation suspending the march of the narrative. It shows the narrator as of two minds about this detail, not knowing whether or not he agrees with what "some maintain." The footnote, moreover, is another manifestation of the cosmic dialogism the story dramatizes. A sundial turned toward the north is an absurdity unless it is there to measure the time by means of Apollo in his guise as a Hyperborean or ultra-northern sun-god.

14. King James Version, as are the following quotations from the Bible. The numbering of psalms is of course different in the Vulgate.

15. See Edgar Allan Poe, "The Facts in the Case of M. Valdemar," *Works*, ed. James A. Harrison (New York: Thomas Y. Crowell, 1902), 6:163. I thank Stephen Barney for help with the Latin.

16. See *Fiction and Repetition* (Cambridge: Harvard University Press, 1982), esp. 1–21.

17. My Bible glosses "Apollyon" in the margin as follows: "That is to say, a destroyer." *The Holy Bible, Containing the Old and New Testaments . . . King James Version* (London and New York: Collins' Clear-Type Press, 1959), New Testament, 243.

18. Friedrich Nietzsche, *The Birth of Tragedy*, trans. Walter Kaufmann, ed. cit., 130, trans. slightly changed; "Dionysus redet die Sprache des Apollo, Apollo aber schliesslich die Sprache des Dionysus," *Die Geburt des Tragödie*, Kritische Studienausgabe, ed. Giorgio Colli and Mazzino Montinari, ed. cit., 1:140.

19. Kaufman trans. The Dionysian artist, says Nietzsche, has identified himself "mit dem Ur-Einen, seinem Schmerz und Widerspruch" (Kritische Studienausgabe, ed. cit., 1:43–44).

20. The reference is to Apollo's flaying of the faun Marsyas when the faun bests him in a musical competition.

21. The figure of stammaring is Nietzsche's own. See Carol Jacobs's admirable discussion of this in her essay on "Nietzsche: The Stammering Text: The Fragmentary Studies Preliminary to *The Birth of Tragedy*," *The Dissimulating Harmony* (Baltimore: Johns Hopkins University Press, 1978), 1–22.

22. See Carol Jacobs's analysis of these, op. cit.

23. Friedrich Nietzsche, *Werke*, ed. Karl Schlecta (Munich: Carl Hanser, 1966), 3:1350; "Ariadne, I love you. Dionysus," *The Selected Letters of Friedrich Nietzsche*, trans. and ed. Christopher Middleton (Chicago: University of Chicago Press, 1969), 346.

24. For discussions of this see not only Carol Jacobs's essay, referred to above, but also Paul de Man, "Genesis and Genealogy (Nietzsche)," *Allegories of Reading*, ed. cit., 79–102.

25. W. B. Yeats, *Poems*, Variorum ed., 612, ll. 30–32.

26. *Webster's New World Dictionary.*

27. Ibid.

28. "Above the table . . . hung the picture which [Gregor Samsa] had recently cut out of an illustrated magazine and put into a pretty gilt frame. It showed a lady, with a fur cap on and a fur stole, sitting upright and holding out to the spectator a huge fur muff into which the whole of her forearm had vanished [und einen schweren Pelzmuff, in dem ihr ganzer Unterarm verschwunden war, dem Beschauer entgegenhob]!" (Franz Kafka, *Das Urteil und Andere Erzählungen* [Frankfurt am Main: Fischer, 1952], 19; *Selected Short Stories*, ed. cit., 19).

29. See above, p. 61.

30. *The Complete Signet Classic Shakespeare*, ed. cit., 551.

31. Anthropologists nowadays have an obligation to show their "subjects" what they have written about them, but that was not always the case.

32. See Martin Dodsworth, "Women without Men at Cranford," *Essays in Criticism* 13, no. 12 (April 1963): 135.

33. See my discussion of these in "Anastomosis," *Ariadne's Thread*, ed. cit., 200–202.

Coda

1. Williams, *Pictures from Breugel and Other Poems* (Norfolk, Conn.: New Directions., 1962), 154.

2. Benjamin, "The Storyteller," *Illuminations*, trans. Harry Zohn (New York: Schocken, 1969), 94, 101. Here is the German original: "Der Tod ist die Sanktion von

allem, was der Erzähler berichten kann. Vom Tode hat er seine Autorität geliehen. . . . Nicht darum also ist der Roman bedeutend, weil er, etwa lehrreich, ein fremdes Schicksal uns darstellt, sondern weil dieses fremde Schicksal kraft der Flamme, von der es verzehrt wird, die Wärme an uns abgibt, die wir aus unserem eigenen nie gewinnen. Das was den Leser zum Roman zieht, ist die Hoffnung, sein fröstelndes Leben an einem Tod, von dem er liest, zu wärmen" ("Der Erzähler," *Illuminationen* [Frankfurt am Main: Suhrkamp, 1969], 421, 428).

3. See Sigmund Freud, *Jenseits des Lustprinzips*, ed. cit., 248–49, *Beyond the Pleasure Principle*, ed. cit., 71–74: "[The life substance must] make ever more complicated *détours* [Umwegen] before reaching its aim of death. . . . What we are left with is the fact that the organism wishes to die only in its own fashion [der Organismus nur auf seine Weise sterben will]. . . . These germ-cells, therefore, work against the death of the living substance and succeed in winning for it what we can only regard as potential immortality [als potentielle Unsterblichkeit], though that may mean no more than a lengthening of the road to death [nur eine Verlängerung des Todesweges bedeutet]."

4. Kierkegaard, *The Concept of Irony, with Constant Reference to Socrates*, trans. Lee M. Capel (Bloomington, Ind.: Indiana University Press, 1968), 270.

5. Matthew Arnold, "The Buried Life," ll. 72–76, *The Poems*, ed. Kenneth Allott (London: Longmans, 1965), 274.

WORKS CITED

Adkins, Arthur W. H. *Merit and Responsibility: A Study in Greek Values*. Oxford: Oxford University Press, 1960.

Ahl, Frederick. *Sophocles' Oedipus: Evidence and Self-Conviction*. Ithaca: Cornell University Press, 1991.

Albert, Georgia. "Understanding Irony: Three *essais* on Friedrich Schlegel." *MLN* 108, no. 5 (December 1993): 825–48.

Alter, Robert. *Partial Magic: The Novel as a Self-Conscious Genre*. Berkeley: University of California Press, 1975.

Ammons, A. R. *Collected Poems: 1951–1971*. New York: Norton, 1972.

Aristotle. *Aristotle on the Art of Poetry*. Translated by Lane Cooper. Ithaca: Cornell University Press, 1947.

———. *Poetics*. Translated by Gerard F. Else. Ann Arbor: University of Michigan Press, 1970.

———. *The Poetics*. Translated by W. Hamilton Fyfe. Loeb Classical Library. Cambridge: Harvard University Press, 1991.

———. *The Rhetoric*. Translated by Lane Cooper. New York: Appleton-Century, 1932.

Arnold, Matthew. *The Poems*. Edited by Kenneth Allott. London: Longmans, 1965.

Augustine. *The Confessions*. Translated by Edward B. Pusey. New York: Pocket Books, 1952.

Austin, J. L. *How to Do Things with Words*. Oxford: Oxford University Press, 1980.

Bakhtin, Mikhail. *The Dialogic Imagination*. Translated by Caryl Emerson and Michael Holquist. Austin: University of Texas Press, 1981.

———. *Problems of Dostoevsky's Poetics*. Translated by Caryl Emerson. Minneapolis: University of Minnesota Press, 1984.

Balzac, Honoré de. *La Peau de chagrin*. Edited by Maurice Allem. Paris: Garnier, 1950.

Barthes, Roland. "L'Effet du réel." *Communications*, no. 11 (1968): 84–89.

Benjamin, Walter. *Illuminationen*. Frankfurt: Suhrkamp, 1969.

————. *Illuminations.* Translated by Harry Zohn. New York: Schocken, 1969.

Borges, Jorge Louis. "Death and the Compass." In *Ficciones,* trans. Anthony Kerrigan, 129–41. New York: Grove Press, 1963.

————. "La muerte y la brujula." In *Ficciones,* 147–63. Madrid: Alianza Editorial: 1982.

Browning, Robert. *The Complete Poetical Works.* Boston: Houghton Mifflin, 1895.

Butcher, S. H. *Aristotle's Theory of Poetry and Fine Art, with a Critical Text and Translation of the Poetics.* New York: Dover, 1951.

Chase, Cynthia. "The Decomposition of the Elephants: Double-Reading *Daniel Deronda.*" In *Decomposing Figures: Rhetorical Readings in the Romantic Tradition,* 157–74. Baltimore: Johns Hopkins University Press, 1986.

————."Oedipal Textuality: Reading Freud's Reading of Oedipus." In *Decomposing Figures: Rhetorical Readings in the Romantic Tradition,* 175–95. Baltimore: Johns Hopkins University Press, 1986.

Cohen, Tom. *Ideology and Inscription: Cultural Critique after Benjamin, de Man, and Bakhtin.* Cambridge: Cambridge University Press, 1998.

————. "The Ideology of Dialogue: The Bakhtin/de Man (Dis)Connection." *Cultural Critique* 33 (Spring 1996): 41–86.

————. "*Othello,* Bakhtin, and the death(s) of dialogue." In *Anti-Mimesis from Plato to Hitchcock,* 11–44. Cambridge: Cambridge University Press, 1994.

————. "'Well!': Voloshinov's Double-Talk." *Sub-Stance* 21, no. 2 (Fall 1992): 91–106.

Damisch, Hubert. "La Danse de Thésée." *Tel Quel,* no. 26 (Summer 1966): 60–68.

Davin, Felix. Preface to "*Etudes philosophiques.*" Vol. 6 in *La Comédie humaine,* by Honoré de Balzac, 681–710. Paris: Seuil, 1966.

De Man, Paul. *Allegories of Reading.* New Haven: Yale University Press, 1979.

————. "The Concept of Irony." In *Aesthetic Ideology,* ed. Andrzej Warminski, 163–84. Minneapolis: University of Minnesota Press, 1996.

————."Dialogue and Dialogism." In *The Resistance to Theory,* 106–14. Minneapolis: University of Minnesota Press, 1986.

————. "The Rhetoric of Temporality, II: Irony." In *Blindness and Insight,* 2nd ed., 208–28. Minneapolis: University of Minnesota Press, 1983.

Derrida, Jacques. "Donner la mort." In *L'Éthique du don: Jacques Derrida et la pensée du don,* 11–108. Edited by Jean-Michel Rabaté and Michael Wetzel. Paris: Métaillé-Transition, 1992.

————. "Le Facteur de la vérité." In *La Carte postale,* 439–524. Paris: Aubier-Flammarion, 1980.

————. *The Gift of Death*. Translated by David Wills. Chicago: University of Chicago Press, 1995.

————. *Glas*. Paris: Galilée, 1974.

————. *Glas*. Translated by John P. Leavey, Jr., and Richard Rand. Lincoln: University of Nebraska Press, 1986.

————. "Hors livre: Préfaces." In *La Dissémination*, 7–67. Paris: Seuil, 1972.

————. *Limited Inc*. Evanston, Ill.: Northwestern University Press, 1988.

————. "La Mythologie blanche." In *Marges de la philosophie*, 247–324. Paris: Minuit, 1972.

————. *La Vérité en peinture*. Paris: Flammarion, 1978.

————. "Signature événement contexte." In *Marges de la philosophie*, 365–93. Paris: Minuit, 1972.

————. *The Truth in Painting*. Translated by Geoff Bennington and Ian McLeod. Chicago: University of Chicago Press, 1987.

————. "White Mythology." In *Margins of Philosophy*, trans. Alan Bass, 207–71. Chicago: University of Chicago Press, 1982.

Dickens, Charles. *Little Dorrit*. London: Oxford University Press, 1953.

————. *Oliver Twist*. Edited by Kathleen Tillotson. Oxford: Clarendon Press of Oxford University Press, 1966.

————. *The Posthumous Papers of the Pickwick Club*. Harmondsworth: Penguin, 1972.

Dodsworth, Martin. "Women without Men at Cranford." *Essays in Criticism* 13 (April 1963): 132–45.

Eliot, George. *Daniel Deronda*. Harmondsworth: Penguin, 1967.

————. *Middlemarch*. Harmondsworth: Penguin, 1974.

Emerson, Ralph Waldo. "Circles." In *Essays: First Series*, vol. 2 in *Collected Works*, ed. Joseph Slater et al., 177–90. Cambridge, Mass.: Belknap Press of Harvard University Press, 1979.

Empson, William. *The Structure of Complex Words*. Cambridge, Mass.: Harvard University Press, 1989.

Erlich, Victor. *Russian Formalism: History-Doctrine*. 4th ed. The Hague: Mouton, 1980.

Faulkner, William. *Absalom, Absalom!* New York: Vintage, 1972.

Forster, John. *The Life of Charles Dickens*. 3 vols. London: Chapman and Hall, 1872.

Freud, Sigmund. *Beyond the Pleasure Principle*. Translated by James Strachey. New York: Bantam, 1967.

————. *The Complete Letters . . . to Wilhelm Fliess*. Translated by and edited by Jeffrey Moussaieff Masson. Cambridge: Harvard University Press, 1985.

———. *A General Introduction to Psycho-Analysis*. Translated by Joan Riviere. New York: Liveright, 1935.

———. *The Interpretation of Dreams*. Vol. 4 in *Works*, ed. James Strachey. Standard Edition. London: Hogarth Press and Institute of Psycho-Analysis, 1953.

———. *Jenseits des Lustprinzips*. Freud-Studienausgabe. Vol. 3. Frankfurt am Main: Fischer, 1989.

———. "The Uncanny." Vol. 4 in *Collected Papers*, trans. Alex Strachey, 368–407. New York: Basic Books, 1959.

Friedman, Alan. *The Turn of the Novel*. New York: Oxford University Press, 1966.

Garrett, Peter K. *Scene and Symbol from George Eliot to James Joyce: Studies in Changing Fictional Mode*. New Haven: Yale University Press, 1969.

Gaskell, Elizabeth. *Cranford; The Cage at Cranford; The Moorland Cottage*. World's Classics ed. London: Oxford University Press, 1965.

Genette, Gérard. "Discours du récit." In *Figures III*, 65–273. Paris: Seuil, 1972.

———. "Frontières du récit." In *Figures II*, 49–69. Paris: Seuil, 1969.

———. *Narrative Discourse*. Translated by Jane E. Lewin. Ithaca: Cornell University Press, 1980.

———. *Palimpsestes*. Paris: Seuil, 1982.

Goethe, Johann Wolfgang von. *Elective Affinities*. Translated by James Anthony Froude and R. Dillon Boylan. New York: Frederick Ungar, 1962.

———. *Die Wahlverwandtschaften*. Munich: Deutscher Taschenbuch Verlag, 1975.

Goodheart, Sandor. "Oedipus and Laius' Many Murders." *diacritics* 8, no. 1 (March 1978): 55–71.

Gordon, Paul. *The Critical Double*. Tuscaloosa: University of Alabama Press, 1995.

Goux, Jean-Joseph. *Oedipus: Philosopher*. Translated by Catherine Porter. Stanford: Stanford University Press, 1993.

Green, André. *Un Oeil en trop: le Complexe d'Oedipe dans la tragédie*. Paris: Minuit, 1969.

Hamacher, Werner. "*Lingua Amissa*: The Messianism of Commodity-Language and Derrida's *Specters of Marx*." In *Ghostly Demarcations: A Symposium on Jacques Derrida's Specters of Marx*, ed. Michael Sprinker. London and New York: Verso, 1998.

———. "Position Exposed: Friedrich Schlegel's Poetological Transposition of Fichte's Absolute Proposition." In *Premises*, trans. Peter Fenves, 222–60. Cambridge: Harvard University Press, 1996.

Hardy, Thomas. *Complete Poems*. Edited by James Gibson. London: Macmillan, 1976.

———. *The Life and Death of the Mayor of Casterbridge*. London: Macmillan, 1975.

————. *The Return of the Native.* New Wessex paperback ed. London: Macmillan, 1974.

Heidegger, Martin. "Das Ding." In *Vorträge und Aufsätze,* 37–59. Pfullingen: Neske, 1954.

————. "The Origin of the Work of Art." In *Poetry, Language, Thought,* trans. Albert Hofstadter, 15–87. New York: Harper and Row, 1971.

————. "The Thing." In *Poetry, Language, Thought,* trans. Albert Hofstadter, 163–86. New York: Harper and Row, 1971.

————. "Der Ursprung des Kunstwerkes." In *Holzwege,* 7–68. Frankfurt am Main: Klostermann, 1972.

Heine, Heinrich. "Die Götter im Exil." Vol. 5, pt. 1, in *Sämtliche Schriften.* Munich: Hanser, 1975.

Hertz, Neil. *The End of the Line.* New York: Columbia University Press, 1985.

Hölderlin, Friedrich. "In Lieblicher Bläue . . . / In Lovely Blueness . . . ." In *Poems and Fragments,* trans. Michael Hamburger, 600–605. Cambridge: Cambridge University Press, 1980.

————. *Remarques sur Oedipe/Remarques sur Antigone.* Translated by François Fédier. Paris: Bibliotheque 10/18, 1965.

Hopkins, Gerard Manley. *Further Letters of Gerard Manley Hopkins.* Edited by C. C. Abbott. London: Oxford University Press, 1956.

————. *Sermons and Devotional Writings.* Edited by Christopher Devlin. London: Oxford University Press, 1959.

————. "The Wreck of the Deutschland." In *The Poems,* ed. W. H. Gardner and N. H. MacKenzie, 4th ed., 51–63. London: Oxford University Press, 1967.

Iser, Wolfgang. *The Act of Reading: A Theory of Aesthetic Response.* London: Routledge and Kegan Paul, 1978.

Jacobs, Carol. "Nietzsche: The Stammering Text: The Fragmentary Studies Preliminary to *The Birth of Tragedy.*" In *The Dissimulating Harmony,* 1–22. Baltimore: Johns Hopkins University Press, 1978.

James, Henry. "The Aspern Papers." In *Novels and Tales of Henry James* (reprint, New York Edition of 1907–9), ed. Leon Edel, 12:3–143. New York: Augustus M. Kelley, 1971.

———— "Glasses." In *The Complete Tales,* ed. Leon Edel, 9:317–70. Philadelphia: J. B. Lippincott, 1964.

————. Preface to *The Golden Bowl.* In *Novels and Tales of Henry James* (reprint, New York Edition of 1907–9), 23:v–xxv. New York: Augustus M. Kelley, 1971.

————. Preface to *Roderick Hudson*. In *Novels and Tales of Henry James* (reprint, New York Edition of 1907–9), 1:v–xx. New York: Augustus M. Kelley, 1971.

Jones, John. *On Aristotle and Greek Tragedy*. London: Chatto and Windus, 1967.

Joyce, James. *Finnegans Wake*. New York: Viking, 1947.

————. *Ulysses*. Harmondsworth: Penguin, 1971.

Kafka, Franz. *The Diaries . . . 1910–1913*. Edited by Max Brod. Translated by Joseph Kresh. London: Secker and Warburg, 1948.

————. "The Judgment." In *Selected Short Stories*, trans. Willa and Edwin Muir, 3–18. New York: Modern Library, 1952.

————. *Tagebücher 1910–23*. Edited by Max Brod. Frankfurt: S. Fischer, 1986.

————. *Das Urteil und Andere Erzählungen*. Frankfurt am Main: Fischer, 1952.

Kaiser, Wolfgang. *The Grotesque*. Translated by Ulrich Weisstein. Gloucester: Peter Smith, 1968.

Kermode, Frank. *The Sense of an Ending*. New York: Oxford University Press, 1967.

Kierkegaard, Søren. *The Concept of Irony*. Translated by Howard V. Hong and Edna H. Hong. Princeton: Princeton University Press, 1992.

————. *The Concept of Irony, with Constant Reference to Socrates*. Translated by Lee M. Capel. Bloomington: Indiana University Press, 1968.

————. *Either/Or*. Translated by Walter Lowrie, rev. Howard A. Johnson. Garden City, N.Y.: Doubleday Anchor, 1959.

————. *Either/Or*. Translated by David F. Swenson and Lillian Marvin Swenson. Princeton: Princeton University Press, 1971.

Knox, Bernard M. W. *Oedipus at Thebes: Sophocles' Tragic Hero and His Time*. New Haven: Yale University Press, 1957.

————. *Studies in Sophoclean Tragedy*. Berkeley: University of California Press, 1964.

Lacan, Jacques. "Le Séminaire sur 'la Lettre volée.'" In *Écrits*, 11–61. Paris: Seuil, 1966.

Lacoue-Labarthe, Philippe. "La Césure du speculatif." In Friedrich Hölderlin, trans., *L'Antigone de Sophocle suivi de La Césure du speculatif par Philippe Lacoue-Labarthe*, 183–223. Paris: Christian Bourgois, 1978.

————. "Typographie." In *Mimesis des articulations*, 167–270. Paris: Aubier-Flammarion, 1975.

————. "Typography." In *Typography: Mimesis, Philosophy, Politics*, 43–138. Cambridge: Harvard University Press, 1989.

Lawrence, D. H. *Women in Love*. Cambridge: Cambridge University Press, 1987.

————. *Women in Love*. New York: Modern Library, n.d.

————. *Women in Love*. Edited by David Farmer, Lindeth Vasey, and John Worthen. Intro. and notes by Mark Kinkead-Weekes. Harmondsworth: Penguin, 1995.

Lear, Jonathan. *Aristotle: The Desire to Understand*. Cambridge: Cambridge University Press, 1988.

Lévi-Strauss, Claude. "The Structural Study of Myth." In *Structural Anthropology*, 202–28. Garden City, N.Y.: Doubleday-Anchor, 1967.

Marcus, Steven. *Dickens: From Pickwick to Dombey*. New York: Basic Books, 1965.

Marx, Karl. *Capital*. Translated by Samuel Moore and Edward Aveling. New York: International Publishers, 1974.

Miller, J. Hillis. *Ariadne's Thread*. New Haven: Yale University Press, 1992.

————. *Black Holes*. Stanford: Stanford University Press, 1999.

————. "Catachreses for Chaos: Irony and Myth in Friedrich Schlegel." In *Revenge of the Aesthetic*, ed. Michael Clark. Berkeley and Los Angeles: University of California Press, 1999.

————. "The Critic as Host." In *Theory Now and Then*, 143–70. Hemel Hempstead: Harvester Wheatsheaf, 1991.

————. *Fiction and Repetition*. Cambridge: Harvard University Press, 1982.

————. "A Guest in the House: Reply to Shlomith Rimmon-Kenan's Reply." *Poetics Today* 2 (Winter 1980/81): 189–91.

————. *Illustration*. Cambridge: Harvard University Press, 1992.

————. "'Le Mensonge, le mensonge parfait': Théories du mensonge chez Proust et Derrida." Translated by Yasmine Van den Wijngaert, aided by Chantal Zabus and Cécile Hayez. In *Passions de la littérature*, ed. Michel Lisse, 405–20. Paris: Galilée. 1999.

————. "Prosopopoeia in Hardy and Stevens." In *Tropes, Parables, Performatives*, 245–59. New York: Harvester Wheatsheaf, 1990.

————. "Re-Reading Re-Vision: James and Benjamin." In *The Ethics of Reading*, 101–22. New York: Columbia University Press, 1987.

————. "Stevens' Rock and Criticism as Cure: II." *Georgia Review* 30, no. 2 (Summer 1976): 330–48. Reprinted in *Theory Now and Then*, 117–31. Hemel Hempstead: Harvester Wheatsheaf, 1991.

————. *Topographies*. Stanford: Stanford University Press, 1995.

Muller, John P., and William J. Richardson, eds. *The Purloined Poe: Lacan, Derrida and Psychoanalytic Reading*. Baltimore: Johns Hopkins University Press, 1988.

Newmark, Kevin. "L'Absolu littéraire: Friedrich Schlegel and the Myth of Irony." *MLN* 107, no. 5 (December 1992): 905–30.

Nietzsche, Friedrich. *The Birth of Tragedy and The Case of Wagner.* Translated by Walter Kaufmann. New York: Vintage, 1967.

———. *Die Geburt der Tragödie.* Vol. 1 in *Sämtliche Werke,* ed. Giorgio Colli and Mazzino Montinari. Kritische Studienausgabe. Munich: Deutscher Taschenbuch Verlag, 1988. Berlin: De Gruyter, 1988.

———. *Nachlass.* Vol. 12 in *Sämtliche Werke,* ed. Giorgio Colli and Mazzino Montinari. Kritische Studienausgabe. Munich: Deutscher Taschenbuch Verlag, 1988. Berlin: De Gruyter, 1988.

———. *The Selected Letters.* Translated by and edited by Christopher Middleton. Chicago: University of Chicago Press, 1969.

———. *Werke.* Edited by Karl Schlecta. 3 vols. Munich: Carl Hanser, 1966.

———. *The Will to Power.* Translated by Walter Kaufmann and R. J. Hollingdale. New York: Vintage, 1968.

Nüsse, Heinrich. *Die Sprachtheorie Friedrich Schlegels.* Heidelberg: Carl Winter, Universitätsverlag, 1962.

Pater, Walter. "Apollo in Picardy." In *Imaginary Portraits,* ed. Eugene J. Brzenk, 185–205. New York: Harper and Row, 1964.

———. *The Renaissance.* Edited by Donald L. Hill. Berkeley: University of California Press, 1980.

Paulson, Ronald. *Hogarth's Graphic Works.* 2 vols. New Haven: Yale University Press, 1970.

Plato. *Republic.* Translated by Paul Shorey. In *The Collected Dialogues,* ed. Edith Hamilton and Huntington Cairns, 575–844. Bollingen ed. Princeton: Princeton University Press, 1961.

Poe, Edgar Allan. "The Facts in the Case of M. Valdemar." Vol. 6 in *Works,* ed. James A. Harrison, 154–66. New York: Thomas Y. Crowell, 1902.

Polheim, Karl Konrad. *Die Arabesque: Ansichten und Ideen aus Friedrich Schlegels Poetik.* Munich: F. Schöningh, 1966.

Price, Martin. "The Irrelevant Detail and the Emergence of Form." In *Aspects of Narrative,* 69–91. New York: Columbia University Press, 1971.

Proust, Marcel. *À la recherche du temps perdu.* Edited by Jean-Yves Tadié. Pléiade ed. Paris: Gallimard, 1989.

———. *Remembrance of Things Past.* Translated by C. K. Scott Moncrieff, Terence Kilmartin, and Andreas Mayor. New York: Vintage, 1982.

Ricoeur, Paul. *Temps et récit.* Vol. 1. Paris: Seuil, 1983.

———. *Time and Narrative.* Translated by Kathleen McLaughlin and David Pellauer. Chicago: University of Chicago Press, 1984.

Rimmon-Kenan, Shlomith. *The Concept of Ambiguity: The Example of Henry James.* Chicago: University of Chicago Press, 1977.

———. "Deconstructive Reflections on Deconstruction." *Poetics Today* 2 (Winter 1980/81): 185–88.

Rousseau, Jean-Jacques. *Oeuvres complètes.* Edited by Bernard Gagnebin and Marcel Raymond. 4 vols. Pléiade ed. Paris: Gallimard, 1964.

Ruskin, John. *Ariadne Florentina.* In *Lectures on Landscape/Michel Angelo and Tintoret/The Lark's Nest/Ariadne Florentina,* vol. 22 in *Works,* ed. E. T. Cook and Alexander Wedderburn, 289–490. New York: Longmans, Green, and Co., 1906.

Said, Edward W. *Beginnings.* New York: Basic Books, 1975.

Schlegel, Friedrich. "Brief über den Roman." In *Gespräch über die Poesie.* In *Kritische Schriften,* 508–18. Munich: Carl Hanser, 1964.

———. "Fragmente." In *Kritische Schriften,* 5–108. Munich: Carl Hanser, 1964.

———. "Letter about the Novel." In *Dialogue on Poetry and Literary Aphorisms,* 94–104. Translated by Ernst Behler and Roman Struc. University Park: Pennsylvania State University Press, 1968.

———. "On Incomprehensibility." In *German Aesthetic and Literary Criticism: The Romantic Ironists and Goethe,* ed. Kathleen Wheeler, 32–40. Cambridge: Cambridge University Press, 1984.

———. *Philosophical Fragments.* Translated by Peter Firchow. Minneapolis: University of Minnesota Press, 1991.

———. "Rede über die Mythologie." In *Gespräch über die Poesie. Kritische Schriften,* 496–503. Munich: Carl Hanser, 1964.

———. "Talk on Mythology." In *Dialogue on Poetry and Literary Aphorisms,* trans. Ernst Behler and Roman Struc, 81–88. University Park: Pennsylvania State University Press, 1968.

———. "Über die Unverständlichkeit." In *Kritische Schriften,* 530–42. Munich: Carl Hanser, 1964.

———. "Über Lessing." In *Kritische Schriften,* 346–83. Munich: Carl Hanser, 1964.

Shakespeare, William. *Troilus and Cressida*. Edited by H. V. Hillebrand and T. W. Baldwin. New Variorum ed. Philadelphia: Lippincott, 1953.

———. *Troilus and Cressida*. Edited by Daniel Seltzer. In *The Complete Signet Classic Shakespeare*, 999–1049. New York: Harcourt Brace Jovanovich, 1972.

Sophocles. *Oedipus the King*. Translated by and commentary Thomas Gould. Englewood Cliffs: Prentice-Hall, 1970.

———. *Oedipus the King*. Translated by Bernard M. W. Knox. New York: Pocket Books–Simon and Schuster, 1972.

———. *Oedipus the King*. Translated by David Grene. In *Sophocles I: Three Tragedies*, ed. David Grene and Richard Lattimore. Chicago: University of Chicago Press, 1954.

———. *Oedipus the King*. In Sophocles, *Oedipus the King; Oedipus at Colonus; Antigone*, trans. F. Storr. Loeb Classical Library. Cambridge: Harvard University Press, 1981.

———. *Oedipus the King*. In *The Three Theban Plays*, trans. Robert Fagles. Harmondsworth: Penguin, 1984.

Sterne, Laurence. *The Life and Times of Tristram Shandy*. Harmondsworth: Penguin, 1967.

———. *Tristram Shandy*. Edited by Howard Anderson. Norton Critical ed. New York: Norton, 1980.

Stevens, Wallace. *Collected Poems*. New York: Vintage, 1990.

Sussman, Henry. *The Aesthetic Contract: Statutes of Art and Intellectual Work in Modernity*. Stanford: Stanford University Press. 1997.

Todorov, Tsvetan. "The Structural Analysis of Literature: The Tales of Henry James." In *Structuralism: An Introduction*, ed. David Robey, 73–103. Oxford: Clarendon Press of Oxford University Press, 1973.

Trollope, Anthony. *An Autobiography*. Edited by David Skilton. London: Penguin, 1996.

———. *Is He Popenjoy?*. World's Classics ed. London: Oxford University Press, 1944.

———. *The Last Chronicle of Barset*. World's Classics ed. London: Oxford University Press, 1961.

———. *The Warden*. World's Classics ed. London: Oxford University Press, 1963.

Valéry, Paul. "Introduction à la Méthode de Léonard de Vinci." In *Oeuvres*, ed. Jean Hytier, 1:1153–99. Pléiade ed. Paris: Gallimard, 1957.

———. "Poésie et pensée abstraite." In *Oeuvres*, ed. Jean Hytier, 1:1314–39. Pléiade ed. Paris: Gallimard, 1957.

Vernant, Jean-Pierre, and Pierre Vidal-Naquet. *Myth and Tragedy in Ancient Greece*. Translated by Janet Lloyd. Brighton, Sussex: Harvester Press, 1981.

Villiers de l'Isle-Adam, Philippe Auguste. *Axël.* Paris: Maison Quantin, 1890.

———. *Axel.* Translated by June Guicharnaud. Englewood Cliffs, N.J.: Prentice-Hall, 1970.

Weber, Samuel. "Benjamin's 'Task of the Translator.'" Unpublished essay.

———. *Unwrapping Balzac: A Reading of La Peau de chagrin.* Toronto: University of Toronto Press, 1979.

Williams, William Carlos. *Pictures from Breugel and Other Poems.* Norfolk, Conn.: New Directions, 1962.

Winter, Sarah. "Lacanian Psychoanalysis at Colonus." In *Freud and the Institutionalization of Psychoanalytical Knowledge: Profession, Discipline, Culture.* Stanford: Stanford University Press, 1998.

Wordsworth, William. *The Prelude.* Edited by Ernest de Selincourt. 2nd ed. revised by Helen Darbishire. Oxford: Clarendon Press, 1959.

Yeats, W. B. *Autobiography.* Garden City, N.Y.: Doubleday Anchor, 1958.

———. *The Poems.* Edited by Richard J. Finneran. New York: Macmillan, 1983.

———. *The Variorum Edition of the Poems.* Edited by Peter Allt and Russell K. Alspach. New York: Macmillan, 1977.

INDEX